Animal Lives Matter

Animal Lives Matter provides a comprehensive analysis of the legal, philosophical, and ethical aspects of animal rights. It argues that the subject extends beyond the matter of our obligations towards animals, to include our wider responsibilities for protecting the environment. Drawing on numerous moral, political, legal, religious, and philosophical theories including utilitarianism, deontology, rights theory, social contractarianism, and the capabilities approach, the author meticulously examines the questions of sentience, speciesism, personhood, and human exceptionalism. Lucid, nuanced, and academically rigorous, this important book will be an essential resource for scholars of law, politics, philosophy, ethics, as well as policy makers and the general reader.

Raymond Wacks, Emeritus Professor of Law and Legal Theory, is the author of 15 books, and editor of 10. Several of his works have been translated into more than a dozen languages. His books include *Personal Information: Privacy and the Law*; *Privacy and Media Freedom*; *Privacy: A Very Short Introduction*; *Law: A Very Short Introduction*; and *Justice: A Beginner's Guide*. Among his most recent publications are *Protecting Personal Information: The Right to Privacy Reconsidered*, *COVID-19 and Public Policy in the Digital Age*, and *National Security in the New World Order: Government and the Technology of Information* (with Andrea Monti). The sixth edition of his *Understanding Jurisprudence: An Introduction to Legal Theory* was published in 2021, as was *The Rule of Law Under Fire?*

Animal Lives Matter

The Continuing Quest for Justice

Raymond Wacks

Routledge
Taylor & Francis Group
LONDON AND NEW YORK

Designed cover image: Courtesy of Tim Phillips, Animal Defenders International

First published 2024
by Routledge
4 Park Square, Milton Park, Abingdon, Oxon OX14 4RN

and by Routledge
605 Third Avenue, New York, NY 10158

Routledge is an imprint of the Taylor & Francis Group, an informa business

British Library Cataloguing-in-Publication Data
A catalogue record for this book is available from the British Library

ISBN: 978-1-032-57312-0 (hbk)
ISBN: 978-1-032-70084-7 (pbk)
ISBN: 978-1-032-70257-5 (ebk)

DOI: 10.4324/9781032702575

Typeset in Sabon LT Pro
by KnowledgeWorks Global Ltd.

For the many creatures, great and small, with whom
I have been fortunate to share my life.

'The time will come when men such as I will look upon the murder of animals as they now look on the murder of men.'

Leonardo da Vinci

Contents

1 Introduction

We harm them. They seldom harm us. We eat them. They rarely eat us. We abuse them. They never abuse us. For most of human history our conceit has ordained that animals exist for us, to do with them as we please. We employ them for sport, entertainment, experiments, and work; their lives are broken by inhumane methods of slaughter, transport, battery farming, and more.[1]

Their legal status in most countries differs little from a chair or a desk. They are regarded as property—to be owned, bought and sold, and disposed of at the whim of their owner.[2] Nor are they generally considered 'persons' in the eyes of the law. These two perceptions, as we shall see, constitute major impediments to the recognition of the rights of animals and the effective protection against the suffering they are compelled to endure.

There is, of course, in many countries, anti-cruelty legislation that seeks to curtail the worst excesses of their maltreatment. Additionally, several jurisdictions have enacted statutes that are calculated to promote more compassionate treatment of animals, particularly in farming, scientific experimentation, and abattoirs. International and regional declarations, as well as constitutional pronouncements, purport to ameliorate their lives.

There can be little doubt that as a species *homo sapiens*' record leaves a great deal to be desired. Despite the advances in the protection of human

1 The United States alone kills more than 8 billion animals a year for food: 23 million are slaughtered daily, or almost 16,000 per minute, 260 every second, Gary L Francione, 'Animals—Property or Persons?' in Cass R Sunstein and Martha C Nussbaum, eds, *Animal Rights: Current Debates and New Directions* (New York: Oxford University Press, 2004), 108, 109. According to the World Animal Foundation, in 2021 almost 83 billion animals were killed across the world. More than 100 million are killed annually by hunters in the United States; about 1.5 billion cows are killed per year; 34.36 million cows and 3.5 million pigs are killed for food. Globally more than 73 billion chickens are killed, 2.1 billion fish are caught daily, and 749 million geese, 52 million Guinea fowl, and more than 500 million goats were slaughtered. In the United States, more than 20 million animals die each year on their way to abattoirs. See worldanimalfoundation.org. The UN Food and Agricultural Organisation (FAO) reports that some 4.3 billion ducks, 572 million rabbits, 627 million turkeys, were killed for food in 2021. This inventory is far from complete.

2 Think of the term 'livestock'.

DOI: 10.4324/9781032702575-1

rights, animals continue to suffer at our hands in mostly atrocious conditions. Moreover, 'long before the Industrial Revolution, Homo sapiens held the record among all organisms for driving the most plant and animal species to their extinctions. We have the dubious distinction of being the deadliest species in the annals of biology'.[3]

The chief concern of the pages that follow is not the depredation we have wrought on the planet,[4] though this defilement is unavoidably touched on, but our signal failure to treat our fellow creatures with compassion and respect. There are obviously numerous humans who are exceptions to this general criticism. Many welfare organisations and charities work indefatigably to protect, rescue, and tend to the needs of wounded, abandoned, and abused animals of every kind. And individuals across the world support their efforts or at least express their affection and concern for nonhumans in countless ways.

But virtue has its limits. Many maintain an uncomfortable conflict between concern for animals, on the one hand, and the outcome that they know are the results of animal suffering, on the other hand. The conditions under which battery hens are kept, for example, are notoriously inhumane, yet those professing to care for their fellow creatures will consume their meat and eggs with equanimity. This so-called 'meat paradox' or 'omnivore's akrasia'[5] is a classic illustration of the cognitive dissonance that pervades the subject of not only this but also many moral dilemmas which injustice spawns. Turning a blind eye is an activity that is not confined to the present subject.

In the face of the cruelty of animal suffering, one must seek to avoid the twin sins of sanctimony and sentimentalism. Equally, one should attempt to preserve a degree of detachment. In attempting to elucidate a complex ethical problem one must, as far as possible, avoid falling prey to emotive stimuli that may influence an objective analysis. This is particularly difficult when the subject concerns the suffering inflicted on others, human or nonhuman. I have strong feelings on both scores, but I trust that my examination of this contentious issue is as impartial as it is possible to be when confronted with

3 Yuval Noah Harari, *Sapiens: A Brief History of Humankind* (London: Vintage, 2024), 74.

4 The world's 7.6 billion people represent just 0.01 per cent of all living things, according to the study. Yet since the dawn of civilisation, humanity has caused the loss of 83 per cent of all wild mammals and half of plants, while livestock kept by humans abounds. Farmed poultry today makes up 70 per cent of all birds on the planet, with just 30 per cent being wild. The picture is even more stark for mammals—60 per cent of all mammals on earth are livestock, mostly cattle and pigs, 36 per cent are human, and just 4 per cent are wild animals, Yinon Bar-On, Rob Phillips, and Ron Milo, 'The biomass distribution on Earth' (2018) 115 *Proceedings of the National Academy of Sciences* (*PNAS*) 6506.

5 'Akrasia' refers to a situation, where one believes in a fact or value x, and yet acts against that fact or value, Elisa Aaltola, 'The Meat Paradox, Omnivore's Akrasia, and Animal Ethics' (2019) 9 *Animals* 1125. See too Robyn M Engel, Carrie C Silver, Christin L Veeder and Ron E Banks, 'Cognitive Dissonance in Laboratory Animal Medicine and Implications for Animal Welfare' (2020) 59 *Journal of the American Association for Laboratory Animal Science* 132.

cruelty, exploitation, and pain. This is not an easy undertaking. Anyone who has witnessed the horrors of the wildlife markets in China[6] and elsewhere in Asia, or stepped inside a laboratory in which experiments are conducted on mammals, or observed videos depicting the maltreatment of animals in abattoirs and elsewhere would require a constitution of steel not to feel nauseated, distraught, and angry.

Consider the case of bear farming in China and Vietnam. The plight of thousands of endangered Asiatic black bears is particularly disquieting. After being trapped in the wild, they are confined in tiny wire cages no bigger than the size of their own bodies. Metal catheters up to 7 inches long are inserted into their abdomens in order to 'milk' them of their bile for use in Oriental medicines and preparations. Many spend their entire lives (which may last up to twenty years) subjected to this torment. In the minds of some otherwise intelligent people, this unspeakable practice is defended on the ground that these creatures are mere objects; therefore the question of their wellbeing, let alone whether they can be said to have rights, simply does not arise.[7]

It is occasionally asserted that concern for animals is misdirected, and it trivialises human suffering by its devotion to the alleviation of nonhuman misery. Indeed one writer claims that the popular movement in support of animal rights is a 'reflection of moral decadence'.[8] This argument seems to be driven by the idea that those who are engaged in animal rights or welfare activities either subordinate human interests to animal interests, or that they have a pathological indifference towards human beings.[9] This seems specious; if those who direct their compassion towards animals are to be charged with diminished sympathy for the plight of their fellow humans, their crime might instead be their ire and resentment at the treatment they inflict on their fellow

6 It is thought, but not yet conclusively demonstrated, that COVID-19 originated from a Wuhan 'wet market' where wild animals, including, birds, rabbits, bats, pangolins, and snakes, are traded illegally. The suffering of these creatures is unspeakable: 'A smorgasbord of dogs being boiled alive, bats served on sticks like lollipops, kittens slaughtered, rats fried and giant snakes carved up for human consumption, with the blood splattering everywhere. There are no hygiene standards. Cross-contamination is rampant. The animal cruelty is off the scale. Bears, tigers, wolf cubs, crocodiles, hedgehogs and turtles are not spared in this notorious wildlife food trade, either'. See news.com.au which contains horrifying videos that are extremely difficult to watch. See Andrea Monti and Raymond Wacks, *COVID-19 and Public Policy in the Digital Age* (Abingdon: Routledge, 2021); Amanda Whitfort, 'Evaluating China's Draft Animal Protection Law' (2012) 34 *Sydney Law Review* 347.

7 Some 300 of these creatures continue to be kept in bile farms. The rescue and subsequent rehabilitation and care of these tortured, often badly injured, creatures by the group, *AnimalsAsia*, is little short of heroic. To witness the bears recuperating after their initial terror on being released is among the most moving experiences of my life. See animalsasia.org/uk

8 Peter Carruthers, *The Animals Issue: Moral Theory in Practice* (Cambridge: Cambridge University Press, 1992), xi.

9 For some 'there is no real difference in the basic grounds on which we should condemn man's inhumanity to animals and man's inhumanity to man', TLS Sprigge, 'Metaphysics, Physicalism, and Animal Rights' (1979) 22 *Inquiry* 101, 103.

nonhumans. In fact, individuals involved in the animal welfare movement are frequently dedicated as well to the alleviation of suffering of oppressed or disadvantaged humans.[10] And even if this were not so, our concern for animals is inseparable from our unease about the ravages we continue to inflict on our environment, and the consequences of this damage on all living things. In relation to the use of live animals in experiments, for instance (discussed in the following section), it is sometimes said that science is somehow value-neutral.[11] This provides a handy device by which scientists may be blinded from the suffering of animals and deny them subjective awareness and moral status.[12]

Cruelty to animals and indifference to the extinction of endangered species is sometimes defended in the name of cultural or ethical relativism. This is a neglected issue that warrants greater attention; I return to it in Chapter 5. It is true that, as in the case of human rights, 'since people are more likely to observe normative propositions if they believe them to be sanctioned by their own cultural standards, observance of human rights standards can be improved through the enhancement of the cultural legitimacy of those standards'.[13] Yet, all too often, these arguments merely camouflage injustice. Where suffering is caused (and especially where international norms are infringed), we should resist such claims.

In pursuit of cogent arguments to support my conclusions, I have, in the relevant chapters, presented accounts of philosophical concepts or theories that either support or invalidate these views. I am strongly of the view that, while sentiment often dictates our moral opinions, principled reasoning grounded in rational thought generally provides dependable guidance to how we should

10 There is a strong connection between the feminist and the anti-vivisection campaigns of the nineteenth century in Britain. See O Banks, *Faces of Feminism* (Oxford: Blackwell, 1986), 81–2, quoted in L Birke, *Women, Feminism and Biology: The Feminist Challenge* (Brighton: Harvester, 1986), 120. CJ Adams, *Neither Man Nor Beast: Feminism and the Defense of Animals* (New York: Lantern Books, reprint, 2015).

11 'It is in the name of science, and with the specious bribe of release from all our ills, that we have been cajoled and threatened and insulted into permitting the continued torture of our kindred and the continued blunting of the sensibilities of those who come to work in our laboratories. Let no-one rely on common decency in such a situation: the pressure of one's professional peer-group, the atmosphere of dismissive tolerance of all outside the clan, the calm assumption that this is what we do, are all far too strong for most of us to resist'. Stephen Clark, *The Moral Status of Animals*, 141–2. See too Max Ricard, *A Plea for the Animals: The Moral, Philosophical, and Evolutionary Imperative to Treat All Beings with Compassion* (Boulder, CO: Shambhala Publications, 2016).

12 '[A]nimals have been allowed to suffer in research not through cruelty, but rather, because consideration of suffering is forgotten in the thrill of the pursuit, by nature ultimately ruthless, complemented by an ideology which discounts the cogency of moral reflection in scientific activity and denies the meaningfulness of attributing feelings to animals, and is coupled with practical pressures'. Bernard E Rollin, *The Unheeded Cry: Animal Consciousness, Animal Pain and Science* (Oxford: Oxford University Press, 1989).

13 AA An'Naim, 'Problems of Universal Cultural Legitimacy for Human Rights' in AA An'Naim and F Deng, eds, *Human Rights in Africa: Cross-Cultural Perspectives* (Washington, DC: Brookings Institution, 1990), 331.

act. In order better to understand the various arguments postulated about our moral obligations, or lack thereof, towards animals, it is important to see them in the setting of the wider philosophical theories from which they are derived. I make no assumptions about my readers; those familiar with the theoretical terrain may wish to skip these introductory accounts and proceed directly to the section that attempts to apply them to my discussion of whether, or to what extent, they advance the cause of protecting the wellbeing of animals.

Scepticism of metaphysical and constitutional pontification is, however, no bad thing in this and other spheres of policy. With regard to animal rights, Judge Richard Posner expresses his misgivings in his typically forthright manner:

> We should be able to agree without help from philosophers and constitutional theorists that gratuitous cruelty is bad—condemnation is built into the word 'gratuitous'—and few of us are either so sadistic or so indifferent to animal suffering, that we are unwilling to incur at least modest costs to prevent gratuitous cruelty to animals; and anyone who supposes that philosophers and constitutional theorists can persuade people to incur huge costs to protect the interests of strangers is surely deluded.[14]

Nevertheless, in the hope that what follows will illuminate the deliberations generated by our treatment of fellow creatures, I have, as an introduction to these chapters, provided an outline of the essentials of each of such theories or concepts.

Experiments on animals

Animals are subjected to a variety of biomedical experiments, as well as being used for other purposes:

> They are used to measure the effects of toxins, drugs, diseases, radiation, bullets, and various forms of physical and psychological deprivation. We burn, poison, irradiate, blind, starve, and electrocute them. They are purposely riddled with diseases such as cancer and infections such as pneumonia. We deprive them of sleep, keep them in solitary confinement, remove their limbs and eyes, addict them to drugs, force them to withdraw from drug addiction, and cage them for the duration of their lives. If they do not die during experimental procedures, we almost always kill them immediately afterward, or we recycle them for other experiments or tests and then kill them.[15]

14 Richard A Posner, 'Animal Rights: Legal, Philosophical, and Pragmatic Perspectives' and RA Epstein, 'Animals as Objects or Subjects of Rights', in Cass R Sunstein and Martha C Nussbaum, eds, *Animal Rights: Current Debates and New Directions* (New York: Oxford University Press, 2004). This assertion comes close to self-refutation; while in denigrating philosophical theories, is Posner not himself adopting one? Pragmatism, perhaps?

15 Gary L Francione, op cit, 109–110.

Controlled to a greater or lesser extent by legislation in several countries,[16] and the 1991 European Convention for the Protection of Vertebrate Animals used for Experimental and other Scientific Purposes,[17] the question of its ethical acceptability remains problematic. Its intractability resides in the perceived benefits—to both humans and nonhumans—that this research allegedly produces. Approximately 100 million animals are used in laboratories around the world annually. Though many procedures inflict pain and distress on animals (which I have been sickened to witness), it is worth noting that some do not. Nor will all be 'sacrificed', the researcher's euphemism for killing.[18] Moreover, it is hard to deny the fact that eating animals 'is responsible for a vastly greater quantity of death and suffering than experimentation'.[19]

Animals are widely used to test the efficacy and toxicity of new drugs. I first researched this distressing subject in 1996[20]; almost thirty years later I had assumed that the reprehensible LD50 test—introduced in 1927—was no longer in use. (LD stands for lethal dose; it seeks to establish the single dose required to kill 50 per cent of test animals.) I was wrong. It takes the lives of about 80,000 animals annually in the EU alone. Rats, rabbits, and primates are the principal victims.[21] It has been argued that the significant differences between humans and animals render a good deal of these experiments of dubious value and possibly even dangerous. One scientist concluded:

> [S]ince animal-based research is unable to combat our major health problems and, more dangerously, often diverts attention from the study of humans, the real choice is not between animals and people, rather it is between good science and bad science. In medical research animal experiments are generally bad science because they tell us about animals,

16 https://en.wikipedia.org/wiki/Animal_testing_regulations

17 Directive 2010/63/EU imposes rigorous welfare and ethical standards.

18 Other euphemisms used by experimenters describe animals as being 'dispatched', 'terminated', 'cervically dislocated', 'exsanguinated', 'decapitated', or 'put down'. Whole rooms are 'depopulated' or simply 'cleaned'. In a survey of 15 laboratories, the animals themselves were routinely reified as 'controls', 'recipients', 'donors', 'carriers', 'bleeders', and so on, A Arluke, 'Trapped in a Guilt Cage' (1992) *New Scientist*, 4 April, 33, 35.

19 Rosemary Rodd, *Biology, Ethics, and Animals* (Oxford: Clarendon Press, 1990), 145. But in extreme cases certain 'experiments' cause significantly greater suffering to individual animals than is the result of meat-eating.

20 Raymond, Wacks, 'Sacrificed for Science: Are Animal Experiments Morally Defensible?' in Gerhold K Becker, ed in association with James P Buchanan, *Changing Nature's Course: The Ethical Challenge of Biotechnology* (Hong Kong: Hong Kong University Press, 1996).

21 It was recently revealed that numerous macaque monkeys were being flown into Manchester from breeding facilities in Mauritius and Vietnam. Some are kept in holding facilities in Barcelona and then tend to be flown into Manchester from Barcelona and Paris. There they are allegedly sent to laboratories where they become subjects of various experiments. The monkey awaiting transport to a laboratory pictured on the cover of the paperback edition of this book is one of them. https://manchestermill.co.uk/p/the-secret-flights-manchester-animal-testing

> usually under artificial conditions, when we really need to know about people.[19]

Whatever the benefits of animal experiments, unless one is to adopt a strict utilitarian position (which I consider in Chapter 6), the pain and distress it causes to its victims call for some justification. Peter Singer famously does so from an act-utilitarian standpoint. His central argument is that in calculating the consequences of our actions, the pain suffered or pleasure enjoyed by animals counts no less than our own. To regard their experience is in some way inferior to ours is 'speciesism'. Animals have moral worth; their lives are not simply expendable or to be exploited for our own ends. Singer does not claim that the lives of humans and animals have equal worth or that they call for identical treatment—except in respect of the capacity to experience pleasure and pain. Animals need not be *treated* equally, but they are entitled to equal *consideration.*

Thus, he asserts, animal experiments are justifiable, provided their pain is restricted to a minimum, and the research is highly likely to produce aggregate benefits outweighing individual suffering. His test is whether it would be morally acceptable to perform such experiments on mentally retarded human orphans.[22] If not, it would be 'speciesist' to inflict pain on animals of similar intelligence.[23]

Singer's illustrious utilitarian antecedent, Jeremy Bentham, generally assumed that any form of animal use that increases human welfare is permissible, as long as it is not wanton. This is a position that he held consistently throughout his life, as demonstrated by a letter written in 1825 to the editor of the *Morning Chronicle*, a newspaper known for its stinging criticisms of animal welfare legislation:

> Sir—I never have seen, nor ever can see, any objection to the putting of dogs and other inferior animals to pain, in the way of medical experiment, when that experiment has a determinate object, beneficial to mankind, accompanied with a fair prospect of the accomplishment of it. But I have a decided and insuperable objection to the putting of them to pain without any such view.[24]

22 Peter Singer, *Practical Ethics* (Cambridge: Cambridge University Press, 1979). For a similar argument from pain and suffering see Stephen RL Clarke, *The Moral Status of Animals* (Oxford: Clarendon Press, 1977).

23 'The laudatory achievements of science, including the many genuine benefits obtained for both humans and animals, do not justify the unjust means used to secure them. . . (T)he rights view does not call for the cessation of scientific research. Such research should go on—but not at the expense of laboratory animals', Tom Regan, *The Case for Animal Rights* (London: Routledge, 1984), 397.

24 Quoted by Johannes Kniess, 'Bentham on Animal Welfare' (2019) 27 *British Journal for the History of Philosophy* 556, 560.

Act-utilitarianism (considered in Chapter 6) does not, however, lead ineluctably to an anti-animal posture. RG Frey, for example, argues that in the case of painful experiments on animals, to rely upon the appeal to benefit to justify such practices, requires some reason which demonstrates that we are not morally entitled to do to humans what we do in our laboratories to animals. And he is unable to discover any argument to support the proposition that, no matter how low its quality, a human life is more valuable than an animal life:

> I myself have and know nothing with which to satisfy this need (for such an argument); that is, I have and know nothing which enables me to say, a priori, that a human life of any quality, however low, is more valuable than an animal life of any quality, however high. Perhaps some readers think that they can satisfy this need: I am receptive to suggestions.[25]

As am I.

Many experiments on animals are unnecessary. Alternatives often exist. The use of tissue culture, *in vitro* methods, mathematical and chemical modelling, computer simulation, and human volunteers is not uncommon, but is far from being generally accepted, even though the 'number of major contributions that replacement techniques have made to Nobel Prize-winning research is astonishing'.[26] Inadequate funding for alternative methods and researchers' hostility have, at least in the past, conspired against what is misleadingly and unfairly described as the 'anti-science' posture of advocates of animal welfare. Cruelty aside, in today's world of advanced technology, the whole process seems anachronistic. One hopes that the Nobel laureate in medicine and physiology, Sir Peter Medawar, was correct when he declared in 1972: 'the use of experimental animals on the present scale is a temporary episode in biological and medical history'.[27] There is no escape from a simple fact:

> The use of animals in laboratory research and experiments that are painful, invasive, or fatal is unjustifiable, and even barbaric. It is an obvious case of treating animals as mere means to our ends, as well as being

25 RG Frey, *Rights, Killing, and Suffering* (Oxford: Basil Blackwell, 1983), 115.

26 M Stephens, 'Replacing Animal Experiments' in G Langley, ed, *Animal Experimentation: The Consensus Changes*, (Basingstoke: Macmillan, 1989) 111. He quotes (at 88) Professor Sir George Pickering, former Professor of Medicine at Oxford who in 1964 wrote: 'The idea, as I understand it, is that fundamental truths are revealed in laboratory experiments on lower animals and are then applied to the problems of the sick patient. Having been myself trained as a physiologist I feel in a way competent to assess such a claim. It is plain nonsense', George Pickering, 'Physician and Scientist (1964) 2 *British Medical Journal*. 1615. See too Aysha Akhtar, 'The Flaws and Human Harms of Animal Experimentation' (2015) 24 *Cambridge Quarterly of Healthcare Ethics* 407.

27 Quoted by M Stephens, 'Replacing Animal Experiments' in G Langley, ed, *Animal Experimentation: The Consensus Changes* (Basingstoke: Macmillan, 1989), 165.

> immeasurably cruel. We do not have the right to treat our fellow creatures in this way ... Don't ask yourself whether you think it is worth it to torture and kill animals to save human lives. Ask yourself whether you think it is worth it to torture and kill animals to *extend* human lives.[28]

As mentioned, legislation to control and regulate the use of animals for experiments exists in a number of countries.[29] The Nuffield Council on Bioethics, an independent body in the United Kingdom, published in 2005 report entitled *The Ethics of Research Involving Animals* which examines the arguments regarding whether animal research yields useful results. It recommends that its predictability and transferability should be evaluated more comprehensively, especially in controversial areas. Frequently encountered ethical questions are considered in seeking to understand what the basis of the disagreements in respect of the moral justification of animal research. Its central proposal is the adoption of the 3Rs: refinement, reduction, and replacement: replacing animal research with non-animal methods, reducing the numbers of animals, and refining experiments to reduce harms and improve welfare—as the guiding principles regulating animal research.[30]

Recently, slightly more far-reaching principles have been formulated which specify the following six principles.[31] The first are 'Principles of Social Benefit' where these benefits are medical and related to health:

1 The Principle of No Alternative Method.
2 The Principle of Expected Net Benefit (to human beings).
3 The Principle of Sufficient Value to Justify Harm (to animals).

These principles require that animal research be done only when there's no alternative to using animals. Furthermore, since animal research sometimes misleads in many ways, resulting in harms to humans, the research must be expected adequately to benefit human beings. Moreover, these benefits must

28 Christine M Korsgaard, *Fellow Creatures: Our Obligations to the Other Animals* (Oxford: Oxford University Press, 2018), 228, 230. Stress supplied. See too Sue Donaldson and Will Kymlicka, *Zoopolis: A Political Theory of Animal Rights* (Oxford: Oxford University Press, 2011), 43.

29 The U.S.' Animal Welfare Act of 1966 (amended eight times between 1970 and 2013) is not intended to control research, but the amendment in 1985 requires the establishment of Animal Care and Use Committees at institutions where experiments are conducted. For a useful summary of the controls, see J Hampson, quoted in Gill Langley, ed, *Animal Experimentation: The Consensus Changes* (London: Palgrave Macmillan, 1989), 229–240.

30 Nuffield Council on Bioethics (2005) http://www.nuffieldbioethics.org/assets/pdfs/The-ethics-of-research-involving-animals-full-report.pdf

31 Tom L Beauchamp and David DeGrazia, *Principles of Animal Research Ethics* (New York: Oxford University Press, 2020).

be significant enough to justify harming animals. The second group of principles is called 'Principles of Animal Welfare':

1 The Principle of No Unnecessary Harm.
2 The Principle of Basic Needs (of animals must be met).
3 The Principle of Upper Limits to Harm.

The United Kingdom's Animals (Scientific Procedures) Act 1986 (amended in 2012) establishes an elaborate system of licensing and inspection operated by a government department. In particular, it requires researchers to demonstrate that the potential results of their experiments are sufficiently significant to justify the use of animals, that their proposed research could not be done without live animals, and that the minimum number of animals will be used.[32]

Legislation plainly cannot stand on its own. Even if enforced, it needs to be buttressed by a programme of education and a consciousness of and support for its moral purpose. Without the endorsement and commitment of government and researchers, it is likely to have only limited effect. There are a number of fundamental practical changes that need to take place in the approach to animal experiments. Firstly, ethical committees (whose members are not confined to scientists) are essential; in particular, since the central criterion of acceptability is (or ought to be) the 'benefits' of the proposed experiment, those who will allegedly enjoy the principal advantages of the research ought to be involved in determining the meaning of what often looks like a precarious weasel-word. Secondly, it is vital that the public (whose taxes tend to support such scientific ends) have access to information on experiments. Participation in ethical committees would assist, but there is plainly a requirement for comprehensible accounts of the nature, purpose, and controls exercised over experiments. Thirdly, a good deal of repetition, pain, and pointless experiments could be avoided if experimenters included in their published papers details of alternatives to the use of animals in the particular experiment, the adverse effects associated with certain procedures, special signs of suffering, results of early failures (to prevent other scientists from repeating them), and painkillers used.

Recreational hunting

Killing animals for sport barely raises an eyebrow in most countries. In the United States, it is estimated that more than 100 million animals die each year at the hands of hunters. Accurate statistics for the world are not easy to

32 Researchers often raise what seems a genuine point about the difficulty of predicting (and hence specifying, as required by Section 5 of the Act) the value of many proposed research projects. The evidence is fairly strong that a high proportion of experiments (41 per cent in one survey) bears 'no relation whatever to the disease that it later helped to prevent, diagnose, treat or alleviate', Julius Comroe and Robert Dripps, quoted by Michael Allen Fox, *The Case for Animal Experimentation* (London: University of California Press, 1986), 140.

obtain, though it is perhaps in the region of at least thrice that figure.[33] In the European Union, more than 52 million wild birds are legally shot by hunters. This includes several severely endangered species such as migratory birds. In Germany, for example, hundreds of thousands of protected lapwings, snipes, turtle doves, and skylarks are shot in France and southern Europe on their way to wintering grounds in the autumn. Every year German and British hunters kill many thousands of woodcocks and Arctic geese from Scandinavia and Eastern Europe.[34]

Hunters inflict pain and suffering on animals who are not adapted to defend themselves against bullets, traps, and other cruel killing devices. Hunting destroys animal families and habitats, and often leaves abandon young, dependent animals behind to starve to death. When I confront hunters with these facts, they insist that they kill only large males, or that any wounded creatures are swiftly despatched. One, however, a seasoned wild boar hunter, grew so repelled by the injuries sustained by his prey and the dogs that harass the quarry that he gave up the 'sport', telling me that it was an odious and barbaric activity.

While many other creatures are hunted in the United Kingdom, the question of fox hunting is emblematic of the impassioned debate is a major political matter. Fox hunting was banned by the Hunting Act 2004 in England and Wales, and the Protection of Wild Mammals (Scotland) Act 2002 in Scotland. But there is compelling evidence to suggest that the legislation is flouted. In England and Wales 'trail hunting' was devised as an alternative to the killing of foxes. The hunt follows a pre-laid trail rather than searching for and chasing the animal. Again, there is considerable evidence to confirm that this is being used as a ploy to conceal unlawful fox hunting. Prior to the passage of these statutes, the Burns report in 2000 suggested that registered hunts had killed between 21,000 and 25,000 foxes each year.[35] While opinion polls show an overwhelming majority against fox hunting, the subject is unlikely to fade from the manifestos of political parties.

33 'With an arsenal of rifles, shotguns, muzzleloaders, handguns, bows and arrows, hunters kill more than 200 million animals yearly—and likely crippling, orphaning, and harassing millions more. The annual death toll in the US includes 42 million mourning doves, 30 million squirrels, 28 million quail, 25 million rabbits, 20 million pheasants, 14 million ducks, 6 million deer, and thousands of geese, bears, moose, elk, antelope, swans, cougars, turkeys, wolves, foxes, coyotes, bobcats, boars, and other woodland inhabitants. Hunters also frequently use food and electronic callers to lure unsuspecting animals in front of their weapons. The truth is, the animal, no matter how well-adapted to escaping natural predators she or he may be, has virtually no way to escape death once he or she is in the cross hairs of a scope mounted on a rifle or a crossbow', https://www.idausa.org/campaign/wild-animals-and-habitats/hunting/

34 Committee Against Bird Slaughter (CABS) https://www.komitee.de/en/campaigns-and-operations/

35 *Report of the Committee of Inquiry into Hunting with Dogs in England and Wales*, HMSO, 9 June 2000.

The activity is fiercely championed, not only by its practitioners but also by many who regard it as a noble rural tradition. To investigate this claim I shall test the argument postulated by the late Roger Scruton, a philosopher I have long admired. His defence is among the most elegant and beguiling. Describing his love for the 'sport of kings', he depicts it as an essential feature of English country life.[36] He portrays its beauty, its contribution to the preservation of the countryside, and the social equality it sustains. There is, however, little compassion for the quarry to which he contends the hunter adopts a 'quasi-religious attitude':

> The hunted animal is hunted as an individual. But the hunted species is elevated to divine status as the totem, and a kind of mystical union of the tribe with its totem seals the pact between them for ever ... For the brief moment of the chase [the fox] is an individual ... Once killed, however, he returns to his archetypal condition, reassuming his nature as The Fox, whom the huntsman knows and loves, and whose eternal recurrence is his deep desire.[37]

It may seem somewhat incongruous to love a creature whose violent death you ardently pursue. But, in lyrical prose, he declares that to relate to animals 'as wild things' we must see them 'as we see nature when the divine idea shines through to us', and this is never more likely to happen than when hunting amid the herd and the pack, on the lively scent of a fox who streams through the hedgerows, staking out the landscape with a matrix of primeval desire'.[38] He describes too the love between huntsman and the animals—horses and hounds—that are accessories in the chase.

The terror, distress, and killing of the fox are, of course, secondary to the claimed virtues of the activity. But, for Scruton, animals have neither rights nor duties. If they did, 'lions would be murderers, cuckoos usurpers, mice burglars, and magpies thieves'. Moreover, the fox would be the worst of criminals worthy of the death penalty because they kill not only for food, 'but with a wanton appetite for death and destruction ... [T]o treat animals as moral beings is to mistreat them – it is to make demands which they could not satisfy, since they cannot understand them as demands'.[39] It does not follow, however, that we have a licence to treat animals as we wish:

> When a beaten fox, driven from covert into the open, sees that he cannot cross to safety and so turns back to his death, his despairing movements

36 Roger Scruton, *On Hunting* (London: Yellow Jersey Press, 1998).
37 Op cit, 75–76.
38 Op cit, 79.
39 Op cit, 132.

are utterly pitiable. His eyes are no longer alert, his crafty expression has vanished ... In that moment the individual is all: for unlike the species he must die. If you could save him you would.[40] But he will not be saved because 'the pleasure of hunting comes in spite of death, and not because of it'.[41]

Scruton's spirited defence is largely, and unashamedly, humancentric[42]; his genuine love of hunting is almost palpable. But, in seeking to justify the practice, he commits at least four unexpected and uncharacteristic, fallacies. Firstly, he rightly condemns trophy hunters and the cruelty of fishing and factory farming; he does so in order to demonstrate that, unlike these activities, the hunted fox is 'given a chance' to escape his fate. To justify X by asserting that Y is worse is the logical fallacy of relative privation. It is, of course, true that there is no shortage of practices that cause animals pain, suffering, and death. It is also true that shooting a lion from the safety of a vehicle 'and to gloat in triumph as the victim drops to the ground in agony'[43] is repugnant, but does the fox really have a fair prospect to escape his killing when pursued by a pack of crazed dogs and a group of fervent hunters on excited horses?

Secondly, he says hunting 'awakens a lively and unsentimental sympathy for animal, of a kind unknown to the lover of pets'.[44] Are all pet lovers really incapable of an unsentimental attitude towards their animals? Here he seems to commit the informal fallacy of hasty generalisation. Thirdly, he asserts that 'the fox will gain nothing from the abolition of hunting ... [which] *might* offer the fox the best form of coexistence with humans who have no other motive to protect him or to conserve his habitat ... [and] hunting discriminates against the old and diseased. For it is not easy to catch a healthy fox ...'[45] This is surely mere speculation, and the 'might' is an appeal to probability: the logical fallacy of assuming the truth of a proposition because it might possibly be the case: *possibiliter ergo probabiliter*. Fourthly, he declares that apart from hunting the fox, 'humans ... have no other motive to protect him or to conserve his habitat'.[46] This is far from uncontentious, and surprisingly constitutes the logical fallacy of *ipse dixit*: an assertion lacking proof.

40 Op cit, 132–133.
41 Op cit, 137.
42 Hunting with hounds 'is the beginning of a new relation to the natural world: the relation which stems from our role as dominant species, able to conscript other species to our purposes, and to exploit their instincts', 75.
43 Op cit, 138. More than 125,000 animals are killed annually by trophy hunters. It is argued that trophy hunting is saving various species in Africa.
44 Op cit, 83.
45 Op cit, 134–135. Stress supplied.
46 Op cit, 135.

The related question of poaching, especially of elephants for their tusks and rhinos for their horns often overlooks the corruption involved.[47] It hardly requires stating that once corruption infiltrates the judiciary, the rule of law, the administration of justice, and the prospect of a fair trial are severely undermined.[48] The bribing of judicial officers is far from uncommon in many jurisdictions; nor is political corruption. Interventions may be violent, principally when committed by members of organised crime. But judicial corruption is a particularly pernicious phenomenon. Moreover, when judges and magistrates, the very apotheosis of justice and the rule of law are corrupt, anti-corruption strategies are deprived of the tools to increase the risks and reduce the benefits of corruption and to penalise corrupt acts:

> The resulting distortions, including the impunity of corrupt individuals, undermine the rule of law, foster public cynicism about the integrity of government, and thus impair essential capacities for sound economic, social and political development. Conversely, strengthening judicial integrity and related capacities to combat corruption can have enormous benefits.[49]

Beasts of burden

'Working animals', a term that camouflages numerous forms of exploitation and abuse, have long been a feature of human society. Horses, donkeys, mules, oxen and buffaloes, camels, llamas, yaks and elephants are among the

47 Some 35,000 elephants are killed in Botswana alone per year. 'Poachers masquerading as rangers, magistrates allegedly taking bribes from kingpins and lenient sentences handed out to ruthless criminals - this is the current state of South Africa's rhino crisis, according to campaigners'. The *Independent* was told 'For the last decade corruption has been driving rhinos into extinction, and it's just getting worse. The kingpins call the shots; we run the intel, they get arrested, but then they always get bail and never go to jail'. The kingpins were able to 'rule' because of the 'dirty officers and magistrates on their payroll'. South Africa is home to 80 per cent of Africa's rhino population, but there are only some 25,000 left, and roughly a thousand are killed every year for their horns. *The Independent*, 17 June 2021 Poachers, corruption and cash: Inside South Africa's new rhino crisis, | The Independent

48 See G Brooks, 'Judicial Corruption: Magistrates, Judges and Prosecutors' in *Criminal Justice and Corruption: State Power, Privatization and Legitimacy* (London, Palgrave Macmillan, 2019).

49 The USAID Program Brief, *Reducing Corruption in the Judiciary*, Office of Democracy and Governance, 2009, available at https://pdf.usaid.gov/pdf_docs/Pnadq106.pdf. Rescuing the rule of law from the clutches of corrupt judges poses the awkward problem of avoiding interference with judicial independence while investigating the suspects. There are no simple solutions. A number of obvious measures could reduce judicial sleaze including education, increased transparency of the court process, fair conditions of employment for judges and court workers, public information campaigns highlighting the problem of corruption, and the enactment and application of anti-corruption norms and regulations. These need to be accompanied by the dismissal of judges found to have accepted bribes or who are guilty of other forms of corruption. The creation of an independent body to monitor judicial conduct is plainly a necessary weapon in the campaign. See Raymond Wacks, *The Rule of Law Under Fire?* (Oxford: Hart Publishing, 2021), Ch 20.

most visible members of the workforce of approximately 300 million animals across the globe. Canines are employed as sniffer dogs to detect, for example, drugs or land mines, as guide dogs, guard dogs, and rescue dogs. Donkeys, whose numbers continue to rise, account for approximately 42 million, are especially prone to cruelty and maltreatment, accounting for the many sanctuaries that rescue sick and injured creatures.[50] Their circumstances often include long hours with little rest, being kept in poor conditions, underfed, badly shod, enduring lameness, ill-fitting harnesses, saddles and yokes, being kept tethered or hobbled, carrying or pulling excessively heavy loads, inhumane training methods, lack of shade, water, cruel handling, and lack of veterinary care.

They are frequently forced to undertake labour that strains their small bodies to breaking point. They are cheap to buy and are therefore treated poorly. Since a new donkey is often less expensive than the cost of veterinary care, sick or injured donkeys are often tied to posts without food or water and left to die. It is common for stray donkeys to be abused for fun. In Spain and Greece, for example they are employed as 'donkey taxis'; they are exposed to high temperatures with little or no shelter, food, or water and are repeatedly required to carry overweight humans. At night, they typically have their feet tied together to prevent them from escaping their suffering. Nor is it uncommon to find pet donkeys left to fend for themselves in backyards. They are regularly found with deformed and crippled feet as a result of laminitis, emaciated bodies from parasite infestation, dental problems, or lack of food. Other pet donkeys are overfed and suffer from severe obesity.

Their property status is epitomised by their disposal—when they grow too old, exhausted, or infirm to continue working; in Greece they are thrown from mountain tops. One need only look at the many images online of these emaciated creatures to apprehend the extent of their distress.

The so-called working animals bear this exploitation with fortitude; they are long-suffering and characteristically 'patient, submissive, and meek'.[51] And yet, unlike human workers, they are afforded no labour rights, a deficit

50 In the United Kingdom, for example, the Donkey Sanctuary has grown from a charity rescuing donkeys from neglect and abuse to an international animal welfare organisation with ten sanctuaries across the country that provide lifelong care to over 7,000 donkeys and mules. It reaches some 1.8 million donkeys and mules through its work in 35 countries: https://www.thedonkeysanctuary.org.uk/ See too World Animal Net www.worldanimal.net/

51 These words attract quotation marks as they are a translation of the renowned South African poet, Jan FE Cilliers' (1865–1940) poem, 'Die Ossewa' (The Ox Wagon) which eloquently captures, in the phrase 'geduldig, gedienstig, gedwee', the compliant character of these beasts as they drag the huge wagons, the yokes pressing on their shoulders, on the trek across the inhospitable country in the burning heat. The poem ends, 'and the bones of their weary legs will eventually lie far away buried in the veld'. I was unsure how best to translate 'gedwee', but I could not have asked for a better authority than the Nobel laureate, JM Coetzee, who helpfully suggested 'meek' which, he revealed to me, is how the word is rendered in the Afrikaans version of the Sermon on the Mount. My thanks to him.

that necessitates change that could entail that animal workers are guaranteed essential rights including the 'right to representation by a labour union, the right to a decent standard of remuneration, the right to healthy and safe working conditions, the right to rest and leisure and the right to a decent retirement'.[52]

*

The rest of this book pursues the following route. Chapter 2 explores the leading philosophical, religious, and cultural attitudes whose, often sharply different, conceptions of the moral status of animals continue to pervade contemporary thinking on the subject. Chapters 3 and 4 are devoted to a consideration of the paramount question of animal rights, its supporters, and detractors. Chapter 5 examines the evolving interest in whether human rights might be extended to sentient creatures. At the heart of the consideration of animal welfare is the disagreement between utilitarians and deontologists which is the subject of Chapter 6. A similar divergence exists among devotees of a welfarist approach to animal protection, and those who regard reform as ineffective, and champion the abolitionist cause; each standpoint is explored in Chapter 7 and 8, respectively. A desire to concentrate on the actual factors that contribute to the flourishing of nonhumans drives the capabilities approach that I discuss in Chapter 9. The attempts to base our moral duties to animals on some form of hypothetical contract are the subject of Chapter 10, while I consider the proposal that animals merit membership of the political community in Chapter 11. Chapter 12 moves to an analysis of the legal and constitutional measures that have been enacted to protect animals in a number of jurisdictions. I attempt to draw the threads together in my concluding chapter (Chapter 13), and suggest how animals' lives might best be defended and enhanced.

52 Alisdair Cochrane, 'Labour Rights for Animals' in Robert Garner and Siobhan O'Sullivan, eds, *The Political Turn in Animal Ethics* (Lanham MD: Rowan and Littlefied, 2016), 27. See too Charlotte E Blattner, Kendra Coulter, and Will Kymlicka, eds, *Animal Labour: A New Frontier of Interspecies Justice?* (Oxford: Oxford University Press, 2019); Donaldson and Kymlicka, op cit, Ch 5.

2 Ethical foundations

Our relationship with animals has long been the subject of moral deliberation from a variety of philosophical and religious perspectives, which are expressed in the cultural attitudes and social practices of communities. Western ideas, as articulated especially by Aristotle, have shaped belief systems with important consequences for nonhuman creatures. Non-Western philosophy and religions, most strikingly, Jainism, Hinduism, and Buddhism, represent a markedly dissimilar outlook regarding our moral obligations to animals.

In this chapter, I offer a brief account of some of the early thinking that has dominated human/animal relations for centuries.[1] My purpose is to demonstrate and, I hope, illuminate, those ideas that continue to permeate much contemporary perceptions and practice. The accounts of more modern thinkers and jurists are, of course, surveyed in later chapters. I resist digging too deeply into the distant historical past where there are, for instance, in the Code of Hammurabi (c 1750 BC) rules concerning the treatment, and more particularly, the liability of animals. Nor do I, explore, except for the most pertinent scriptural injunctions that in any event, infuse modern thinking about our relations with animals.[2]

It seems important to note the distinction between the philosophical ideas whose influence continues to shape current attitudes towards the treatment of animals, on the one hand, and the religious teaching which, in practice, may exert only peripheral authority in the countries where they hold varying degrees of sway, on the other hand. Among the first, one would clearly include especially Immanuel Kant and Jeremy Bentham whose attitudes towards animals will become evident (and which are further discussed in Chapter 6). Any generalised judgement about the influence of religious teaching and doctrine

1 I can here only touch on the major theorists whose influence has been greatest. For a more comprehensive treatment of these thinkers, with generous extracts from their work, including Marx, Machiavelli, Berkeley, Hegel, Herder, Pope, Nietzsche, Fichte, Sidgwick, Horkheimer, Godwin, and several others, see Paul AB Clarke and Andrew Linzey, eds, *Political Theory and Animal Rights* (London: Pluto Press, 1990). Similarly, my account of the religious and cultural approaches is necessarily selective and brief.

2 For a magisterial account from earliest times to the present day, see Stephen M Wise, 'The Legal Thinghood of Nonhuman Animals' (1996) 23 *Environmental Affairs* 471.

DOI: 10.4324/9781032702575-2

that comprise the second category is more complex. Some of these principles are styled 'laws', but this is to exaggerate their authority, at least in most existing societies. Nevertheless, as I shall suggest below, they do encapsulate a number of prevailing approaches to human relations with nonhuman creatures. Certain religious dogma, however, I have placed in the first group. The naturalist philosophy of St Thomas Aquinas, as will become clear in the following section, continues to exert considerable influence with regard to the conceptual framework of the Catholic outlook towards animals.[3] His teachings are further discussed in Chapter 9.

Ancient Greek philosophers used a number of conceptual tools upon which to found their attitude to good conduct. These included the notions of moral (ευδαιμονία) and *ethos* (ἦθος), and *ethics* (δέον). Moral principles were perceived to be either the standard of conduct that individuals have fashioned for themselves, or as the cluster of duties that a society requires of its members. Moral behaviour is required if social groups are to achieve stability. *Ethos* is defined as the character, sentiment, or temperament of a person, community, or institution regarded as a natural endowment; it stimulates manners and customs.

It is Aristotle whose analysis still endures and whose influence on our thinking about the place of nonhumans in society will be evident in the chapters that follow. Following Plato, he considers the ethical virtues (including justice, temperance, and courage) as rational, emotional, and social skills. If we are to live well, we must understand how values such as friendship, pleasure, virtue, wealth, and honour form a coherent whole. By learning general rules, we develop the practical wisdom to behave in the most rational way. We also require emotional and social skills to put into practice our general understanding of wellbeing. Essential to his discussion of virtue is the quest for the 'Golden Mean'. If justice is a virtue, he argues, it must be a kind of mean: a halfway point between two extremes, one of excess and the other of deficiency. So, for example, the virtue of courage, if present in excess, becomes recklessness; and if deficient, it takes the form of cowardice. Our lives are replete with moral dilemmas. But there is no particular imperative that we can apply to them all. Our obligations cannot be frozen in a code that is all-encompassing. This is the core of the 'doctrine of the mean'. Aristotelean virtue ethics thus avoids the inflexible forms of duty embraced by both

3 It is difficult to summarise the attitude of Christianity to animals. Each church adopts a slightly different interpretation of Jesus' compassion towards nonhumans. The creation narrative in Genesis spurns a variety of constructions, none of which seems conclusive. Peter Singer argues that it has provided a justification for the idea that animals exist for human purposes: Peter Singer, *Animal Liberation Now* (New York: Harper Collins, 2023)—a view disputed by, amongst others, Andrew Linzey, *Creatures of the Same God* (Brooklyn, NY: Lantern Books, 2009), Bernard Rollin, *Animal Rights and Human Morality* 3rd edn (Amherst, NY: Prometheus Books, 2006), and Norm Phelps, *Animal Rights According to the Bible* (Brooklyn, NY: Lantern Books, 2002). See too Jonathan M Cahill, 'Grounded in Love: A Theistic Account of Animal Rights' (2016) 6 *Journal of Animal Ethics* 67.

deontologists such as Kant, and consequentialists such as Bentham (discussed in the following section).

Aristotle emphasises the importance of both character and virtue. Character is a state of being. If I am a kind person, I have the right feelings towards others. But our character or inner temperament also influences our deeds. The virtue ethics approach associated with Aristotle looks to the question of what constitutes a good life, and what kind of person we ought to be. In other words, he was more concerned with good action, rather than right action. The purpose, or *telos*, of social and political associations is to promote this good action, and as such, he regarded virtue above any other social distinction or hierarchy, such as wealth or descent:

> Those who contribute most to an association of this character, *i.e.* who contribute most to good action, have a greater share in the polis and should therefore, in justice, receive a larger recognition from it than those who are equal to them (or even greater) in free birth and descent, but unequal in civic excellence, or than those who surpass them in wealth but are, surpassed by them in excellence.[4]

It is only through politics that we achieve and express our complete human nature. We are designed for political engagement since we have the capacity for language which enables us to articulate, debate, and distinguish between good and bad, just and unjust. By exercising these abilities, we learn how to become virtuous: 'Moral excellence comes about as a result of habit. We become just by doing just acts, temperate by doing temperate acts, brave by doing brave acts'.[5]

The subject of slavery is frequently employed as an analogy to the persecution of animals (and is a question considered in later chapters of this book). Opprobrium commonly attaches to Aristotle's justification of slavery as a feature of justice. Modern sensibilities are strongly opposed to this institution, but it was an essential aspect of the Athenian state. Justice, according to Aristotle, is a question of fit: it is about allowing individuals to realise their true nature. In order for slavery to be just, not only must it be necessary, it should also be natural. It is natural because certain individuals are suited by their nature to be slaves. Its necessity comes from the freedom it affords citizens to participate in political life while their slaves attend to menial tasks at home. Where, however, free men have been forced into slavery (in the case, for example, of prisoners of war), their slavery is unjust. Thus, where a slave is not naturally predisposed to his predicament, his master has no right to compel him to continue his enslavement.

4 Aristotle, *Politics*, transl by H Rackham (Cambridge, MA: Harvard University Press, 1950), Book II, Chapter I.

5 Aristotle, *Nichomachean Ethics*, transl by WD Ross (Oxford: Oxford University Press, 1980), Book II, Chapter I.

Aristotle is emphatic that those who are inferior intellectually and morally are appropriately treated as political and social inferiors in a properly ordered *polis*. He argues that certain individuals are naturally superior and therefore fit to rule, while others are naturally inferior and thus suited to be ruled by others. Men, he asserts, are naturally superior to women, and hence more fit to rule. Indeed, it is their own interests that women are controlled by men in the same way that 'natural slaves' are governed by the 'naturally free'. In this respect, his account of justice fails to respect all individuals as rational free agents. By concentrating on the manner in which persons are *un*equal, his theory is difficult to accept in our age of equality and human rights.

In respect of animals, Aristotle recognises a close affinity between us and them, accepting that both have souls. Unlike Plato, however, his conception of a soul is not a discrete spiritual entity that can envisage a higher dominion of transcendent truth, or that can transmigrate from one species to another. Instead, for him the soul is the animating form of a living being or its internal governing principle. An animal's soul constitutes its nature as final cause, guiding it to the ends that it seeks in its life. The soul is therefore a more important gauge of its nature than the matter of which it is made. He imagines an animal's soul as regulating the harmonious operation of its bodily parts. Comparing the animal organism to a well-governed commonwealth, he says that the soul is 'situated in a central origin of authority over the body', with the other parts each living by 'structural attachment' to it and performing their own functions. There is, in other words, a substantial resemblance between humans and animals.[6]

Animals act, he maintains, without mediating rational processes, which can obscure both intention and action. They are moved not by thought but by desire, which may include elements of intellect, imagination, purpose, wish, and appetite. Unlike us, animals act 'by nature and also for a purpose':

> When the desirable result is effected invariably or normally, it is not an incidental or chance occurrence.... It is absurd to suppose that there is no purpose [*heneka*] because in nature we can never detect the moving power in the act of deliberation.[7]

Despite his acknowledgement that animals exist for the use of humans, his theory of *telos* validates the conviction that animals exist for us, and that plants exist for animals. Farmed animals fulfil their *telos* more fully than wild animals. A wild animal may be hunted by humans and be captured or killed, whereas a farmed animal has its whole life humanly ordered. In

6 David Grumett, 'Aristotle's Ethics and Farm Animal Welfare' (2019) 32 *Journal of Agricultural and Environmental Ethics* 321. I draw on this helpful essay here.

7 Aristotle, *Physics*, transl by PH Wicksteed and FM Cornford (Volume 2) (London: Heinemann, 1929–1934), 2.8, 199b24–27.

the same way that the soul directs the body, and reason governs passion, so animals should be governed by humans. There is, in other words, a *scala naturae* according to which, no justification is required for our superiority over animals.

Aristotle famously defined the good of a thing as that at which it aims.[8] This aim, and its associated good, is a consequence of function, which, in the case of farmed species is, in its most general terms, sentient life.[9] This life is ruled by the soul's vegetative faculty which nourishes its body and thereby contributes to the excellence with which it fulfils its function.[10] A living being enjoys a good life when it is possible to adopt a perspective extending across its whole lifespan[11]:

> From this it follows that only at the end of its life, whether this is a result of slaughter or humane killing, may an animal be said to have lived a good life. Aristotle develops a rich understanding of goodness, including animal purpose and the value added by husbandry that has the potential to inform the concept of a good life currently used in animal welfare.[12]

The Romans were not renowned for evincing compassion towards animals, indeed the influence of Roman law was paramount in advancing the conception of animals as property—I discuss this factor in Chapter 4. The rise of Christianity was little different; with the conspicuous exception of St Francis of Assisi, the patron saint of animals, the received wisdom was resolutely anthropomorphic. Aristotelean ethical theory strongly influenced the authoritative influential teachings of the Dominican, St Thomas Aquinas, whose main work *Summa Theologiae* contains the most comprehensive statement of Christian doctrine on the subject.[13] The thirteenth century witnessed the development of European city-states. The Pope's authority over these states was hampered through want of a theological stance in respect of the exercise of secular power. Previously, the foremost Christian thinker of the day, St Augustine, had merely endorsed the biblical exhortation to 'render ... unto Caesar the things which are Caesar's'. But Aquinas deployed Aristotle's philosophy in an effort to reconcile secular and Christian authority. He argued that Christianity was a stage in the development of humanity that was unavailable to the Greeks. The *polis* in which we were destined to live was therefore Christian.

8 Aristotle, *Nichomachean Ethics*, 1.1, 1094a1–3.
9 Op cit, 1.7, 1098a2–4.
10 Op cit, 1.13, 1102a34–b12.
11 Op cit, 1.7, 1098a18–19.
12 David Grumett, op cit, 328.
13 See John Finnis, *Aquinas: Moral, Political, and Legal Theory* (Oxford: Oxford University Press, 1998); Sean Coyle, 'Natural Law in Aquinas and Suarez' (2017) 8 *Jurisprudence* 319.

For Aquinas, natural law is merely one element of divine providence: it is a 'participation' in the eternal law—the rational plan that orders all creation. In other words, it is the means by which rational beings participate in the eternal law. Secondly, when human beings 'receive' natural law, its content comprises the principles of practical rationality by which human action is to be judged as either reasonable or unreasonable. Indeed, for Aquinas it is this characteristic of natural law that justifies its description as 'law', for law, he claims, consists in rules of action declared by one who protects the interests of the community: since God defends and protects the universe, His decision to create rational beings with the capacity to act freely in accordance with reason entitles entitles us to regard these principles as constituting 'law'.[14]

The tenets of natural law are binding on us, Aquinas contends, because—as rational beings—we are guided towards them by nature; they point us towards the good, as well as certain specific goods. Moreover, these principles are known to us by virtue of our nature: we demonstrate this knowledge in our inherent aspiration to achieve the various goods that natural law exhorts us to pursue. We are able to discern the essence of practical knowledge, though the precise practical consequences of that understanding may often be difficult to determine. And, Aquinas acknowledges, our passion or malevolence may obstruct their application. At the heart of Aquinas's elucidation of natural law is the elementary idea that good be done and evil avoided. Given his theological context of objective moral truth, Aquinas contends that we have a continuing duty to seek the good. We know intuitively what constitutes the good: it includes life, knowledge, procreation, society, and reasonable conduct. For him the good is prior to the right. Whether an act is right is less important than whether it achieves or is some good. We are, he suggests, capable of reasoning from these principles about goods to practical means by which to realise these goods.

The status of animals in his ethical schema, however, is unequivocally subordinated to the interests of humans. They are not 'rational creatures':

> There is no sin in using a thing for the purpose for which it is.... Hence it is that just as in the generation of a man there is first a living thing, then an animal, and lastly a man, so too things, like the plants, which merely have life, are all alike for animals, and all animals are for man. Wherefore it is not unlawful if man use plants for the good of animals, and animals for the good of man, as the Philosopher [Aristotle] states.[15] Now the most necessary use would seem to consist in the fact that animals use plants, and men use animals, for food,

14 In Chapter 5, I examine the broader question of natural rights, and revisit the Thomist tradition and its relevance to human rights and their possible extension to animals.

15 Aristotle, *Politics*, I, 3.

> and this cannot be done unless these be deprived of life: wherefore it is lawful both to take life from plants for the use of animals, and from animals for the use of men.... [T]his is in keeping with the commandment of God Himself: for it is written[16]: 'Behold I have given you every herb ... and all trees ... to be your meat, and to all beasts of the earth': and again[17]: 'Everything that moveth and liveth shall be meat to you.' According to the Divine ordinance the life of animals and plants is preserved not for themselves but for man.... Dumb animals and plants are devoid of the life of reason whereby to set themselves in motion; they are moved, as it were by another, by a kind of natural impulse, a sign of which is that they are naturally enslaved and accommodated to the uses of others.[18]

In short, being kind or sympathetic to animals is justified merely because cruelty towards them may induce humans to be unkind to each other. Aquinas defends hunting as just and natural; animals are our property: we have unrestricted dominion over them. He also dismisses the possibility of friendship with 'irrational creatures'; they have no fellowship with rational humans, but we can love them out of charity if we consider them as the good things that we desire for others, and for our own use.[19]

In the modern period, the most extreme human-centric position was adopted by René Descartes who notoriously pronounced animals as being nothing more than automata, machines. Since they lacked a rational soul, they could not be self-conscious beings. They may cry in pain when violently attacked, but it does not follow that they are experiencing pain. They may be more complex mechanisms than a clock, but that is only because they were manufactured by God rather than by humans.[20] This callous disregard for animal suffering facilitated or even encouraged, Peter Singer observes, the widespread practice in Europe of vivisection, allowing 'the experimenters to dismiss any qualms they might feel' and this Cartesian insouciance is evident

16 *Genesis* 1:29–30.

17 *Genesis* 9:3.

18 Aquinas, 'Summa Theologica' in *The Summa Theologica of St Thomas Aquinas*, 2nd edn (London: Burns, Oates and Washbourne, 1922) Question 96.

19 Aquinas, 'Summa Theologica' in *The Summa Theologica of St Thomas Aquinas* (New York: Benziger Bros, 1918) Part 1, Questions 64.1 and 65.3. Similarly, St Augustine justifies the killing of animals on the ground that they 'have no rational association' with us, and hence any moral relationship with them is impossible. St Augustine, *The City of God*, transl by M Dods (Edinburgh: TT Clark, 1877) Book I, 31.

20 René Descartes, *Discourse on Method*, transl by J Veitch (Assam: East India Publishing Company, 2021), Volume 5. Leibniz took issue with the question of animal souls, '[It] may be said that not only the soul (the mirror of an indestructible universe) is indestructible, but also the animal itself is indestructible, though its mechanism may often perish in part and take off or put on an organic slough', GW Leibniz, *A Treatise of Human Nature* (Oxford: Clarendon Press, 1888), Book I, 176.

in an account of activities at the Jansenist seminary of Port Royal in the late seventeenth century:

> They administered beatings to dogs with perfect indifference, and made fun of those who pitied the creatures as if they felt pain. They said the animals were clocks, that the cries they emitted when struck were only the noise of a little spring that had been touched, but that the whole body was without feeling. They nailed poor animals up on boards by their four paws to vivisect them and see the circulation of blood which was a great subject of conversation.[21]

The Aristotelian–Thomist view was, however, not without its critics. The Enlightenment engendered a degree of empathy for creatures, notably in the writing of David Hume who contended that 'beasts are endow'd with thought and reason as well as man'.[22] And both Thomas Hobbes[23] and John Locke[24] cleave, to a greater or lesser extent, to the same standpoint.

Hobbes claims that every act we perform, though ostensibly kind or altruistic, is actually self-serving. My compassion is simply an enactment of my power. Any account of human action, including morality, must acknowledge our fundamental self-interest. In *Leviathan*, he reflects on how we might behave in a state of nature, before the formation of any government. He recognises that we are essentially equal, mentally and physically: even the weakest has the strength to kill the strongest. But this equality, he submits, spawns disagreement. And we tend to disagree for three main reasons: competition (for limited supplies of material possessions), distrust, and glory (we remain hostile in order to preserve our powerful reputations). As a consequence of our inclination towards discord, Hobbes concludes that we are in a natural state of perpetual war of all against all, where no morality exists, and all live in constant fear:

> In such condition, there is no place for industry, because the fruit thereof is uncertain; and consequently no culture of the earth, no navigation, nor use of the commodities that may be imported by sea; no

21 Nicholas Fontaine, *Memoires pour server A l'histoire de Port-Royal*, Volume 2 (Cologne, 1738), 52–53, quoted in L Rosenfield, *From Beast-Machine to Man-Machine: The Theme of Animal Souls in French Letters from Descartes to La Metttrie* (New York: Oxford University Press, 1940). Quoted by Peter Singer, *Animal Liberation Now* (New York: Harper Collins, 2023), 228, 333.

22 David Hume, *A Treatise of Human Nature* (Oxford: Clarendon Press, 1888), Book I, 176.

23 Thomas Hobbes, '*De Cive*' in William Molesworth, ed, *The English Works of Thomas Hobbes of Malmesbury* (London: John Bohn, 1841), Volume 2, 63–75.

24 Locke asserts that no-one has the freedom to 'to destroy himself, or so much as any creature in his possession' unless 'some nobler use, than its bare preservation calls for it', John Locke, *The Second Treatise of Government* in *John Locke: Two Treatises of Government,* Peter Laslett, ed (Cambridge: Cambridge University Press, 1988), 270–271.

> commodious building, no instruments of moving and removing such things as require much force; no knowledge of the face of the earth, no account of time, no arts, no letters, no society; and which is worst of all, continual fear and danger of violent death; and the life of people, solitary, poor, nasty, brutish, and short.

The social contract is therefore required by which we surrender our natural freedom in order to create an orderly society. But such a contract with animals is impossible hence we can have no duties towards them:

> [O]ur dominion thereof over beasts, hath its original [*sic*] from the right of nature, not from divine positive right. For if such a right had not been before the publishing of the Sacred Scriptures, no man by right might have killed a beast for his food, but he to whom the divine pleasure was made manifest by holy writ; a most hard condition for men indeed, whom the beasts might devour without injury, and yet they might not destroy them. Forasmuch therefore as it proceeds from the right of nature, that a beast may kill a man, it is also by the same right that a man may slay a beast.[25]

Locke argues that the social contract suffers from an important flaw: in this state of nature property was inadequately protected. For Locke, therefore (especially in *Two Treatises of Civil Government*), in order to rectify this defect in an otherwise idyllic natural state that man forfeited, under a social contract, some of his freedom. Strongly suggestive of Aquinas's central postulates, Locke's theory rests on an account of man's rights and obligations under God. He thus regards the treatment of animals as ordained by God:

> God's super-eminent superiority gave Him a right over everything. It followed that His inferiors enjoyed a right only in terms of the aspect and extent granted by Him.... [M]ankind enjoyed a right to the earth and its creatures because God decided it was so.... On this basis, then, rights would be grants made from God.[26]

Rare glimmers of sympathy for the plight of animals manifest themselves in some of the works of Rousseau[27] and Voltaire.[28]

It is, however, Immanuel Kant whose instrumental view of animals (to which I return in Chapter 6) constitutes a repudiation of the view that animals are owed direct moral duties. For Kant, justice is intimately bound up with duty. To

25 Op cit, 113–114.
26 Op cit, 246.
27 Jean-Jacques Rousseau, 'Second Discourse' in *The Social Contract and Discourses* (London: Dent, 1913), 178–180.
28 Voltaire 'Betes' in *Dictionnaire Philosophique* (Wentworth Press, 2019).

say that we have duties of justice to other persons is to say that they have rights against us. Basing justice on duty means that Kant regards what is right as independent of what we consider to be good. Justice requires respect for the right, regardless of difficult circumstances and desirable and undesirable consequences. Persons have the right to be respected as individuals—as ends in themselves. The priority of right, according to Kant, arises from the freedom that individuals have in their relations between each other; it has nothing to do with achieving happiness. Justice and right come before all other values because they stem from the idea of freedom which, in turn, is a prerequisite of all human ends.

The categorical imperative is the mainspring of his conception of moral duty owed by rational beings. I discuss this concept in greater detail in Chapter 3; suffice it here to say that it stimulates us to act for the sake of an act itself: 'Act only according to that maxim whereby you can at the same time will that it should become a universal law'. In other words, act as if your values should apply to all. It is its second iteration that commentators have suggested may be construed to apply to animals: 'So act that you use humanity, in your own person as well as in the person of any other, always at the same time as an end, never merely as a means'.

But his preoccupation with acting morally does not, however, lead him to extend kindness to non-rational beings. That is because:

> Beings the existence of which rests not on our will but on nature, if they are beings without reason, have only a relative worth, as means, and are therefore called *things*, whereas rational beings are called *persons* because their nature already marks them as an end in itself, that is, as something that may not be used merely as a means.[29]

Treating persons as means, Kant insists, violates their dignity because every human being possesses dignity as an end in itself. This echoes Aristotle's view that humans are rational beings. And it is only towards other rational being that we owe direct moral duties:

> As far as reason alone can judge, a human being has duties only to human beings (himself and others), since his duty to any subject is moral constraint by that subject's will. Hence the constraining (binding) subject must, first, be a person;.... A human being can therefore have no duty to any beings other than human beings; and if he represents to himself that he has such duties ... [h]e is led to this misunderstanding by mistaking his duty with regard to other beings for a duty to those beings.[30]

29 Immanuel Kant, *Groundwork of the Metaphysics of Morals* transl by Mary Gregor (Cambridge: Cambridge University Press, 1998), 4, 428.

30 Immanuel Kant, *The Metaphysics of Morals*, transl by Mary Gregor (Cambridge: Cambridge University Press, 1996), 6, 422.

While Kant withholds moral status from animals, he does not espouse the Cartesian position that regards them as unconscious automata. He acknowledges that the animals are sentient creatures susceptible to both pleasure and pain, who have discernible interests, and whose lives may be good or bad according to the criteria applicable to them as members of the animal kingdom. Moreover, even if animals lack reason and consequently do not pursue their interests rationally, they still consciously respond to environmental signals so as to pursue their interests.[31] But because they lack the autonomous rational wills that furnish human beings with their moral standing, the only duties we have towards them are indirect duties. This means that, although we should avoid harming animals, we should do so because feelings of compassion and love towards them help us to act morally towards other humans. In other words, this indirect duty of kindness is merely instrumental in fostering ethical conduct to other people:

> If a man shoots his dog because the animal is no longer capable of service, he does not fail in his duty to the dog, for the dog cannot judge, but his act is inhuman and damages in himself that humanity which it is his duty to show towards mankind. If he is not to stifle his human feelings, he must practice kindness towards animals, for he who is cruel to animals becomes hard also in his dealings with men.[32]

This enigmatic reasoning is shown by Christine Korsgaard, in an intricate reconstruction of Kant, to be unstable.[33] The fact that we are, according to Kant, the only creatures that are capable of owing duties because we can exercise choice and engage in ethical reflection, does not entail that we are the only creatures that can be the object of duties. In other words, it is possible with Kant's formulation to separate those creatures that possess duties (humans) from those who are the objects of duties (nonhumans). It does not follow, Korsgaard argues, that exercising choice is an activity that necessarily

31 Immanuel Kant, *Critique of Judgment*, transl by WS Pluhar (Indianapolis, IN: Hackett Publishing Company, 1987), 5, 457.

32 Immanuel Kant, *Lectures on Ethics*, transl by Louis Infield (New York: Harper and Row, 1963), 239.

33 Christine M Korsgaard, *Fellow Creatures: Our Obligations to the Other Animals* (Oxford: Oxford University Press, 2018). For another excellent, elaborate interpretation of Kantian strictures that block direct duties to animals, see Michael Cholbi, 'A Direct Kantian Duty to Animals' (2014) 52 *The Southern Journal of Philosophy* 338, who argues that animal welfare belongs to an axiological category that Kant overlooks, that is, it consists of non-derivative values that are neither conditioned nor unconditioned because their value is independent of its relation to rational willing; animal welfare, not animals as such, has non-derivative value: 'Animal welfare is neither unconditionally good nor a source of dignity. However, animal welfare is an end in itself because it is a non-derivative and final good. Thus, there exists a direct duty to promote animal welfare. This duty is imperfect and operates according to a consequentialist logic', 358.

involves autonomous will; ethical thinking may apply to our concerns about, for instance, our bodily needs and desires. In this sense, therefore, we are no different from animals. And, she contends, we ought to reject the proposition that 'ought to implies can'. We should accept the distinction between what we ought to do and what we can do. Failure to do so opens the door to the contention that we cannot owe duties to animals because we could not fulfil them if we did. The main problem with this form of thinking is that, at least on the basis of Kantian reasoning:

> [O]ur duty is not to achieve the good, but to treat individuals in a way that accords with their value as ends in themselves. Those duties are owed not just to abstract representatives of the group 'animals' but to the particular animals with whom we ourselves interact. They are owed not to *all* of the animals, but to *each* of the animals, one by one as *individuals*.[34]

This interpretation—with its important combination of two elements—animals-as-ends, on the one hand, and the recognition of animals as individuals with needs and desires, on the other hand, seems to rescue Kant's view from its apparent speciesist, anthropocentricism that denies direct duties to animals.[35]

Seeking a champion of the cause of animal welfare—although not animal rights—many have looked to the swashbuckling utilitarian reformer, Jeremy Bentham, whose statement that our general moral duty to minimise suffering extends to avoiding the suffering of animals is frequently cited. He had an 'extraordinary combination of a fly's eye for detail, with an eagle's eye for illuminating generalizations',[36] and devoted himself to uncovering what he regarded as the shibboleths of his age and to creating a comprehensive theory of law, logic, politics, and psychology, founded on the principle of utility which I discuss in Chapter 6. His unrelenting, often devastating, assault on the received wisdom of his day is magnificent in its caustic power, for, as John Stuart Mill described it, Bentham found the battering-ram more useful than

34 Op cit, 218. Stress supplied. See too Emer O'Hagan, 'Animals, Agency, and Obligation in Kantian Ethics' (2009) 35 *Social Theory and Practice* 544.

35 Paola Cavalieri detects a *non sequitur* when Kant introduces a category of 'beings whose existence does not depend on our will but on nature', *Groundwork of the Metaphysics of Morals* transl by Mary Gregor (Cambridge: Cambridge University Press, 1998), 45, and then uses this will/nature dichotomy 'to shift surreptitiously from the opposition to between objects of reason and objects of inclination to the quite different opposition between rational beings and non-rational beings'. Paola Cavalieri, *The Animal Question: Why Nonhuman Animals Deserve Human Rights* (Oxford: Oxford University Press, 2001), 54. A simple answer to the 'tangle of difficulties' might be to enquire whether we would consent to be used as a means to the ends of a person stronger and more intelligent than us, op cit, 58.

36 HLA Hart, *Essays on Bentham: Studies on Jurisprudence and Political Theory* (Oxford: Clarendon Press, 1982), 4.

the builder's trowel.[37] Moved by the spirit of the Enlightenment, Bentham sought to expose the law to the cold light of reason.

While he recognises that the interests of sentient animals warrant protection on account of their vulnerability to suffering, Bentham nevertheless opines:

> If the being eaten were all, there is very good reason why we should be suffered to eat such of them as we like to eat: we are the better for it, and they are never the worse. They have none of these long-protracted anticipations of future misery, which we have. The death they suffer in our hands commonly is, and always may be, a speedier and by that means a less painful one, than that which would await them in the inevitable course of nature. If the being killed were all, there is very good reason why we should be suffered to kill such as molest us: we should be the worse for their living, and they are never the worse for being dead. But is there any reason why we should be suffered to torment them? Not any that I can see.[38]

This betrays a combination of ignorance and insensitivity that undermines his apparent sympathy for sentient suffering declared in the celebrated passage above. Animals led to the slaughter manifestly suffered fear and anxiety in his day. It exhibits, as Cavalieri puts it, 'the classical ... distinction between benevolence and justice. The injunction against tormenting is usually tied to benevolence ... while the prohibition on taking life tends to be connected to the higher ethical sphere of justice'.[39] In other words, and a similar position is evident in the utilitarian tenets of Mill and Sidgwick, there is no retreat from the speciesist standpoint of the theorists who precede them.

Other religions and traditions

Legal systems are in many cases bound up with their religious roots which may be profound and resilient. The Roman Catholic Church, for example, has the longest, continuously operating legal system in the Western world. The influence of religion is palpable in the case of Western legal systems:

> [B]asic institutions, concepts, and values ... have their sources in religious rituals, liturgies, and doctrines of the eleventh and twelfth centuries, reflecting new attitudes toward death, sin, punishment, forgiveness, and salvation, as well as new assumptions concerning the relationship of the divine to the human and of faith to reason.[40]

37 Quoted in Gerald J Postema, *Bentham and the Common Law Tradition* (Oxford: Clarendon Press, 1986), 148.

38 Jeremy Bentham, *An Introduction to the Principles of Morals and Legislation*, JH Burns and HLA Hart, eds (London: The Athlone Press, 1970.)

39 Paola Cavalieri, op cit, 65–66.

40 Harold J Berman, *Law and Revolution: The Formation of the Western Legal Tradition* (Boston, MA: Harvard University Press, 1995), 165.

Ecclesiastical law in twelfth century Europe played an important role in a number of fields. Ecclesiastical courts claimed jurisdiction over a wide range of matters, including heresy, fornication, homosexuality, adultery, defamation, and perjury. Canon law still governs several churches, especially the Roman Catholic Church, the Eastern Orthodox Church, and the Anglican Communion of Churches. The rise of secularism has not entirely extinguished the impact of religious law. While the jurisdiction of Western legislatures and courts over exclusively religious matters is often curtailed, many legal systems incorporate religious law or delegate to religious institutions matters of a domestic nature. Of course, at least in Western societies, a hallmark of legal systems is the separation between church and state.

Several religious legal traditions coexist with state systems of law, while some have actually been adopted as state law. The most significant are Talmudic, Islamic, and Hindu law. All three derive their authority from a divine source: the exposition of religious doctrine as revealed in the Talmud, Koran, and Vedas, respectively. All have influenced secular law in a variety of ways. For example, Talmudic law had a significant impact on Western commercial, civil, and criminal law. Islamic (or *sharia*) law is based largely on the teachings of the Koran. It extends to all aspects of life, not merely those that pertain to the state or society. It is observed, to a greater or lesser extent, by more than one-fifth of the population of the world, some 1.3 billion people.

Both Judaic and Islamic texts exhibit significant concern for the welfare of animals.[41] As mentioned, the epithet 'law' is generally applied to describe these directives, but, in the modern context, they are mostly more accurately regarded as moral codes or traditional tenets of a particular faith.

Judaism treats animals as property, and pursues a balance between their interests in not suffering, and human interests in their use. Traditionally, Jewish law permitted a broad spectrum of pain-inflicting conduct on the grounds that it was in legitimate human interests. Judaism teaches that animals are part of God's creation, have feelings and relationships, and should therefore be treated with compassion. Humans are directed to avoid *tza'ar ba'alei chayim*—causing

41 My principal sources are Y Michael Barilan 'The Vision of Vegetarianism and Peace: Rabbi Kook on the Ethical Treatment of Animals' (2004) 17 *History of the Human Sciences* 69; JD Bleich, 'Judaism and Animal Experimentation' (1986) 22 *Tradition* 1; Joshua Cahan, '*Tza'ar Ba'alei Ḥayim* in the Marketplace of Values' (2014) 65 *Conservative Judaism* 30; Samier Saeed, 'Squashing the Beef: Why American Animal Rights Advocates Should Start Liking Jewish and Islamic Law' (2022) 42 *Columbia Journal of Environmental Law* 521; Nazrul Islam and Saidul Islam, 'Human-Animal Relationship: Understanding Animal Rights in the Islamic Ecological Paradigm' (2015) 14 *Journal for the Study of Religions and Ideologies* 96; Nadeem Haque and Al-Hafiz Basheer Ahmad Masrib, 'The Principles of Animal Advocacy in Islam: Four Integrated Ecognitions' (2011) 19 *Society & Animals* 279. See too Mahfouz Azzam, 'Islamic Philosophy on Animal Rights' in Joyce D'Silva and Jacky Turner, eds, *Animals, Ethics and Trade: The Challenge of Animal Sentience* (London: Routledge, 2006); RC Foltz, *Animals in the Islamic Tradition and Muslim Cultures* (Oxford: Oneworld Publications, 2006).

pain to any living creature. The Talmud explicitly imparts that Jews must refrain from causing them pain. Biblical tales employ sympathy to animals to illustrate the virtues of prominent Jewish figures. None the less, Judaism permits the harming or killing animals if it is the only way to satisfy an essential human need. This is based on the anthropomorphic principle that human interests carry greater importance than those of animals; a tenet expressed in Genesis:

> And God blessed them, and God said unto them, Be fruitful, and multiply, and replenish the earth, and subdue it: and have dominion over the fish of the sea, and over the fowl of the air, and over every living thing that moveth upon the earth. And God said, Behold, I have given you every herb bearing seed, which is upon the face of all the earth, and every tree, in the which is the fruit of a tree yielding seed; to you it shall be for meat. And to every beast of the earth, and to every fowl of the air, and to every thing that creepeth upon the earth, wherein there is life, I have given every green herb for meat: and it was so.[42]

There is a consistent abhorrence expressed by rabbis of hunting and animal fights for sport. Leviticus 17:13 instructs Jews to pour out the blood of hunted prey and cover it with earth—an acknowledgement of the opprobriousness of hunting by urging hunters to conceal their shame by hiding the evidence of their carnage. Animal experiments are allowed provided that there is a genuine possibility of benefit to humans, and that no unnecessary pain is caused.[43]

Considerably more contentious—and politically sensitive—are the rules relating to the slaughter of animals prescribed by the strict dietary laws of *kashrut* which are governed by the *shechita*. It is claimed by its adherents that this method of killing reduces suffering.[44] The slaughter must be conducted by a Jew called a *shochet* who has been trained in the laws of *shechita*, animal anatomy and pathology, and serves an apprenticeship with a qualified *shochet*. The slaughter is carried out by cutting the creature's throat with a single stroke from a sharp instrument called a *chalaf*. The incision must sever

42 Genesis 1–3. There are a number of other commands and exhortations, for example, to feed animals before yourself (Deuteronomy 11:15); allowing animals to rest on the Sabbath (Exodus 20:10, and Deuteronomy 5:14); prohibiting the severing a limb from a live animal and eating it (Genesis 9:4) or killing a cow and her calf on the same day (Leviticus 22:28); muzzling an animal threshing corn (Deuteronomy 25:4); and harnessing an ox and donkey together (Deuteronomy 22:10).

43 See JD Bleich, op cit, 1.

44 The argument is sometimes heard that it may actually be less inhumane than the conventional practice of stunning an animal before slaughter in abattoirs. Several extremely disturbing images and videos have appeared that online reveal the horrors of the killing process which, in many cases, seem far from humane. It has therefore generated a debate about which method causes the greater or lesser pain—often disingenuous arguments which tend to deploy the fallacy of relative privation leading to an ethical *cul-de-sac*. Killing animals for food is objectively painful.

the trachea, oesophagus, carotid arteries, and jugular veins. The animal must be allowed to bleed out. The *shochet* is required to inspect the animal afterwards to confirm that the slaughter was properly carried out.

While the practice (which is adopted also by Islamic practice, see later) has long been defended as humane, it has attracted significant condemnation from animal rights groups and others, which has resulted in number of European countries introducing restrictions on its use. Scandinavia, for instance, has enacted legislation requiring that animals be stunned either before or just after their throats being cut. Belgium in 2019 banned the practice. An opinion poll conducted in 2020 revealed that 90 per cent of Europeans supported a ban on slaughter of animals that have not been stunned.[45] The subject clearly raises the question not only of the conflict between animal welfare and religious freedom, but, in their reluctance to proscribe the practice, the desire of some governments to avoid allegations of anti-semitism and Islamophobia, the thorny issue of relativism, cultural and ethical.[46]

Jewish law prohibits the castration of animals, a proscription unique in antiquity. Notably, the anti-cruelty stipulations apply not only to forbid physical harm, but also mental and emotional harm.[47] The animal's property status is not the decisive factor in determining one's obligations: they are owed even to those of an enemy.[48] Similarly, one is required to assist a beast of burden that has fallen or is struggling under the weight of its load, even if it belongs to one's enemy.[49] Cruelty to animals was punishable by flogging, though it is unclear whether 'cruelty' refers solely to a violation of one of the specific commands mentioned above, or mistreatment of animals in general.[50] Tying the legs of animals in a manner causing them pain is prohibited by the *shulchan aruch*.[51]

While these rulings, of which there are several others in similar vein, manifest an authentic concern for the interests of animals, the interests of humans

45 Wojciech Kość, 'Nine out of 10 EU citizens oppose animal slaughter without stunning, poll finds', *The Guardian* 9 Oct 2020. So-called 'ag-gag' laws to prevent whistleblowing about the treatment of animals on farms and abattoirs exist in the United States, Canada, and Australia. They prohibit undercover filming or photography of activity on farms without the consent of their owner. See Jodi Lazare, 'Animal Rights Activism and the Constitution: Are Ag-Gag Laws Justifiable Limits?' (2022) 59 *Osgoode Hall Law Journal* 667.

46 See Carla M Zoethout, 'Ritual Slaughter and the Freedom of Religion: Some Reflections on a Stunning Matter' (2013) 65 *Human Rights Quarterly* 651. This question is beyond the scope of present concerns, but I touch on it in Chapter 5.

47 Gathering eggs from a bird's nest requires that the mother bird be sent away so that it does not witness the removal of her eggs. Boiling an animal's meat in the milk of its mother is prohibited.

48 Elijah Judah Schochet, *Animal Life in Jewish Tradition: Attitudes and Relationships* (Brooklyn, NY: Ktav Publishing House, 1984), 154.

49 Schochet, op cit, 59.

50 Max May, 'Jewish Criminal Law and Legal Procedure' (1940) 31 *Journal of Law and Criminology* 438, 440.

51 Aviva Cantor, 'Scapegoats: Jews, Animals, and Oppression' (2012) 78 *La Ressegna Mensile di Israel* 95, 97. The *Shulchan Arukh* ('Set Table') is the most widely accepted code of Jewish law compiled in the sixteenth century by Rabbi Joseph Karo.

inevitably take precedence where a conflict arises. Nevertheless, as Samier Saeed points out:

> It is also important to note that rabbinic authorities considered the ethical implications of *tza'ar ba'alei chayyim* to outstrip its legal implications. Kindness to animals was considered extremely virtuous and a great distinction of the Jewish people compared to the nations with which they were surrounded in antiquity. It was not uncommon for rabbinic *responsa* to state that a certain practice, such as plucking feathers from a live bird or cutting off a bird's tongue, may be legally permissible to advance some human purpose, but should be avoided because of the cruelty involved. A number of authorities indicate that divine punishment for cruelty to animals is possible even where no violation of the law occurs. Thus, historically, there was a gap between what legal authorities thought was morally condemnable and what they in fact permitted.[52]

Rabbi Schochet maintains that later rabbinic authorities grew 'uncomfortable' with the 'stark' notion that human interests always trumped those of an animal in avoiding pain.[53] Their more sophisticated interpretation of the *tza'ar ba'alei chayyim* distinguished between legitimate and illegitimate use, as well as by examining more closely the extent of pain inflicted on the animal.[54] Saeed suggests that *tza'ar ba'alei chayyim* extends only to the experience of suffering, but not an animal's interest in life.[55] Rabbi Bleich unequivocally states that killing an animal is not a violation of this principle.[56] It does not follow that animals may be killed gratuitously; it would contravene *bal taschit*[57] and the censure attached to hunting for sport.

The driving force of Judaism's treatment of animals is thus the principle of *tza'ar ba'alei chayyim*. Under this overarching norm, animals are perceived as possessing objective moral value because of what they are, and this value is prized in various circumstances.[58] Consequently, Jewish law does not specify broad exceptions for individual cases; rather because of its recognition of the intrinsic worth of animals, it imposes stringent regulation as in the case of the use of animals for food.[59]

Interestingly, Islamic law has no equivalent to the *shochet;* slaughter may be conducted by any mentally competent male or female. The differences

52 Samier Saeed, op cit, 541. Footnotes omitted.
53 Schochet, op cit, 264.
54 Schochet, op cit, 266.
55 Schochet, op cit, 176, 220, 267; Bleich, op cit, 8. Both quote numerous authorities.
56 Bleich, op cit, 10.
57 *Bal taschit* is the prohibition against destroying property without good cause.
58 Oliver A Houck, 'Noah's Second Voyage: The Rights of Nature as Law' (2017) 31 *Tulane Environmental Law Journal* 17, n 8. Quoted by Saeed, op cit, 544.
59 See Louis A Berman, 'The Dietary Laws as Atonements for Flesh-eating' in Roberta Kalechofsky, ed, *Judaism and Animal Rights: Classical and Contemporary Responses: Classical & Contemporary Responses* (Tucson, AZ: 1992) 150, 154.

generally end there; its rules relating to *halal* echoes many of the Judaic principles. The procedures in respect of ritual slaughter (*dhabihah*) are almost identical: prior to slaughter, animals must be rested, fed, and properly cared for; the knife used must be sharp and clean, and, out of consideration to the animal, it should not be sharpened in front of it, and pain to the animal should be minimised.[60] The animal should be carried gently to slaughter and permitted to rest on its side.[61] It must be securely restrained prior to the cut which must pierce the trachea and oesophagus.[62]

The striking similarities between the two religious doctrines extend to a number of prohibitions against, for example, hunting for sport, the separation of male and female animals during the mating season, placing excessive weight on beasts of burden, taking a mother bird's eggs from her nest, and other cruel practices which are encapsulated in the hadith literature in which the Prophet condemned any beating of animals, and issued a total ban on striking and branding them on the face,[63] and 'curses' the maltreatment of animals in general.[64] In respect of the right to use or exploit animals: '[U]nder Islamic Law, these rights are often curtailed quite clearly and sharply, and animal interests often supersede human commercial interests.[65] Ultimately, owners of animals simply do not have an absolute right to manage and dispose of their animals as they see fit'.[66]

Kindness and respect towards animals is believed by a number of Islamic scholars to be fundamental to the faith:

> The philosophical justification and basis for Islamic animal advocacy consists of the following principles, which recognise and uphold inherent ecological values, termed *ecognition*, from *e*cological re*cognition*:

Ecognition 1: All nonhuman animals are a trust from God.
Ecognition 2: *Equigenic rights* do exist and must be maintained.
Ecognition 3: All nonhuman animals live in communities.
Ecognition 4: All nonhuman animals possess personhood.[67]

60 S Nomanul Haq, 'Islam and Ecology: Toward Retrieval and Reconstruction' (2001)130 *Daedalus* 141, 172, quoted by Saeed, op cit.

61 Sarra Tlili, 'Animals Would Follow Shaf'i'ism: Legitimate and Illegitimate Violence to Animals in Medieval Islamic Thought' in Robert Gleave and Istvan Kristo-Nagy, eds. *Violence in Islamic Thought from the Qoran to the Mongols* (Edinburgh: Edinburgh University Press, 2016), 225, 227.

62 Sira Abdul Rahman, 'Religion and Animal Welfare: An Islamic Perspective' (2017) 7 *Animals* 11. See too Phillip Ackerman-Lieberman, 'Comparison Between the Halakha and Shari'a' in Abdelwahab Meddeb and Benjamin Stora, eds, *A History of Jewish-Muslim Relations: From the Origins to the Present Day* (Princeton, NJ: Princeton University Press, 2013).

63 Steven (Musa) Woodward Furber, *Rights and Duties Pertaining to Kept Animals A Case Study in Islamic Law and Ethics* (Abu Dhabi, UAE, Tabah Foundation, 2015).

64 Rahman, ibid.

65 Tlili, op cit, 266.

66 Saeed, op cit, 546.

67 Nadeem Haque and Al-Hafiz Basheer Ahmad Masrib, op cit, 280.

Islam espouses the general principle that animals have an interest in their own bodies and that their produce should be respected. So, for instance, sheep owners do not actually own all the animals' wool; selling it in its entirety is prohibited since cutting the wool down to the sheep's skin would cause the animal pain.[68] Similarly, it is objectionable to milk all of it; some must remain for its young.[69] Indeed Muslim commentators opine that that an owner must provide nourishment to supplement a mother animal's milk if she lacks sufficient to feed her young.[70] The same logic applies to bee hives which may not be completely stripped of their honey.[71]

It does not follow that merely because an animal is fit to perform a particular task without harm, that it may be used for that task. Thus, it is not permitted to ride a cow as if it were a horse, nor should birds be caged.[72]

While both religions Islam denounce animal abuse, the question of enforcement of these benevolent provisions is predictably problematic. There is an inevitable disparity between theory and practice, both in regard to scripture and secular legislation. In Israel, for example, few cases of cruelty have resulted in prosecutions under the 1994 Animal Protection Law.[73] Islam states generally regarded animal cruelty as a matter of criminal law,[74] but the extent to which these enlightened stipulations are converted into actual practice is another matter.

Three concepts central to Hinduism—*karma* and *samsara* (reincarnation), and *ahiṃsā* (non-harming)—form the core of its tradition on the subject of animal wellbeing.[75] It teaches that the divine is present in all

68 Tlili, op cit, 226; Furber, op cit, 27.

69 Furber, op cit, 14, 19.

70 Furber, op cit, 27.

71 Furber, op cit, 26. The provision of water to animals looms large in the texts. Saeed mentions that Umar, Mohammad's second political successor, states that he flogged a man who was about to slaughter a sheep without first providing it with water: James L Wescoat, Jr, 'The "Right of Thirst" for Animals in Islamic Law: A Comparative Approach' (1995) 13 *Society and Space* 637, 643.

72 Haq, op cit, 170, 171.

73 According to the group, *Concern for Helping Animals*: http://www.chai.org.il/en/compassion/legislation_protection.htm (accessed 20 June 2023).

74 Furber, op cit, 2. See too Asmi Wood, 'Animal Welfare Under the Shari'a' (2013) 12 *Macquarie Law Journal* 155.

75 I draw here on Daniel A Dombrowski, *Hartshorne and the Metaphysics of Animal Rights* (Albany, NY: State University of New York Press; 1988); H Roderigues, *Hinduism and Animal Rights* (2015) http://www.mahavidya.ca/2015/06/26/hinduism-and-animal-rights/ (Accessed on 21 June 2023). See too Knut A Jacobsen 'The Institutionalization of the Ethics of "Non-Injury" toward All "Beings" in Ancient India' (1994) 16 *Environmental Ethics* 287; Christopher G Framarin, 'The Moral Standing of Animals and Plants in Manusmṛti' (2014) 64 *Philosophy East and West* 192; Christopher Framarin, 'The argument for Ahiṃsā in the Anuśāsanaparvan of the Mahābhārata' in Neil Dalal, ed, *Asian Perspectives on Animal Ethics: Rethinking the Nonhuman* (London: Routledge 2014).

living beings and that notwithstanding differences in form, ability, intelligence, and self-awareness the presence of the soul in all forms binds all creatures and commands peaceful, respectful coexistence between them.[76] The *Mahabharata* epic poem describes how Yudhishtira rebukes his cousin for carelessly felling a tree to release his anger with the dictum, 'humans should take from this planet only that which is necessary for our survival', and adds that when societies infringe this norm, all of humanity will face the consequences, for all life is interconnected and performs a unique purpose in the world.[77]

Similarly, serious karmic repercussions await those who take an innocent life, cause unnecessary suffering or pain to another life form, or casually endorse such pain and distress. Therefore, it is not only those who kills an animal in the abattoir who will acquire a degree of bad *karma*, but also those who participate in each stage of the process, including the ultimate consumers of its meat. This means that they cannot attain the ultimate Hindu aspiration of *moksa*: freedom from the painful cyclical rebirth that one faces after death. Achieving *moksa* is possible only by recognizing our oneness with the divine which requires attaining an elevated plane of spiritual awareness.[78]

In India many Hindus, predominantly the upper class Brahmins, are vegetarian apparently on moral grounds, to avoid harm to animals.[79] This regime began with the appearance of the Vedas which predates Christianity by thousands of years. The Vedas encourage vegetarianism chiefly because all animals are said to have once been human, or, in accordance with the concept of *karma*, may become human again. Maiming or killing an animal is disparaged because humans share the same life force as animals. On the other hand, sacrificing an animal is permitted where substantial benefits may result.[80]

76 'Hinduism treats many animals and birds with respect.... Reverence for things natural also extends to trees and plants', Valmik Thapar, *Land of the Tiger, A Natural History of the Indian Subcontinent* (Berkeley CA: University of California Press, 1997), quoted by Pankaj Jain, 'Dharma, and Environmental Ethics' (2010) *Union Seminary Quarterly Review*, no page numbers stated.

77 Dharma Krishna, *Mahabharata: The Greatest Spiritual Epic of All Time* (Ashland, OH: Torchlight Publishing, 1999).

78 Ashim K Bhattacharyya, *Hindu Dharma: Introduction to Scriptures and Theology* (Bloomington, IN, iUniverse, Inc., 2006).

79 Margaret Puskar-Pasewicz, ed, *Encyclopedia of Vegetarianism* (Westport: Greenwood Publishing Group, 2010).

80 DA Dombrowski, op cit, 22. Many Hindu festivals call for animal sacrifices, although the creature is not necessarily killed; it is normally a ritualistic, symbolic act which does not harm the animal. The practice is justified by the (somewhat tendentious) claim that no hatred is directed towards the animal, see Tom Regan, *Animal Sacrifices: Religious Perspectives on the Use of Animals in Science* (Philadelphia, PA: Temple University Press, 1987), 202.

Hinduism endows the cow with special status. The animal symbolises the entire animal kingdom as well as motherhood, especially because it provides not only milk, dried dung, and even urine, which is regarded as a cleansing agent.[81] Even non-vegetarian Hindus are unlikely to harm a cow because of the serious *karmic* consequences. In ancient Sanskrit texts, cows were emblematic of the Brahmin; killing or injuring a cow is therefore considered to be equivalent to visiting those harms upon a member of the Brahmin class.[82]

Jainism shares with Hinduism the concepts of *karma*, *samsara*, and *moksa*, but they differ in their interpretation of these concepts.[83] In respect of their attitude to animals, however, Jainist philosophy is perhaps the most radical of all faiths. At its heart is the concept of *ahiṃsā* or non-violence towards all living beings.[84] Only by pursuing a life of non-violence is a Jain able to avoid the endless cycle of reincarnation. In the words of its foremost sage, Mahavira, 'there is no quality of soul more subtle than non-violence and no virtue of spirit greater than reverence for life'. *Ahiṃsā* is normally construed negatively—do not cause harm, but contemporary Jains also interpret it positively—do acts which promote justice, peace, and freedom. He also states: 'Do not injure abuse, oppress, enslave, insult, torment, torture or kill any creature or living being'. Jain monks therefore seek scrupulously to avoid crushing insects under their feet, and cover their faces to avoid unintentionally swallowing flying insects.

Jains are forbidden from performing tasks that cause harm, such as those involving the cutting down of trees, dealing in meat, eggs, dairy, silk, or leather. They may not buy or sell pesticides, weapons; participate in zoos or circuses that use animals. They are lacto-vegetarian (since cows are harmed by the milking process), but are not required to be vegan, though many are. Strict Jains will even avoid eating root vegetables because small creatures may be injured when the plant is picked.

81 Mark Muesse, *The Hindu Traditions: A Concise Introduction* (Minneapolis, MN: Fortress Press, 2011), 81.

82 Wendy Doniger, *The Hindus: An Alternative History* (London: Penguin Books, 2009), 658.

83 See Vilas Adinath Sangave, *Aspects of Jaina Religion*, 3rd edn (Bharatiya Jnanpith, 2001); Christopher Key Chapple, *Nonviolence to Animals, Earth, and Self in Asian Traditions* (Albany, NY: State University of New York Press, 1993).

84 See Sarvepalli Radhakrishnan, 'The Pluralistic Realism of the Jainas' in his *Indian Philosophy* (Oxford: Oxford University Press, 2008); Paul Dundas, *The Jainas* (London and New York: Routledge, 2002).

Reverence for the natural world is a fundamental element of both Buddhism[85] and Native American culture.[86] Fundamental to the former are the 'Four Noble Truths'. The first is the truth or fact of suffering. The second explains the causes of suffering which is mainly the craving for pleasure, for instance, and is also caused by ignorance of the reality that nothing exists independently of all other things. The third truth is the claim that suffering can end and *nirvāṇa* is attainable. The final truth consists in an eightfold path towards achieving this state or way of life.

Buddhists subscribe to the concept of *Ahiṃsā* which, as was mentioned above, is common to both the Brahmins and Jains. For Buddhists, it is interpreted as a prohibition on killing or harming others. The Buddha expounded that those sentient beings presently existing in the animal dominion have been our mothers, brothers, sisters, fathers, children, friends in past rebirths. One cannot therefore draw a firm distinction between moral rules pertaining to animals and those applicable to humans; fundamentally humans and animals belong to a single family. He believed that we have moral duties to animals and therefore disapproved of occupations that entailed the slaughtering of animals, and instructed monks to refrain from wearing animal skins and engaging in conduct which intentionally causes harm to animals.

As in the case of Hinduism, the notion of *karma* is an essential Buddhist precept. In particular, according to the Buddha, those who are cruel or violent will endure a similar fate in a following life. He explicitly singled out butchers and abattoir workers who will themselves be slaughtered in their next life in the same manner as they slaughtered animals.

The thrust of Buddhist ethical thought appears to advise that adherents adopt vegetarianism, but this is not an ineluctable conclusion from the doctrinal texts and historical practice, as Bronwyn Finnigan points out. It is not a simple deduction from the sources. She, however, suggests:

> Since everything exists as relational constituents of an ecological biosphere, if anything has intrinsic value, the entire system does. The modern, industrialised meat-eating industry causes significant ecological damage. Eating meat sustains such practices. So, one should not eat meat. One might also include a reference to the intrinsic badness of suffering and argue that the ecological damage caused by such

85 The literature is vast, see, in particular, Bronwyn Finnigan, 'Madhyamaka Ethics' in D Cozort and JM Shields, eds, *Oxford Handbook of Buddhist Ethics* (Oxford: Oxford University Press, 2017); Peter Harvey, *An Introduction to Buddhist Ethics* (Cambridge: Cambridge University Press, 2000); Tony Page, *Buddhism and Animals* (London: UKAVIS Publications, 1999); James J Stewart, *Vegetarianism and Animal Ethics in Contemporary Buddhism* (Abingdon and New York: Routledge, 2014); Norm Phelps, *The Great Compassion: Buddhism and Animal Rights* (Brooklyn, NY: Lantern Books, 2004).

86 See Howard L Harrod, *The Animals Came Dancing: Native American Sacred Ecology and Animal Kinship*, 2nd edn (Tucson, AZ: University of Arizona Press, 2000); Dave Aftandilian, 'Toward a Native American Theology of Animals: Creek and Cherokee (2011) 61 *CrossCurrents* 191.

> practices is bad because it directly and indirectly results in suffering to the biological entities that are relationally constituted by this system.[87]

This would seem to follow from the five precepts, the first of which interdicts the taking of life. It has been construed to apply to all sentient beings, not merely mammals, but also to invertebrates and insects.[88]

Native Indian[89] approaches to animals and the natural world in general are well-known. The following anecdote captures one aspect of its view:

> Many Yukon First Nations people find the assumption of control inherent in the agricultural metaphor absurd, perhaps even offensive to the animals. At wildlife management meetings, one Kluane First Nation hunter regularly objected to use of the term wildlife management itself. Humans cannot 'manage' wildlife populations, he said. Animals manage themselves; they make their own decisions about when to reproduce, and where to go, decisions that are quite independent of any human desires. Wildlife management, he said, is not about managing animals; it is about managing people.[90]

*

The influence—positive, but mostly negative—exerted by the Western theorists and thinkers described in the first section of this chapter will become evident in the forthcoming pages. It does not require great insight to grasp the unfortunate truth that few of the altruistic precepts embraced by the various religions have found their way into the world we actually inhabit. Perhaps they could be described as noble aspirations; if so, the extent to which they might mobilise attitudes and practice towards animals, or whether other approaches may better achieve justice, are among the principal questions that the following pages seek to answer.

87 Bronwyn Finnegan, 'Buddhism and Animal Ethics' (2017) 12 *Philosophy Compass* (no page number stated). Italics removed.

88 I cannot here explore Daoist philosophy, save to say that it encourages love and compassion (*ci*), the exercise of restraint and frugality (*jian*), and the pursuit of harmony *wuwei*. It teaches that the great transformation brings about a 'Great Unity' in which all things are part of one organic whole, and emphasises the fundamental similarities between humans and nonhumans. It also fosters the kind treatment of others and the prevention of harm to others, including animals, by disturbing their homes or eating their bodies. See Lisa Kemmerer, 'The Great Unity: Daoism, Nonhuman Animals, and Human Ethics' (2009) 7 *Journal for Critical Animal Studies*, 63. See too Livia Kohn, *Cosmos and Community: The Ethical Dimensions of Daoism* (Cambridge: Three Pines, 2004); John Gray, *Straw Dogs: Thoughts on Humans and Other Animals* (London: Granta, 2002), 79–80, 112–114.

89 Sometimes the term 'Amerindian' is used. In Canada 'First Nations' is used to describe indigenous peoples. On African culture see Kai Horsthemke, 'Animals and African Ethics' (2017) 7 *Journal of Animal Ethics* 119. For a discussion of Māori tradition, see SM Mead, *Tikanga Māori: Living by Māori Values* (Wellington: NZ: Huia Publishing, 2003).

90 Paul Nadsdy, *Power, Knowledge, and Aboriginal-State Relations in the Southwest Yukon* (Vancouver, BC: University of British Columbia Press, 2004).

3 Animal rights

The wellbeing of our fellow creatures is frequently characterised as one of 'animal rights', indeed much of the literature employs this phrase somewhat promiscuously, often in the titles of articles and books, without necessarily endorsing the view that granting animals rights is logically or legally practical, or that it constitutes the most effective, or even, the most appropriate, means by which to advance the cause of protecting the interests of nonhumans.[1] Endowing animals with rights has become a battle cry intoned to advance the cause of nonhuman welfare. This is clearly a testament to the power of 'rights talk' which has tended to 'saturate' a good deal of political discourse in general, at least in the West.[2]

This chapter offers first a brief introduction to the concept of rights. This is intended to demonstrate the foundation of the case for animal rights inferred from welfare legislation, as well as the more ambitious claim that animals be accorded human rights (discussed in Chapter 5). I shall assess the hurdles that beset the path towards the recognition of both forms of rights in Chapter 4.

What are rights?

To claim that animals have, or ought to have, rights is to say that such rights are against *us*—humans or human institutions. Unlike us, who have rights against other humans, animals cannot have rights against other animals.

1 Moreover, it is not always clear whether the phrase applies to moral or legal rights. In addition, it occasionally signifies a broader notion of 'human rights', while it is also deployed to denote a general argument for compassion towards animals. As if this conceptual confusion were not enough, the term is sometimes invoked to describe *existing* legal rights of animals, whereas in other contexts it is used as a banner by which to advocate increased rights for nonhumans. For an illuminating discussion of this quandary, see Will Kymlicka and Sue Donaldson, 'Rights' in Lori Gruen, ed, *Critical Terms for Animal Studies* (Chicago: University of Chicago Press, 2018), 320.

2 The metaphor is Nigel Biggar's in his *What's Wrong with Rights?* (Oxford: Oxford University Press, 2020), 334. The West, he asseverates, 'need to get beyond whatever it is that is tying our tongues over duty and virtue. Right-talk is just not enough'. Ibid.

DOI: 10.4324/9781032702575-3

Until we appeared on the scene, they did not need rights; their welfare was not dependent on human conduct.[3] The argument in support of animal rights may therefore be about our *duties* towards animals. But the literature bristles with debate about whether the protection animals receive in law or through regulation generates genuine rights. If so, what is the extent of these rights? Are they rights against the world (so-called real rights or rights *in rem*), or are they personal rights (rights *in personam*) against specific individuals (such as a farmer or the owner of a pet)? This question is rarely asked. Nor, regrettably, is there much clarity or consistency in the use of the term 'right' in the huge literature on the subject. I shall attempt to disentangle some of the confusion in the following paragraphs.

It is important, especially for what follows in our discussion of animal rights, to bear in mind the sources of rights or, to put it another way, how rights are made. The previous chapter touched on the distinction between moral and legal rights. The former may emanate from a religious, customary, or conventional source. The latter may be a creation of public or private law. An example of the former is criminal law, while the latter may arise through the law of contract or tort. Rights may be created by statute or common law. They may be waived or relinquished. The claim that animals have, or ought to be vested with, *human* rights or political rights might also boil down to an argument in support of the fundamental duties we owe them (either because we think all living creatures have certain rights in virtue of their being born, or because, in the case of political rights, that the polity has certain duties towards them).

The utilitarian, as was outlined in Chapter 2, in order to prove the case for treating animals humanely, needs to demonstrate that the consequences of such humaneness outweigh the consequences of any of a number of alternatives, and this may stretch the empirical evidence to breaking-point. The proponent of a rights-based argument, on the other hand, needs to overcome, in particular, the complaint that animals cannot really be said to possess rights.[4]

As the clamour in support of animal rights grows louder, many countries have become increasingly polarised in respect of the extent to which a variety of practices, ranging from fox-hunting to experiments on animals can be justified in a compassionate society. Many shrink from the very notion that an animal is capable of being vested with rights. Yet consider the following conclusion reached in a judgement by an Indian court:

> [W]e hold that circus animals ... are housed in cramped cages, subjected to fear, hunger, pain, not to mention the undignified way of life they have to live, with no respite and the impugned notification has been

3 One might (with only a hint of facetiousness) apply the legal maxim *qui prior est tempore, potior est iure*— generally translated as 'first in time, is first in law'; perhaps it is humans who should question whether it is *we* who should have rights against those who preceded us!

4 I draw here on Raymond Wacks, *Understanding Jurisprudence: An Introduction to Legal Theory*, 6th edn (Oxford: Oxford University Press, 2021), 312–316.

> issued in conformity with ... the values of human life, philosophy of the Constitution.... Though not homosapiens, [*sic*] they are also beings entitled to dignified existence and humane treatment sans cruelty and torture.... Therefore it is our fundamental duty to show compassion to our animal friends, but also to recognise and protect their rights.... If humans are entitled to fundamental rights, why not animals?[5]

Is the idea really so far-fetched? To assert that since animals cannot be the subject of duties, they cannot be 'moral agents' and are thus incapable of being objects of rights is to beg the question about what it takes to be a right-holder. In particular, it presumes a choice-based rather than an interest-based theory of rights.[6] This distinction is considered in the following section.

The concept of a right seems to have emerged only in the Middle Ages, while the notion of a duty is much older, and existed among the Stoics in ancient Greece. The idea of natural rights is closely associated with what we now call human rights, and is the subject of Chapter 5.

Immanuel Kant's exposition of rights is a useful starting point for any account of the concept of a right, although its influence has been somewhat displaced by the systematic analysis of 'jural relations' by the American jurist, Wesley Hohfeld, discussed in what follows. Kant regards a right as having 'peremptory force', that is to say it is related to the justified use of force or coercion. This means that my right, say, to freedom of movement is, in effect, a statement that any coercive attempt to prevent me from going for a walk cannot be justified, but coercion to stop you from obstructing my stroll is defensible. Rights are therefore an essential tool by which to protect freedom.

But a right, according to Kant, has a degree of internal complexity. This might include, for example, my power to waive my protection afforded by the right.[7]

Hohfeld classified a right as follows:

Opposites	right	privilege	power	immunity
	no-right	duty	disability	liability
Correlatives	right	privilege	power	immunity
	duty	no-right	ability	disability

5 *Nair* v *Union of India* (2000) Kerala High Court No 155/1999, quoted by Martha C Nussbaum, *Frontiers of Justice: Disability, Nationality Species Membership* (Cambridge, MA: Belknap Press, 2006), 325.

6 In any event, is it wildly implausible that animals may indeed be subjects of certain duties (for example, a guide dog, sheepdog, or watchdog)?

7 For an example of how a Kantian view of rights might operate in practice, see the judgement of Lord Lindley in the case of *Quinn v Leathem* [1901] AC 495 at 534.

Hohfeld sought to clarify the proposition 'X has a right to do R' which may, in his view, mean one of four things[8]:

- That Y (or anyone else) is under a duty to allow X to do R; this means, in effect, that X has a *claim* against Y. He calls this claim right simply a 'right'.
- That X is free to do or refrain from doing something; Y owes *no duty* to X. He calls this a 'privilege' (though it is often described as a 'liberty').
- That X has a power to do R; X is simply free to do an act which alters legal rights and duties or legal relations in general (for example, sell his property) whether or not he has a claim right or privilege to do so. Hohfeld calls this a 'power'.
- That X is not subject to Y's (or anyone's) power to change X's legal position. He calls this an 'immunity'.

Hohfeld conceived of these four 'rights' having both 'opposites' and 'correlatives' (i.e., the other side of the same coin) as shown in the above table.[9] Thus, to use Hohfeld's own example, if X has a *right* against Y that Y shall stay off X's land, the *correlative* (and equivalent) is that Y is under a *duty* to keep off the land. A *privilege* is the *opposite* of a *duty*, and the *correlative* of a '*no-right*'. Hence, whereas X has a *right* (or *claim*) that Y should stay off his land, X himself has the *privilege* of entering on the land, or, in other words, X does not have a duty to stay off.

It is important to observe that, for Hohfeld, claim rights (i.e., rights in the normal sense) are strictly *correlative* to duties. To say that X has a claim right of some kind is to say that Y (or someone else) owes a certain duty to X. But to say that X has a certain liberty is *not* to say that anyone owes him or her a duty. Thus, if X has a *privilege* (or liberty) to wear a hat, Y does not have a *duty* to X, but a *no-right* that X should not wear a hat. In other words, the *correlative* of a liberty is a no-right. Similarly, the correlative of a power is a liability (i.e., being liable to have one's legal relations changed by another), the correlative of an immunity is a disability (i.e., the inability to change another's legal relations).

8 *Fundamental Legal Conceptions as Applied in Judicial Reasoning*, WW Cook, ed (New Haven, CN and London: Yale University Press, 1964). A key element in his analysis is the doubt he casts on Kant's idea, mentioned above, that rights are both internally complex and have peremptory force. For Kant, the internal complexity of a right derives from the fact that it entails, inter alia, the permissibility of conduct exercising the right, the duty on others not to interfere with its exercise, the power to waive such duty. He conceives rights as conclusive of its inviolability and permissibility. Hohfeld, on the other hand, shows that these features delineated by Kant are, in fact, part of legal rules themselves. In other words, they could not be captured by a single conception of a right, and hence his fourfold classification of the elements of a right.

9 I return to the subject of correlativity in Chapter 4.

But is it true to say that whenever I am under some duty, someone else has a corresponding right? Or vice versa? In the first case, surely it is possible for me to have a duty without you (or anyone else) having a right that I should perform it. In the criminal law, certain duties are imposed upon me but no one has a correlative right to my performing these duties. This is because it is possible for there to be a duty to do something which is not a duty to *someone*; for instance, the duty imposed on a police officer to report offenders—the duty is owed to no one in particular, and, hence, it gives rise to no-right in anyone. There are several other instances of the absence of correlativity of rights and duties in the criminal law: the duty, say, to observe road signs is absent of a corresponding obligation to others and therefore entails no rights vested in anyone. On the other hand, it is, of course, common for me to have a right to do something, without you (or anyone else) having a parallel duty.

And even where someone owes a duty to *someone* to do something, the person to whom he owes such a duty does not necessarily have any corresponding right. Thus, a professor has certain duties towards his or her students, but this may not automatically confer any rights upon them:

> To seek to explain the notion of a right by reference to that of a duty and, hence, to take the absence of a duty as proof of the absence of a right ... is to link up two ideas which are quite independent. Rights are rights in virtue of some title which gives them to us, whereas duties are duties in virtue of some position or authority which lays them on us....[10]

Equally, we generally accept that we owe certain duties to future generations, infants, the senile or comatose, yet many argue that it does not follow from this that they have rights. Yet these criticisms seem to miss the point of Hohfeld's objective. JW Harris offers a spirited defence of Hohfeld's position.[11] It is true that, in order to make sense of legal relations between persons, correlativity is part of the law's lowest common denominator—because every judicial issue involves at least two persons. In practice, therefore, *litigation* gives rise to opposing parties—even where, strictly speaking, the defendant does not owe a duty to the plaintiff (or, as the suing party is now—rather absurdly styled in England and Wales—the 'claimant'). Thus, my duty to pay tax on my income does not necessarily give rise to a right held by another; but the taxman will pursue me in the courts in order to recover tax owing. Hence, the court has to answer the question: does the defendant owe a duty *to the plaintiff*?

In other words, *someone* has to bring the action or, indeed, be sued. Correlatives seem a convenient way of describing the relationship between the

10 Alan R White, *Rights* (Oxford: Clarendon Press, 1984), 72. A neglected monograph.
11 JW Harris, *Legal Philosophies*, 2nd edn (London: Butterworths, 1997), 81–83.

plaintiff's action and the defendant's conduct. But, as Harris concedes, where a court holds that in certain rare circumstances an injunction may be granted by a civil court to restrain a threatened breach of the criminal law, a private person may bring an action only where he has a 'private right'; this must mean that he has a 'private interest'—a non-Hohfeldian, non-relational conception of right. And, on the other hand, there will be cases where a general, uncorrelated 'duty' is the basis for recognizing a certain relationship. Perhaps the answer is that 'judicial reasoning [is] necessarily infused with moral and political ideas about private right and public duty, for which some non-Hohfeldian analysis is essential'.[12]

All four of Hohfeld's elements of a right (which, in modern accounts, are usually called claim-rights, liberties, powers, and immunities) are rights *against a specific person or persons*. Confusion is sometimes generated by the fact that, in Hohfeld's scheme, X's liberty does not occasion any *duty* on Y's part not to interfere. Thus, the fact that X has a liberty (as against Y) to wear a hat does *not* necessitate that Y is under a duty not to interfere with X's wearing a hat. Y would therefore be entitled to *prevent* X from wearing a hat (for example, by buying up the supply of hats and refusing to sell X one).[13]

Joseph Raz and Neil MacCormick have questioned Hohfeld's correlativity thesis by arguing that duties are often imposed in order to *protect* rights rather than merely being correlative to such rights.[14] And it is surely true that when we talk of imposing duties on people (such as the duty to wear seatbelts), we do not think of this duty as being owed to some person or persons. We do not, in other words, normally think that where there is a duty there is a right. They contend that instead of Hohfeld's fourfold dissection, a right contains internal complexity that provides a justification or reason to be weighed against competing factors when determining whether it should be recognised. In short, Kant holds that a right is both internally complex and emanates peremptory force; Hohfeld regards a right as having peremptory force; and Raz and MacCormick consider a right to be internally complex without peremptory force.[15]

12 JW Harris, *Legal Philosophies*, 83.

13 Nigel Simmonds and Joshua Neoh, *Central Issues in Jurisprudence*, 6th edn (London: Sweet & Maxwell, 2022), 318.

14 Joseph Raz argues (as part of a larger defence of freedom) that '[A]ll rights are based on interests', J Raz, *The Morality of Freedom* (Oxford: Clarendon Press, 1986), 191. See too 'Legal Rights' (1984) 4 *Oxford Journal of Legal Studies* 1; *Ethics in the Public Domain: Essays in the Morality of Law and Politics* (Oxford: Clarendon Press, 1995); Neil MacCormick, *Legal Right and Social Democracy: Essays in Legal and Political Philosophy* (Oxford: Clarendon Press, 1982), Ch 8, and 'Rights in Legislation' in PMS Hacker and J Raz, eds, *Law, Morality and Society* (Oxford: Clarendon Press, 1977).

15 See Matthew Kramer, 'Rights without Trimmings' in Matthew Kramer, NE Simmonds, and Hillel Steiner, *A Debate Over Rights: Philosophical Enquiries* (Oxford: Oxford University Press, 1998), 36 ff.

A more general criticism of Hohfeld contends that he fails adequately to analyse the essential *nature* of rights and other legal concepts. JW Harris maintains[16] that we cannot understand the totality of any legal concept frozen in time in a 'momentary legal system'. We employ legal concepts in legal reasoning as part of what he calls the 'doctrine model of rationality'. In other words, all legal concepts exist in a historical context which requires reference to certain fundamental features of the legal system (for instance, our conception of property rights). In addition, criticism is frequently made of Hohfeld's treatment of the concepts of 'duty' and 'power'. In particular, it is argued that he fails to distinguish the various *types* of duty and power: we use these terms in several ways which his analysis tends to neglect.[17]

Theories of rights

There are two major theories of rights: the so-called 'will' (or 'choice') theory and the 'interest' theory. The former (advanced especially by HLA Hart)[18] holds that when I have a right to do something, what is essentially protected is my *choice* whether or not to do it. Every claim-right, it claims, entails that someone has a duty, but not every duty entails a claim-right. It stresses the freedom and individual self-fulfilment that are regarded as essential values which the law ought to guarantee.

The 'interest' theory, on the other hand, most effectively championed by Neil MacCormick,[19] maintains that the purpose of rights is to protect, not individual choice, but certain *interests* of the right-holder. All claim-rights involve duties, and all duties entail claim-rights.[20]

16 *Law and Legal Science: An Enquiry into the Concepts, Legal Rule and Legal System* (Oxford: Clarendon Press, 1979), sect 3.

17 For an interesting alternative analysis of legal rights, see J Raz, 'Legal Rights' (1984) 4 *Oxford Journal of Legal Studies* 1.

18 See HLA Hart, *Essays on Bentham: Studies on Jurisprudence and Political Theory* (Oxford: Clarendon Press, 1982), Ch 7. See too Matthew H Kramer, 'Refining the Interest Theory of Rights' (2010) 55 *American Journal of Jurisprudence* 31, and Visa AJ Kurki, 'Rights, Harming and Wronging: A Restatement of the Interest Theory' (2018) 38 *Oxford Journal of Legal Studies* 430.

19 See *Legal Right and Social Democracy: Essays in Legal and Political Philosophy* (Oxford: Clarendon Press, 1982), Ch 8, and 'Rights in Legislation' in PMS Hacker and J Raz, eds, *Law, Morality and Society* (Oxford: Clarendon Press, 1977).

20 See Matthew H Kramer, 'Do Animals and Dead People Have Legal Rights?' (2001) 14 *Canadian Journal of Law & Jurisprudence* 29. On Kramer's analysis of the interest theory, see, in particular, 'Getting Rights Right' in Matthew H Kramer, ed, *Rights, Wrongs and Responsibilities* (London: Palgrave, 2001). For will theories, see HLA Hart, *Essays on Bentham: Jurisprudence and Political Theory* (Oxford: Clarendon Press, 1982); Hillel Steiner, *An Essay on Rights* (Oxford: Blackwell, 1994); NE Simmonds, 'Rights at the Cutting Edge' in Matthew H Kramer, NE Simmonds, and Hillel Steiner, *A Debate over Rights. Philosophical Enquiries* (Oxford University Press, 1998); and Carl Wellman, *Real Rights* (Oxford: Oxford University Press, 1995).

It is important to observe that most of the advocates of both theories (though not MacCormick) normally accept the *correlativity* of rights and duties; indeed, this is (as will be suggested below) often central to their arguments. In rejecting the will theory, proponents of the interest theory raise two main arguments. First, they disparage the view (at the heart of the will theory) that the essence of a right is the power to waive someone else's duty. Sometimes, they argue, the law *limits* my power of waiver without destroying my substantive right (for example, I cannot consent to murder or contract out of certain rights). Secondly, there is a distinction between the substantive right and the right to *enforce* it. MacCormick gives the instance of children: their rights are exercised by their parents or guardians; how can it be said, therefore, that the right-holder (i.e., the child) has any choice whether or not to waive such rights? It must, he argues, be concluded that children have no rights—which is plainly wrong.[21]

While the will theory, by arguing that the enforcement of Y's duty requires the exercise of will by X (or someone else), rests on the assumption of the correlativity of rights and duties, it is possible to postulate the interest theory (as MacCormick does) independently. Thus, it may be argued that conferring a right on someone (to housing, for example) constitutes an acceptance that the interest represented by that right ought to be recognised and protected. There are two main versions of this theory. One asserts that X has a right whenever he is in a position to benefit from the performance of a duty. The other claims that X has a right whenever the protection of his interest is recognised as a reason for imposing duties—whether or not they are *actually* imposed.[22]

But is *having* an interest the same as something *being* in the interest of X? Alan White thinks not:

> [S]omething can be in the interest of the animate or the inanimate, but only the animate can have (or take) an interest in something—in neither case is there any logical connection between interests and rights.[23]

In other words, something can be in *my* interests (for instance, learning the truth about my past), and, *a fortiori*, something can be in *something's* interest (for instance, turning off your stereo is in the interests of peace and quiet) without its being anyone or anything's right. This argument thus rejects the

21 Matthew Kramer suggests that my duty is correlative to your right when I have breached my duty by affecting your interests. This approach obviates the requirement to consider the wider purposes of the law or to discern the various interests protected by the law, as Raz's account does, Matthew H Kramer, 'Rights without Trimmings' in Matthew H Kramer, NE Simmonds, and Hillel Steiner, op cit, 80–98.

22 A useful account may be found in Tom Campbell, *The Left and Rights: A Conceptual Analysis of the Idea of Socialist Rights* (London: Routledge & Kegan Paul, 1983), Ch 6 and 9.

23 Alan R White, op cit, 103.

proposition that merely because something is for my good, to my benefit, or because I need it gives me a right to it. It is part of a more comprehensive criticism of the very notion of animals as right-holders which I briefly discuss in Chapter 4.

Rights-based theories

Rights occupy a central place in contemporary legal, moral, and political philosophy. Indeed, it is not unreasonable to suggest that the extravagant service which the concept is asked to perform has drained it of much of its meaning.

Ronald Dworkin argues for the primacy of rights over considerations of the general welfare. The epicentre of his 'rights thesis' is his criticism of HLA Hart's model of rules which is founded on the conceptual apartheid of law and morality.[24] For Hart (and other legal positivists), we gain a better understanding of law by maintaining, for the purpose of analysis, a separation between the law as it is and the law as it ought to be. Dworkin repudiates this approach because, he contends, law consists not merely of rules (as Hart claims) but also of what Dworkin calls 'non-rule standards'. When a court decides a difficult or 'hard' case, it draws on these standards—principles and policies—to reach its judgement. There is no 'rule of recognition' (as postulated by legal positivists) to distinguish between legal and moral principles.

A judge in a hard case—where there is no immediately applicable precedent—therefore has to appeal to *principles* which will include his own conception of what is the best interpretation of the 'great network of political structures and decisions of his community'.[25] He must ask 'whether it could form part of a coherent theory justifying the network as a whole'.[26] In other words, there is always one 'right answer' to every legal problem; it is up to the judge to find it. This answer is 'right' in the sense that it coheres best (or 'fits') with the institutional and constitutional history of the law. Legal argument and analysis is therefore interpretative (or, what Dworkin prefers to call, 'interpretive') in character.

The theory is premised on Dworkin's concern that the law ought to 'take rights seriously'. If (as Hart claims) the outcome of a hard case turns on the judge's own view or intuition or the exercise of his 'strong discretion', rights

24 See, in particular, Ronald Dworkin, *Taking Rights Seriously*, new impression with a reply to critics (London: Duckworth, 1978); *A Matter of Principle* (Cambridge, MA and London: Harvard University Press, 1985); *Law's Empire* (Cambridge, MA and London: Belknap Press, 1986). For a detailed account of Dworkin's theory, see Stephen Guest, *Ronald Dworkin*, 3rd edn (Stanford: Stanford Law and Politics, 2012). I have attempted to describe and evaluate its main claims in Raymond Wacks, *Understanding Jurisprudence: An Introduction to Legal Theory*, 6th edn (Oxford: Oxford University Press, 2021), Ch 5. The key elements are discussed in the same volume, Ch 3 and 4.

25 Ronald Dworkin, *Law's Empire* (Cambridge, MA and London: Belknap Press, 1986), 245.

26 Ibid.

are rendered fragile things to be sacrificed by courts at the altar of community interests or other conceptions of the good. Individual rights, if they are to be treated with the respect they deserve, they (i.e., in effect, principles) are to be accorded proper recognition as part of the law. This leads Dworkin (inter alia) to deny the legal positivist separation between law and morals; to reject the proposition that judges either do or should *make* law; to argue that judges must seek 'the soundest theory of law' on which to decide hard cases; and to conclude that, since judges (who are unelected officials) do not make law, the judicial role is democratic and prospective.

Dworkin distinguishes between 'personal' and 'external' preferences. The former refers to those things that I want for *myself*; the latter are the things I want for *others*. So, for example, I may want to be affluent, but not wish others to be. He contends that when we seek to improve the general welfare, external preferences should be excluded—because they undermine the 'basic right to equal concern and respect' which, in his theorem, is a fundamental political right—'a postulate of political morality'.[27] They have this effect because any imposition of external preferences is equivalent to a judgement that those on whom they are imposed are inferior, not to be treated as equals or 'with equal concern and respect':

> Rights cannot be understood as things people have, come what may, no matter what general justification for political decisions is in play. We construct political theories as a package, and the rights that package assigns individuals must vary with what else is in the package. The idea of rights as trumps is a *formal* idea: it fixes the general function of rights within any particular theory that uses the idea at all. We can therefore think about the content of rights at two different levels of analysis. When we are engaged in constructing a general political theory, we must consider what package—what general justification for political decisions together with what rights—is most suitable.... But on other occasions we must take the general scheme of some political theory as fixed and consider what rights are necessary as trumps over the general background justification that theory proposes.[28]

For Dworkin, therefore, no utilitarian view offers an adequate foundation for a theory that takes rights seriously, and only a restricted form of utilitarianism (which excludes external preferences) provides some support for the egalitarianism that is the main appeal of utilitarianism. Dworkin concedes that 'to prevent a catastrophe or even to obtain a clear and major benefit',[29] it may be necessary for individual rights to be overridden. Thus, my right to

27 *Taking Rights Seriously* (London: Duckworth, 1978), 272.
28 *Taking Rights Seriously*, 281.
29 *Taking Rights Seriously*, 192.

free speech may have to give way when the public interest requires it (say, during a state of emergency). But this suggests that there is an implicit recognition that even the most fundamental rights are not immune to the claims of utility—the public interest.

This, in turn, raises the question whether utilitarianism is itself inevitably hostile to individual rights. A utilitarian, as discussed in Chapter 6, is committed to the proposition that all actions are to be judged according to the extent to which they advance or contribute to the general welfare. Does this suggest that he is unable to accommodate rights into his felicific calculus? It has been argued that utilitarianism is compatible with individual rights because when an interest is shown, by reference to the general good, to be worthy of protection, a *right* to that interest may be recognised. But this means, first, that rights are at the mercy of the felicific calculus (a rather fragile guarantee) and, secondly, that rights will always succumb to considerations of the general welfare.

Another way out of the apparent impasse has been offered by Alan Gewirth.[30] Briefly, he argues that we cannot justify—in the interests of the general welfare—the denial of rights to others without accepting the importance of rights. At the very least, in order to persuade another that his or her rights should be denied, the latter should be accorded the right to freedom of thought—so that he or she may consider the argument against the right that is sought to be denied!

Can animals have rights?

We may now, I hope, be in a better position to answer the question posed in the title of this chapter: whether animals are capable of being rights-bearers.[31] I touched above on the shape of this argument which is based, first, on the contention that there is no logical barrier to prevent nonhumans from being accorded rights. It then, secondly, seeks to derive some of these rights from legislative or regulatory provisions that protect the welfare of animals. It is founded on the proposition that statutes that impose a duty on persons not to inflict cruelty on animals (with their normal sanctions for violation) could be said to confer on animals a legal right to humane (i.e., non-cruel) treatment.[32]

30 See, in particular, Alan Gewirth, *Reason and Morality* (Chicago, IL: University of Chicago Press, 1978).

31 A strong case for animals as right-bearers is made by Saskia Stucki, 'Towards a Theory of Legal Animal Rights: Simple and Fundamental Rights' (2020) 40 *Oxford Journal of Legal Studies* 533, and Tom Regan, *The Case for Animal Rights* (London: Routledge, 1984). For assaults on this view, see RG Frey, *Rights, Killing and Suffering: Moral Vegetarianism and Applied Ethics* (Oxford: Basil Blackwell, 1983); Raymond Wacks, review (1986) 49 *Modern Law Review* 403; and Peter Carruthers, *The Animals Issue: Moral Theory in Practice* (Cambridge: Cambridge University Press, 1992).

32 See Joel Feinberg, 'Human Duties and Human Rights', 188–189, and 'The Rights of Animals and Unborn Generations', 159, both reproduced in his *Rights, Justice and the Bounds of Liberty: Essays in Social Philosophy* (Princeton, NJ: Princeton University Press, 1980).

This would seem, *prima facie*, to be a viable argument. At the very least, it suggests that nonhumans have intrinsic, rather than merely instrumental, value justifying their legislative defence. However, this does not constitute legal status as a matter of law.[33] Nor do these putative rights attain the force that is normally associated with rights properly so called. They cannot be considered as 'trumps' in the Dworkinian sense. Indeed, in the case of animals it is, alas, we humans who constantly hold the trump cards against all animals. These attenuated 'rights' thus fall short of the conventional threshold, but this is not because of the lack of correlativity (see later), for, as Saskia Stucki maintains, the duties imposed by such legislation are not regarded as indirect duties *regarding* animals but as direct duties *owed to* the protected animals themselves.[34] It is therefore, she suggests, arguable that such statutory provisions, by protecting animals directly, render them beneficiaries of the duties specified therein: where one is owed a legal duty, a right generally results.[35] This, its advocates argue, means that a right, albeit qualified, inheres in the beneficiaries of those for whom the legislation explicitly provides. Stucki usefully distinguishes between first-order rights (claims and liberties) which affect a person's actual rather than normative conduct, on the one hand and the second-order rights created by powers and immunities which concern other legal relations, on the other. The latter, however, are nevertheless useful in reinforcing the first-order rights of animals. Indeed, several complex rights include immunities: the freedom from the legal power of another (the disability bearer) to alter the immunity holder's rights. Thus, animals' claims and liberties may be strengthened by immunity rights that protect those first-order rights from being annulled, by others.

So, for example, an animal's right not to be treated as property may be described as an immunity that would eradicate the legal powers that accompany the state of legal disposability caused by their status as property; this

33 See, for example, Richard Epstein, 'Animals as Objects, or Subjects, of Rights' in Cass R Sunstein and Martha C Nussbaum, eds, *Animal Rights: Current Debates and New Directions* (Oxford: Oxford University Press, 2005) 144ff; Steven M Wise, 'Legal Rights for Nonhuman Animals: The Case for Chimpanzees and Bonobos' (1996) 2 *Animal Law Review* 179; Gary L Francione, *Animals, Property, and the Law* (Philadelphia, PA: Temple University Press, 1995), 91ff.

34 Saskia Stucki, 'Towards a Theory of Legal Animal Rights: Simple and Fundamental Rights' (2020) 40 *Oxford Journal of Legal Studies* 533 (accessed online, no page numbers stated). See too David Bilchitz, 'Moving Beyond Arbitrariness: The Legal Personhood and Dignity of Non-Human Animals' (2009) 25 *South African Journal of Human Rights* 38, 42–43; Joel Feinberg, 'The Rights of Animals and Unborn Generations' in Joel Feinberg, *Rights, Justice, and the Bounds of Liberty*, 159, 161–162.

35 Matthew H Kramer, 'Legal and Moral Obligation' in Martin P Golding and William A Edmundson, eds, *The Blackwell Guide to the Philosophy of Law and Legal Theory* (Oxford: Blackwell, 2005) 188; Matthew H Kramer, 'Do Animals and Dead People Have Legal Rights?' (2001) 14 *Canadian Journal of Law and Jurisprudence* 29.

could restrict the rights of owners of animals to determine their fate. As passive rights, immunities lend themselves to be regarded as animal rights, because they are postulated as a correlative; in other words, they describe what the person disabled by an animal's immunity right cannot legally do.[36] She, rightly, observes that powers may not be apposite here; unlike immunities, powers need to be exercised not merely enjoyed, though, of course, as is the case with children, humans could act as representatives of animals.[37]

Welfare rights fail to provide the vigorous defence against competing human interests, however, trivial they may be. The quest is plainly to recognise rights that can, *prima facie*, withstand the forces arraigned against them. The ostensible compassion expressed in benevolent welfare laws is inadequate. The ideal would, of course, be the endorsement of animal rights as human rights (examined in Chapter 5). The hurdles that hamper this path, while not insurmountable, are significant, as we shall see, and I express my reservations in that chapter. In any event, there is unquestionably space in which to promote more robust rights that fall short of this ambition.[38] An important means by which to achieve this goal is to extinguish the notion that animals are property, and treat them as legal persons. The concept of legal personhood is widely regarded as a prerequisite of the ability to hold rights properly so called[39]:

> To say that a being is a person is merely to say that the being has morally significant interests, that the principle of equal consideration applies to that being, that the being is not a thing. In a sense we already accept that animals are persons; we claim to reject the view that animals are things and to recognize that, at the very least, animals have a morally significant interest in not suffering. Their status as property, however, has prevented their personhood from being realized.[40]

36 See Matthew H Kramer, 'Rights Without Trimmings' in Matthew H Kramer, NE Simmonds, and Hillel Steiner, op cit, 22.

37 Saskia Stucki, 'Towards a Theory of Legal Animal Rights: Simple and Fundamental Rights' (2020) 40 *Oxford Journal of Legal Studies* 533, n 17. See too HLA Hart, 'Legal Rights' in HLA Hart, *Essays on Bentham: Studies in Jurisprudence and Political Theory* (Oxford: Oxford University Press, 1982), 172, 181–182, 190; Neil MacCormick, 'Rights in Legislation' in PMS Hacker and J Raz, eds, *Law, Morality, and Society: Essays in Honour of HLA Hart* (Oxford: Oxford University Press, 1977), 199. See the following chapter.

38 Anne Peters, 'Liberté, Égalité, Animalité: Human-Animal Comparisons in Law' (2016) 5 *Transnational Environmental Law* 25, 46ff. William A Edmundson, 'Do Animals Need Rights?' (2015) 23 *Journal of Political Philosophy* 345.

39 Gary L Francione, *Animals, Property, and the Law* (Philadelphia, PA: Temple University Press, 1995).

40 Ibid, 'Animals—Property or Persons?' in Cass R Sunstein and Martha C Nussbaum, eds, *Animal Rights: Current Debates and New Directions* (Oxford: Oxford University Press, 2005) 108, 131. See too Steven M Wise, 'Animal Rights, One Step at a Time' in Sunstein and Nussbaum, op cit, 19; Visa AJ Kurki, *A Theory of Legal Personhood* (Oxford: Oxford University Press, 2019).

An analogy is often drawn with slavery. As chattels, slaves were incapable of being vested with rights.[41] And without legal rights they, like animals, generally lacked legal standing by which they were able to enforce the application of the protection afforded by the law, however, weak they may be. Granting legal rights to animals would facilitate enforcement by representatives or guardians acting on their behalf.[42]

Welfare legislation, whether or not it may be construed as the source of putative rights, is predictably trounced by competing human rights or even interests. 'Balancing' is an inescapable feature of the judicial weighing of competing interests; the recognition of fundamental animal rights could help to prevent the routine competition between heavyweight and lightweight contestants.[43] In particular, it might raise the threshold above which suffering is excused or justified by human benefits.[44]

According proper rights to animals—at least in respect of the negative rights against killing and the protection of bodily integrity—would mark a shift towards an acknowledgement that their abuse and exploitation is no longer thrust into the darker reaches of normativity. It would be fanciful to imagine that it could be achieved with a wave of a wand, rather than undertaken 'one step at a time'.[45] Notwithstanding the circumscribed and, many would say, inadequate nature of these adventitious or inferred rights, several impediments obstruct the road to their recognition. These doubts, reservations, and misgivings are explored in Chapter 4.

Rights talk immediately raises the distinction between what a right is, on the one hand, and what rights people actually have, or ought to have, on the other—this is, loosely, the distinction between moral rights and legal rights. The two are often confused, and it is by no means certain that even Hohfeld's

41 See Milton Meltzer, *Slavery: A World History* (Boston, MA: Da Capo Press, 1993); Hugh Thomas, *The Slave Trade: The Story of the Atlantic Slave Trade 1440-1870* (New York: Simon and Schuster, 1997). But, as Richard Posner points out, the rights of Negro slaves in the antebellum South 'at least nominally' included the right not to be gratuitously tortured, wounded, or killed, Richard Posner, op cit, in Cass R Sunstein and Martha C Nussbaum, eds, *Animal Rights: Current Debates and New Directions*, 71.

42 As is already the case in respect of animal welfare legislation where animal protection societies have standing to act for animals. A striking example is the Nonhuman Rights Project founded by Steven M Wise, see https://www.nonhumanrights.org. Such rights would obviously need to include the right of access to courts in order to enforce them. This question is considered further in Chapter 12.

43 The exercise normally entails a test of proportionality which includes criteria of necessity and suitability. Animals predictably fare poorly. See Chapter 12.

44 See Joel Feinberg, 'The Rights of Animals and Unborn Generations' in Joel Feinberg, *Rights, Justice, and the Bounds of Liberty: Essays in Social Philosophy* (Princeton NJ: Princeton University Press, 1980); David Bilchitz, 'Fundamental Rights as Bridging Concepts: Straddling the Boundary Between Ideal Justice and an Imperfect Reality' (2018) 40 *Human Rights Quarterly* 119; Gary L Francione, *Rain Without Thunder: The Ideology of the Animal Rights Movement* (Philadelphia, PA, Temple University Press, 2007).

45 Steven M Wise, 'Animal Rights, One Step at a Time' in Sunstein and Nussbaum, eds, op cit, 19.

influential analysis of rights is applicable to moral rights. It probably is not.[46] A moral right is an entitlement which confers moral liberties on those who have them to do certain things, and the moral constraint on others to abstain from interference.[47] A legal right, on the other hand, is one recognised by the law. Does the same follow in respect of moral rights? I shall briefly consider this testing question, and then address the problem of whether animals, or, to enable me to put the strongest case, 'higher' animals, are capable of being bearers of rights. Or, as HJ McCloskey puts it, '[t] o show that animals possess moral rights, moral rights against persons, it is not sufficient to establish that persons have duties in respect of animals'.[48] His argument rests on the view that there is no strict correlativity of rights, a position generally accepted in respect of *legal* rights. It warrants closer examination. This sort of claim typically proceeds along the following lines:

1 Central to the concept of moral rights is the notion of *exercising* such rights. The paradigm possessor of a right is an actor or potential actor who can act by doing what he is entitled to do, or act by demanding, claiming, requiring what he is entitled to demand or claim, require. In the absence of the possibility of such action in the being towards whom duties are owed, and where the being is not a member of a kind which is normally capable of action, we withhold talk of rights and confine ourselves to talk of duties. Moral rights are ascribed to beings that are capable of moral autonomy, moral self-direction, and self-determination.
2 We can therefore deny the capacity for rights to 'ex-persons' (the brain damaged, or extremely senile) and 'non-persons' (those born with damaged or under-developed brains), but not to 'potential persons' (infants who will become persons). We also deny this capacity to inanimate objects and plants, even though they (like ex-persons and non-persons) may be the object of duties. This is because they cannot exercise rights or have them exercised for them.
3 The capacity to have interests is insufficient to establish a capacity to bear rights. This is because, though nonhumans (including corporate bodies, churches, states, and clubs) may be said to have interests, the idea that nonhuman animals have interests relies on an equation of interests with desires, aims, and beliefs, and it would therefore still need to be shown that the possession of *these* capacities is a ground for the attribution of rights. Moreover, 'rights and interests are completely different things'.[49]

46 See Joseph Raz, 'Legal Rights' (1984) 4 *Oxford Journal of Legal Studies* 1.
47 See HJ McCloskey, 'Moral Rights and Animals' (1978) 22 *Inquiry* 23, 27–28.
48 McCloskey, 'Moral Rights and Animals', 27–28.
49 Ibid, 39. Here McCloskey departs from his earlier view expressed in 'Rights' (1965) 15 *Philosophical Quarterly* 115. See also Tom Regan, 'McCloskey on Why Animals Cannot Have Rights' (1976) 26 *Philosophical Quarterly* 251. Joseph Raz argues (as part of a larger and sophisticated defence of freedom) that '[A]ll rights are based on interests', J Raz, *The Morality of Freedom* (Oxford: Clarendon Press, 1986), 191.

There will be circumstances where a right-bearer may wish to exercise his rights *against* his own interests. Equally it may be in his interests to deprive him of his freedom to exercise rights. And where a putative right-bearer is incapable of expressing his wishes (if he has any), his mind would have to be read. Where he has no mind or will to be read, he cannot be a representation of his rights or the exercising or waiving of moral rights.

4 Since most animals lack the relevant moral capacity, they do not have moral rights. Some animals (whales and dolphins) may be found to have such capacity: it may therefore be 'morally appropriate for us meanwhile to act towards (whales and dolphins) *as if* they are possessors of rights'.[50]

This is a careful argument, but it does not seem to be a particularly convincing one. Indeed, some of its claims do not appear to advance its own case. Thus, it is difficult to see how a right-bearer's inability to express his or her wishes leads ineluctably to the conclusion (in point 3) that he or she has no rights that can be represented. To argue (as McCloskey does)[51] that the paternalism it involves would offend liberal values may call for an examination of those values. Nor is the speculative empirical move (in point 4) a particularly solid foundation for the benevolence towards a limited range of creatures.

Nonhuman animals have interests and needs. In particular, they have a clear interest in avoiding pain and probably also an untimely death. But this does not dispose of the matter. It enables one to reject the will theory of rights—which is plainly less congenial to animals than the interest theory. The main virtue of an interest-based approach is that it more easily facilitates the grounding of *duties* towards animals.[52] MacCormick offers the example of children: their rights are exercised by their parents or guardians; it cannot therefore be argued that the child has a *choice* whether or not to waive its rights. This would lead to the specious conclusion that children have no rights. And a similar point could, of course, be made in relation to animals.

It hardly requires pointing out, but the rights extrapolated from animal welfare legislation exist as a *brutum fulmen*, unless and until they receive judicial recognition. The extent to which lawmakers and judges have been willing to take this step is considered in Chapter 12.

50 McCloskey, 'Moral Rights and Animals', 42–43. McCloskey proposes, instead of a rights-based argument, a justice-based argument in support of animals. A full account would require an analysis of how considerations such as desert, merit, wellbeing, needs, and wishes feature in the structure of a theory of justice towards animals.

51 Ibid, 39.

52 This is not to say, of course, either that all duties derive from rights or that morality is rights-based. See Raz, *The Morality of Freedom*, Ch 7.

4 Rights resistance

The pursuit of limited rights for animals extrapolated from welfare legislation, adumbrated in the previous chapter, encounters predictable resistance from a number of quarters. Some are a consequence of an express or implied attitude or perspective such as a humancentric view of animals and, indeed, the world; others consist in the hostility towards the very concept of rights and, in particular, animal rights.[1] An assortment of antagonisms—philosophical, political, pragmatic, and legal—is raised against its acceptance.

A more ambitious proposal—that animals be accorded human rights—is advanced by some who perceive it to be a logical development of human rights theory and practice. There is, of course, an inevitable overlap between the objections against rights *tout court*, but where they are more pertinent to the disapproval of *human* rights for animals, I shall reserve my discussion of their distinctive nature for Chapter 5 which, I hope, is a more practicable approach.

At first blush, it would appear that the statutory and regulatory protection against the mistreatment of animals and measures to secure their welfare constitutes recognition that rights are created. At the very least, it suggests that nonhumans have intrinsic, rather than merely instrumental, value justifying their legislative defence. Yet this does not approximate to legal status as a matter of law.[2] Nor do these putative 'rights' attain the force that are normally

1 'Must we', asks Jacques Derrida, 'pose the question of our relations with the *animot* in terms of "rights"?' He answers his own question in the negative, based on his general scepticism regarding the nature of rights, Jacques Derrida, *The Animal That Therefore I Am*, Marie-Louise Mallet, ed, transl by David Wills (New York: Fordham University Press, 2008), 88. See too Gary Steiner, *Animals and the Limits of Postmodernism* (New York: Columbia University Press, 2013), 149–151.

2 See, for example, Richard Epstein, 'Animals as Objects, or Subjects, of Rights' in Cass R Sunstein and Martha C Nussbaum, eds, *Animal Rights: Current Debates and New Directions* (Oxford: Oxford University Press, 2005), 144ff; Steven M Wise, 'Legal Rights for Nonhuman Animals: The Case for Chimpanzees and Bonobos' (1996) 2 *Animal Law Review* 179; Gary Francione, *Animals, Property, and the Law* (Philadelphia, PA: Temple University Press), 91ff.

DOI: 10.4324/9781032702575-4

associated with rights properly so called. They cannot be considered 'trumps' in the Dworkinian sense.[3] Indeed, in the case of animals it is, alas, we humans who constantly hold the trump cards against all animals.

These attenuated 'rights' fall short of the conventional threshold not because of the lack of correlativity (see later), for, as mentioned in the previous chapter, the duties imposed by such legislation are not regarded as indirect duties *regarding* animals but as direct duties *owed to* the protected animals themselves.[4] It is therefore, as Stucki contends, arguable that such statutory provisions, by protecting animals directly, render them beneficiaries of the duties specified therein. In other words, where one is owed a legal duty a right will normally accrue.[5]

Consequently, it is arguable that a right, albeit qualified, inheres in the beneficiaries of those for whom the protection in the legislation explicitly provides. The consequence of this limitation, however, is that while subordinate rights of animals (for example, painless killing) is accorded protection, the primary right (not to be killed at all) remains unprotected. And even though we might extrapolate more expansive rights such as the right to life or against torture, they are routinely flouted in practice when they conflict with our welfare or wishes, however, trifling.

In the absence of fully fledged rights, the fragility of the safeguards offered by animal welfare legislation is self-evident. The restricted normative potency of such well-meaning stipulations points to the need for a fundamental shift towards an acceptance of substantively resilient legally recognised rights—ideally along the lines of human rights. If this seems an ambitious or idealistic objective

3 They lack the clout to stand up to a contest against a utilitarian calculus or, *a fortiori*, competing rights. See generally on the fragility of such 'rights' and the broader question of 'legitimate' right-holders, Steven M Wise, 'Hardly a Revolution—The Eligibility of Nonhuman Animals for Dignity-Rights in a Liberal Democracy' (1998) 22 *Vermont Law Review* 793; William A Edmundson, 'Do Animals Need Rights?' (2015) 23 *Journal of Political Philosophy* 345; Thomas G Kelch, 'The Role of the Rational and the Emotive in a Theory of Animal Rights' (1999) 27 *Boston College Environmental Affairs Law Review* 18; Gary L Francione, *Animals, Property, and the Law* (Philadelphia, PA: Temple University Press, 2007); Matthew H Kramer, 'Do Animals and Dead People Have Legal Rights?' (2001) 14 *Canadian Journal of Law and Jurisprudence* 29; Visa AJ Kurki, 'Legal Competence and Legal Power' in Mark McBride, ed, *New Essays on the Nature of Rights* (Abingdon: Hart Publishing, 2017), 46; Tom L Beauchamp, 'Rights Theory and Animal Rights' in Tom L Beauchamp and RG Frey, eds, *The Oxford Handbook of Animal Ethics* (Oxford: Oxford University Press, 2011), 91ff.

4 Saskia Stucki, 'Towards a Theory of Legal Animal Rights: Simple and Fundamental Rights' (2020) 40 *Oxford Journal of Legal Studies* 533. See too David Bilchitz, 'Moving Beyond Arbitrariness: The Legal Personhood and Dignity of Non-Human Animals' (2009) 25 *South African Journal of Human Rights* 38, 42–43; Joel Feinberg, 'The Rights of Animals and Unborn Generations' in Joel Feinberg, *Rights, Justice, and the Bounds of Liberty: Essays in Social Philosophy* (Princeton, NJ: Princeton University Press, 1980), 159, 161–162.

5 Matthew H Kramer, 'Legal and Moral Obligation' in Martin P Golding and William A Edmundson, eds, *The Blackwell Guide to the Philosophy of Law and Legal Theory* (Oxford: Blackwell, 2005), 188.

(a matter to be evaluated in the following chapter), it is worth considering the creation of a sturdier regime of explicitly animal rights.

A constant theme in the argument against nonhumans enjoying rights is the claim that since they cannot be subject to duties, they are incapable of being right-holders. The general question of correlativity was discussed in Chapter 3 where I pointed to the criticism of the Hohfeldian schema. It is simply not the case that every duty gives rise to a right. There can be a duty to do *something* (for example, a judge's duty to decide a case) which is not owed to *someone*, and therefore does not entail any specific right. The Ten Commandments are replete with duties, but no one (apart perhaps from God!) accrues a right. It is often maintained that in early US law, 'the masters of slaves had absolute duties towards them, as toward animals, but the slaves had no rights'.[6] Similarly, as John Stuart Mill mentions, the fact that the law is under a duty to punish a convicted offender does not give him or her a right to be punished! Certain duties that benefit specific persons confer rights only on the intended beneficiaries of those duties.[7] Conversely my right to something does not logically generate a duty in you.[8]

There will always be those, albeit compassionate souls, who remain unconvinced that even the existence of welfare statutes explicitly protecting animals can generate rights:

> We can keep animals from suffering ... without having to grant them rights or the capability of having rights. The legal prohibition on the shooting of various sorts of birds and animals outside restricted seasons confers protection on their freedom, but does not give them a right or assume them to be capable of one.[9]

6 Alan R White, *Rights* (Oxford: Clarendon Press, 1984), 65.

7 See Matthew Kramer, 'Rights Without Trimmings' in Matthew H Kramer, NE Simmonds, and Hillel Steiner, *A Debate Over Rights: Philosophical Enquiries* (Oxford: Oxford University Press, 1998), 85ff; Visa AJ Kurki, 'Rights, Harming and Wronging: A Restatement of the Interest Theory' (2018) 38 *Oxford Journal of Legal Studies* 430, 436ff; David Lyons, 'Rights, Claimants, and Beneficiaries' (1969) 6 *American Philosophical Quarterly* 173.

8 Thus, argues White, my right to treat people in certain ways does not impose upon them a duty to permit themselves to be so treated. 'Still less', he continues, 'does my right to treat animals ... in certain ways lay on them any duty to allow themselves to be so treated, for the idea of their having a duty is absurd', 64.

9 White, op cit, 89. He refers, in a footnote, to the Cruelty to Animals Act 1876, ss 2 and 3 which Feinberg avers confers rights on animals, is not borne out by the language of these sections. This seems to be correct; they proscribe painful experiments, but it is not easy to extrapolate rights granted to the victims. See Joel Feinberg, 'Human Duties and Animal Rights' in Richard Knowles Morris and Michael W Fox, eds, *On the Fifth Day: Animal Rights and Human Ethics* (Moreno Valley, CA: Acropolis Books, 1978). See too Joel Feinberg, 'The Rights of Animals' in T Regan and P Singer, eds, *Animal Rights and Human Obligations* 2nd edn (London: Pearson, 1989). White's book was published in 1984; the UK's Animal Welfare Act 2006 is more positive.

The matter is, of course, one of analytical and statutory interpretation. Does a fox in England acquire rights in virtue of the Hunting Act 2004? If so, it would seem to rest on the view that rights are no more than an 'alternative formulation of duties'.[10] A 'refined and reversed' form of correlativity is suggested by Stucki which

> must show that animal rights are not merely reflexes *created* by animal welfare duties, but rather the *grounds* for such duties. In other words, positive animal welfare duties must be plausibly explained as some kind of codified reflection, or visible manifestation, of 'invisible' background animal rights that give rise to those duties.[11]

This shift away from Hohfeld correlativity enables her to argue, persuasively I think, that, in the way that the existence of children implies that of parents, it is not really 'parents' but rather those who will *later* be called 'parents' when a child is born.[12] In other words, that is really the content of a right. And this facilitates the claim that the basis of a duty is not a right, but an interest that warrants protection which supports the idea that the recognition of animals' welfare in animal welfare statutes constitutes the grounds for imposing a duty on others, and hence gives rise to the recognition—at least in theory—of the rights of the animals thereby protected.[13]

Is it, however, too sanguine to regard these adventitious 'rights' as genuine rights? At best, they extend to the avoidance of pain and suffering caused by cruel practices of slaughter and inhumane forms of experiments.[14] An authentic, substantive right not to be killed at all remains well out of reach, as do the fundamental rights to dignity or against torture. In any event, as with rights in general, they are defeasible when weighed against competing

10 HLA Hart, 'Legal Rights' in HLA Hart, *Essays on Bentham: Studies in Jurisprudence and Political Theory* (Oxford: Oxford University Press), 181–182, 190. See too Neil MacCormick, 'Rights in Legislation' (n 43) 199. 'Rights in Legislation' in PMS Hacker and J Raz, eds, *Law, Morality, and Society: Essays in Honour of HLA Hart* (Oxford: Oxford University Press, 1977), 198ff. Cf Joseph Raz, 'Legal Rights' (1984) 4 *Oxford Journal of Legal Studies* 1, 12.

11 Saskia Stucki, 'Towards a Theory of Legal Animal Rights: Simple and Fundamental Rights' (2020) 40 *Oxford Journal of Legal Studies* 533.

12 The analogy is Alan Gewirth's in *Human Rights: Essays on Justification and Applications* (Chicago, IL: University of Chicago Press, 1982), 14.

13 It matters not that such rights are implied rather than explicitly expressed, see Neil MacCormick, 'Rights in Legislation' in PMS Hacker and J Raz, eds, *Law, Morality, and Society: Essays in Honour of HLA Hart* (Oxford: Oxford University Press, 1977), 191–192; Joseph Raz, 'Legal Rights' (1984) 4 *Oxford Journal of Legal Studies* 1, 13–14. But, needless to add, such recognition awaits judicial approval.

14 But see Cass R Sunstein, 'Standing for Animals (with Notes on Animal Rights)' (2000) 47 *UCLA Law Review* 133.

rights or interests; the tests of proportionality and necessity often extinguish or undermine *prima facie* rights,[15] especially, of course, where animals are the potential beneficiaries.[16]

The indifference or even hostility towards animal rights exhibited by certain religious doctrine and philosophical thinking was explored in Chapter 2. I suggested there that it may be necessary to engage in a form of 'constructive interpretation'[17] to avoid too superficial an understanding of these sources.[18] In addition to such ethical doubts, there are a number of reservations about the very idea that animals have, or ought to have, rights. At their heart is the humancentric or anthropocentric outlook that regards, *a priori*, the very idea of nonhumans acquiring rights as anathema. Some of the further objections flow directly or indirectly from this premise. Others relate more explicitly to the standard legal prerequisites for holding rights which, so it is contended, animals fail to satisfy, or they are based upon various deficiencies of rights themselves. There are, I think, the following six main obstructions or, in some cases, predispositions, that beset the path.

Anthropocentrism

A morality whose premise is human-centred, that assumes 'man is the measure of all things', and that rights accrue only to humans, inexorably creates a species barrier outside of which nonhumans reside. Generally labelled 'speciesism', it captures the conceit of an anthropocentric standpoint's assumption that criteria are required by which to determine what constitutes a

15 I consider some of the difficulties encountered by courts when engaged in the balancing exercise between Articles 8 and 10 of the European Convention on Human Rights, see Raymond Wacks, *Privacy and Media Freedom* (Oxford: Oxford University Press, 2013), *passim*. See too Tom L Beauchamp, 'Rights Theory and Animal Rights' in Tom L Beauchamp and RG Frey, eds, *The Oxford Handbook of Animal Ethics* (Oxford: Oxford University Press, 2011); Matthew H Kramer, 'Do Animals and Dead People Have Legal Rights?' (2001) 14 *Cambridge Journal of Law and Jurisprudence* 29; William A Edmundson, 'Do Animals Need Rights?' (2015) 23 *Journal of Political Philosophy* 346.

16 See, for example, Steven M Wise, 'Hardly a Revolution—The Eligibility of Nonhuman Animals for Dignity-Rights in a Liberal Democracy' (1998) 22 *Vermont Law Review* 793; Joel Feinberg, 'The Rights of Animals and Unborn Generations' in Joel Feinberg, *Rights, Justice, and the Bounds of Liberty: Essays in Social Philosophy* (Princeton NJ: Princeton University Press, 1980), 159; Gary L Francione, *Animals, Property, and the Law* (Philadelphia, PA: Temple University Press, 2007).

17 An approach that is central to Ronald Dworkin's right thesis developed especially in *Law's Empire* (Cambridge, MA and London: Belknap Press, 1986). See too Raymond Wacks, 'Law's Umpire: Judges, Truth, and Moral Accountability' in Peter Koller and André-Jean Arnaud, eds, *Law, Justice, and Culture* (Stuttgart: Franz Steiner Verlag, 1998), 37.

18 This is what I take to be the primary endeavour of Christine Korsgaard's (re)interpretation of Kant in her admirable *Fellow Creatures: Our Obligations to the Other Animals* (Oxford University Press, 2018) which I considered in Chapter 2.

'human'. This obviously constitutes a major stumbling block that thwarts the moral and legal endeavour to confer rights on animals.[19]

To satisfy some test in order to be treated as right-bearing subjects, animals become, in effect, quasi-humans. Their distinctive identity is, for the purpose of moral 'assessment' suspended and then, in all likelihood, lost altogether.[20] The claim that anthropocentrism is inevitable[21] is questioned by those who contend that the hubris of bestowing rights on the basis of a human-oriented qualification (under which higher primates are most likely to pass) is antithetical to the just treatment of nonhumans. It relies, in part, on the requirement of 'personhood' which is discussed in the following section.[22]

An anthropocentrist could, of course, argue that

> [T]he best approach to the question of animal rights is a humancentric one that appeals to our developing knowledge and sentiments about animals and that eschews on the one hand philosophical argument and on the other hand a legal-formalist approach to the issue....[23]

How might such a case be made? Judge Posner's first step is to deny the claim by many rights advocates[24] that cognitive capacity is a necessary or sufficient condition of having rights. Does a one-day-old foetus not have rights, he asks. And most people, he asserts, would find it 'downright offensive' to give more rights to monkeys than 'retarded people'.[25] Moreover, slaves had cognitive capacity but no rights. Legal rights, he contends, are instrumental

19 Some anthropocentric positions are based on the alleged irrationality of the case for animal rights. See Richard A Posner, 'Animal Rights: Legal, Philosophical, and Pragmatic Perspectives' and RA Epstein, 'Animals as Objects or Subjects of Rights', in Cass R Sunstein and Martha C Nussbaum, eds, *Rights: Current Debates and New Directions* (New York: Oxford University Press, 2004). For a compelling critique of this view, see Gary Steiner, *Animals and the Limits of Postmodernism* (New York: Columbia University Press, 2013), 134–147.

20 For example, Giorgio Agamben asks us to see animals as degraded humans, Giorgio Agamben, *The Open: Man and Animal*, transl by K Attell (Stanford, CA: Stanford University Press, 2004). See too his *Homo Sacer: Sovereign Power and Bare Life*, transl by D Heller-Roazen (Stanford, CA: Stanford University Press, 1998). Cf Rob Boddice, 'The End of Anthropocentrism' in Rob Boddice, ed, *Anthropocentrism: Humans, Animals, Environments* (Leiden: Brill, 2011), 1; Matthew Calarco, *Thinking Through Animals: Identity, Indifference, Indistinction* (Stanford, CA: Stanford University Press, 2015).

21 Boddice, *passim*, op cit.

22 I consider the question of human exceptionalism in relation to human rights in the next chapter.

23 Richard A Posner, 'Animal Rights: Legal, Philosophical, and Pragmatic Perspectives' in Cass R Sunstein and Martha C Nussbaum, eds, *Rights: Current Debates and New Directions* (New York: Oxford University Press, 2004), 51. See too RA Epstein, 'Animals as Objects or Subjects of Rights', in Sunstein and Nussbaum, op cit, 143.

24 His principal target here is Steven M Wise, *Rattling the Cage: Toward Legal Rights for Animals*, reprinted (Lebanon, IN:Da Capo Press, 2001).

25 Op cit, 56.

in securing civil liberties; they are, in large part, enjoyed by voters. Animals do not belong to this enfranchised group. The most effective way to protect animals is therefore by prohibiting their maltreatment: 'we don't need the vocabulary of rights, which is ... just an impediment to clear thought as well as a provocation in some legal and philosophical quarters'.[26] Nor is he persuaded by the utilitarian position (which I discuss in Chapter 6) that regards the life of a healthy pig as worthier of legal protection than that of a severely retarded human being—a proposition he finds 'unpalatable even bizarre'.[27]

There is, he says, no 'metric' that would facilitate the approaches to animal rights 'to be commensurated and conflicts among them to be resolved'.[28] An ethical theory approach that even implicitly equates the life of a human with a nonhuman is 'weird' and 'insane'.[29] But the absence of a 'metric' is surely 'a feature of ethical theories generally: there is no universally agreed upon metaethical standpoint that can resolve all conflicts between different theories'.[30] He concludes that a humancentric approach which pays attention to the facts[31] along with the combination of empathy and animal welfare laws are sufficient to protect animals against suffering:

> The humancentric approach establishes continuity between the animal rights movement and the love of pets, both seen as founded on sentiment rather than on philosophical idealism, and by so doing the approach helps explain the movement, parallel to the animal rights movement, to award damages for emotional suffering to pet owners whose pets are killed or injured by negligence or other (human) misconduct.[32]

Posner's speciesist pragmatism is dismissed by Peter Singer as implausible for the following reasons.[33] First, he repudiates the speciesism that drives Posner's rationale for his approach. No sufficient justification exists for regarding species membership as the basis for protecting one group of creatures to the exclusion of another. From this, he argues, it does not follow that all animals have the same rights as us; it would be absurd to grant them voting rights, but nor would it be less absurd to give that right to babies or severely

26 Op cit, 59.
27 Op cit, 60.
28 Op cit, 63.
29 Op cit, 69.
30 Gary Steiner, *Animals and the Limits of Postmodernism* (New York: Columbia University Press, 2013), 134.
31 In particular, preferring humans to animals 'is a fact deeply rooted in our current thinking and feeling, a fact based on beliefs that can change but not a fact that can be shaken by philosophy.... If we were cats, we would put cats first.... Reason doesn't enter', 67.
32 Op cit, 72–73.
33 Peter Singer, 'Ethics Beyond Species and Beyond Instincts' in Cass R Sunstein and Martha C Nussbaum, eds, *Animal Rights: Current Debates and New Directions* (New York: Oxford University Press, 2004), 78, 83.

retarded humans. Nevertheless, we treat these humans with equal consideration; we don't, for example, eat them or experiment on them. Yet we do these things to animals that possess greater self-awareness than they do. Instead of a gap between humans and animals, there is an overlap in the possession of any valuable characteristic by individuals of different species. To regard humans as superior is prejudice[34]:

> The only acceptable limit to our moral concern is the point at which there is no awareness of pain or pleasure and no conscious preferences of any kind. That is why pigs are objects of moral concern, but lettuces are not.[35]

Singer also contests Posner's rejection of the relevance and power of moral argument. He argues that the decisive factor in moral judgement is that one accepts constraints on the extent to which one prefers one's own interests. In other words, moral reasoning is distinguished by the universalisability of its principles. Posner, he suggests, is driven to accepting the position that moral argument should be powerless against the strong instincts at the heart of the test of universalisability. Many such instincts relating to animals, Singer argues, cannot survive this test because we instinctively treat animals in ways that are in our interests, not theirs. Nor is it necessarily true that factual errors, as Posner claims, account for our moral instincts; we sometimes need to change these instincts that are not a consequence of factual errors.[36]

Posner's conviction that moral argument is ineffective against our instincts is disputed by Singer. If it were the case, he asks, how would he explain the progress in the field of race relations, crimes against humanity, homosexuality, and other moral issues? Philosophers, Singer contends, have played an important role in these movements, including the animal rights lobby.[37] Finally, Singer repudiates Posner's idea that the wellbeing of animals would be better protected if they were treated as property rather than endowing them with rights. Approximately ten billion animals are raised for food annually in the United States, mostly in wretched factory-farm conditions. How, Singer asks, does their status as property improve their lot?[38]

Both Posner and Richard Epstein base their rights-scepticism on moral instinct or intuition which they claim trumps rational thought. But, however, 'tenacious' these sentiments may be, they are always susceptible to reasoned

34 Singer, op cit, 79.
35 Op cit, 80.
36 Op cit, 84.
37 He quotes (op cit, 86) the view of a political scientist who describes the effect that academic philosophers have had in the animal rights crusade as 'a sustained attempt ... to change radically the status afforded to animals in moral thinking', Robert Garner, *Animals, Politics and Morality* (Manchester: Manchester University Press, 1993), 1–2.
38 Op cit, 90.

argument. And, as in the case of women and slaves, rational thinking changed our view of their moral—and eventually—their legal status.[39] The analogy with slaves is resisted largely on the ground that unlike animals, they were moral agents.

The line between sentiment and reason is not fixed.[40] Moreover, reason

> puts us in a position to recognize a fundamental kinship with animals, a kinship forged out of the mortality that we share with them ... it originates in a feeling of vulnerability and mortality that we share with other sentient beings.... As regards our relationship to animals, much of the work of reason in this connection consists in undoing a set of prejudices that long ago became reified into tenacious 'moral convictions'.[41]

Richard Epstein's humancentrism draws on Roman law (to which I return in the following section) which endowed humans with rights on the ground that they were born in a state of natural freedom. They were therefore regarded as 'natural persons' unlike animals. For Epstein, the analogy with women and slaves is invoked to justify this distinction, although they were treated as free men when their humanity was eventually recognised.[42]

There are two forms of anthropocentrism that are so deep-seated they pass almost unnoticed. The first proceeds on the assumption that because a practice is traditional, it cannot be questioned. For example, fox hunting has long been a feature of country life in England; to oppose it on compassionate grounds is, its supporters assert, to assail a venerable custom that gives pleasure to many. One might employ this argument to justify bull-baiting if it were still the common entertainment it once was in England. In the very town where I now reside, the Bull Run was celebrated annually. When the Society for the Protection of Animals (SPCA) led a campaign against the practice in 1833, locals defended their ancient custom as a 'traditional, manly, English sport; inspiring courage, agility and presence of mind under danger', claiming that it was less cruel than fox hunting. The local newspaper queried: 'Who or what is this London Society that, usurping the place of constituted

39 No one 'ever gave a thought to slaves, no more in the West than in the East. Everywhere the way of life depended on them. One cannot say they were accepted as such, for there was no acceptance. Everyone used them; no one paid attention to them'. Edith Hamilton, *The Echo of Greece* (Toronto: Foul Play Press, 1964), 28, 1957 edition quoted by Wise, op cit, 489.

40 So-called 'non-cognitivism in ethics' claims that in moral reasoning there can be no rational solutions: we cannot *objectively* know what is right or wrong. It is closely associated with David Hume in his *Treatise of Human Nature*.

41 Gary Steiner, op cit, 138. See too his *Animals and the Moral Community: Mental Life, Moral Status, and Kinship* (New York: Columbia University Press, 2008).

42 See Steven M Wise's fine historical analysis: 'The Legal Thinghood of Nonhuman Animals' (1996) 23 *Environmental Affairs* 471.

authorities, presumes to interfere with our ancient amusement?'[43] To respond that the law has long proscribed bear- and bull-baiting would be met by the answer that fox hunting is also now unlawful in England, Scotland, and Wales.[44]

The second form of anthropocentrism is even more pernicious. There is a strain of *machismo* that regards certain kinds of sympathy for animals to be a sign of faintheartedness (an echo of the description of bull-baiting in Stamford as 'manly') or a left wing plot 'to punish the upper class'.[45] Several years ago, an article appeared in the British magazine, *The Spectator*, which described how the author, a Mr Hume, and his friends working in an abattoir enjoyed spraying the blood of headless chickens at each other. My letter to the editor was published the following week:

> Sir: There is a fashionable tendency in conservative thought that, sadly, is increasingly reflected in your pages. It consists in both deriding those who protest against animal suffering and rejoicing in this savagery with puerile bravado. Amid graphic accounts of mindless barbarism, we are invited to dismiss the idea of concern for animals as deluded wimpishness. Tough guys are unmoved by, even enjoy, cruelty: 'shooting each other with the spray from headless chickens in real-life zap zone'.
>
> The foundation of Mr Hume's argument is specious and dangerous. If animals are 'filthy' and too 'dim' to exercise rights, Mr Hume would presumably deny similar rights to newly born, senile or demented human animals.

43 Robert Chambers, *The Book of Days: A Miscellany of Popular Antiquities in Connection with the Calendar*, Volume 2 (W & R Chambers Ltd, 1864), 575. The Elizabethans, including the Queen, enjoyed watching bears being baited by mastiffs which, when they grew tired, were replaced by others until they have mauled it to death—'a sport very pleasant' according to Thomas Platter, see Clare Williams, ed, *Thomas Platter's Travels in England 1599* (London: Jonathan Cape, 1937). Blind bears were 'whipped into a fury to entertain the crowds', see Ian Mortimer, *The Time Traveller's Guide to Elizabethan England* (London: Vintage, 2013), 335, see too 334–336. Similar bloodshed was inflicted on bulls by packs of dogs. For graphic descriptions (requiring a strong constitution), see HWL Emmison, *Elizabethan Life: Home, Work and Land* (Essex Record Office, 1976). Extraordinarily, it was unlawful *not* to indulge in bull-baiting. So ingrained in the culture was this 'sport' that every town boasted a bull-ring. Shakespeare mentions both activities in *The Merry Wives of Windsor* and *Twelfth Night*. See too Giles E Dawson, 'London's Bull-Baiting and Bear-Baiting arena in 1562' (1974) 15 *Shakespeare Quarterly* 97.

44 Fox hunting was banned by the Hunting Act 2004 in England and Wales, and the Protection of Wild Mammals (Scotland) Act 2002 in Scotland. See Chapter 1.

45 Roger Scruton, *How to Be a Conservative* (London: Bloomsbury, 2014), 9. See too his *On Hunting* (London, Yellow Jersey Press, 1998). More recently, he wrote: 'It is difficult for many people today to understand how you can be bound by a code of honour and sympathy to an animal that you are intending to kill; but this is exactly what was once understood by chivalry and it is perhaps a function of sport to cultivate the spirit of chivalry in those who engage in it', *The Guardian*, 28 November 2004.

> His assertion that 'animals are idiotically endowed with rights that are really the preserve of people' not only confuses the descriptive with the normative (as does much of his piece), but also glibly neglects the possibility of alternatives to 'rights' that might afford a satisfactory legal and moral basis for securing animal welfare.
>
> Let us reject the fatuous political correctness that seeks to conceal the truth or distort the unpalatable. Where, however, it happens to coincide with compassion and sensitivity towards our fellow creatures, we should not be too chicken to face up to our ethical duties.[46]

Both tradition and masculinity conceal an immanent human-centred indifference to animal welfare, let alone rights.

Gratuitous cruelty is not, however, confined to the past. Cockfighting, dog fighting, bullfighting, bull-running, and several other forms of 'entertainment' persist in many parts of the world. A particularly egregious example was uncovered by the BBC in June 2023. A sadistic monkey 'torture ring' stretching from Indonesia to the United States involved hundreds of customers in the United States, United Kingdom, and elsewhere paying Indonesians to torment baby long-tailed macaques on video. The network is said to have begun on YouTube and moved to private groups on the Telegram app where some have more than a thousand members. Clients devise ideas for the most barbaric forms of torture and killing, and pay to watch the barbarity on their screens. The purpose is to create bespoke films, in which these creatures are abused, tortured, and sometimes killed. At least 20 individuals are currently under investigation, including two key suspects being probed by the US Department of Homeland Security. The BBC managed to track down the torturers in Indonesia, as well as distributors and customers in the United States.

One has been identified as a grandmother in her forties who is known in the community as 'sadistic'. The other is a ringleader known as 'Mr Ape' who confessed to the BBC that he had killed at least four monkeys and tortured many more, and admitted that he had commissioned 'extremely brutal' videos. The grandmother's phone was found to contain approximately 100 torture videos, as well as evidence that she had paid for the creation of some of the most extreme videos produced. Indonesian police have arrested and charged two suspects.[47]

46 *The Spectator*, 2 September 2000.

47 *BBC News* https://www.bbc.co.uk/news/world-65951188 (accessed on 21 June 2023). Storey and 'Mr Ape' have (at the time of writing) yet to be charged, but they, along with at least three other key targets, face up to seven years in prison. Asep Yadi Nurul Hikmah was charged with animal torture and the sale of a protected species and was sentenced to three years in jail. M Ajis Rasjana was sentenced to eight months' jail, the maximum sentence in Indonesia for torturing an animal.

Animals as property

If animals are not persons, what are they? Roman law was clear; they were property. Its influence, especially of the Byzantine Emperor, Justinian's codification, was considerable, and, as I now sketch, this commodification of animals remains an important impediment to the recognition of animal rights.

The proprietary relationship between humans and animals is deeply ingrained in our social and legal order. I own my pets; the farmer is the owner of his livestock, and so on. It is a situation that has barely changed over the centuries. The world, according to the ancients, was divinely created for humans in a 'Great Chain of Being'. This inevitably relegated animals to nonhumans which, in effect, meant property, an attitude that continued to pervade the law for centuries. Descartes, for example, (in)famously described animals as machines.[48] In the absence of a rational soul, he asserted, animals were incapable of being self-conscious beings.[49]

But it is Roman law whose influence was paramount in advancing the conception of animals as property. During the period of the so-called classical jurists, between the first century BC and the middle of the third century AD, Roman law achieved a condition of considerable sophistication. Between AD 529 and 534, Justinian ordered the creation of a systematic, comprehensive codification. The three resulting books, the *Corpus Juris Civilis* (comprising the Digest, Codex, and Institutes), were to be treated as definitive: a conclusive statement of the law that required no interpretation.

Its meticulous detail proved to be its strength. More than 600 years after the fall of the Western Roman Empire, Europe witnessed a revival in the study of Roman law. And Justinian's codification was at its heart. Its contradictions and complexity were an unexpected advantage, since, despite the emperor's fantasy of finality, the rules were susceptible to interpretation and adaptation to suit the requirements of the time. In this way, Roman civil law spread throughout most of Europe. By the eighteenth century, however, it was recognised that more concise codes were called for. Justinian's collation was replaced by several codes that sought brevity, accessibility, and exhaustiveness. The Napoleonic code of 1804 came close to fulfilling these lofty aspirations. It was exported by colonisation to large tracts of Western and Southern Europe and thence

48 Perhaps 'the great cogitator would have been nearer the truth if he had described himself as a machine', John Gray, *Straw Dogs: Thoughts on Humans and Other Animals* (London: Granta, 2002), 188. He explains: 'Consciousness may be the human attribute that machines can most easily produce. It may be in their capacity for consciousness that humans and the machines ... are most alike'.

49 The premise of his position was the Aristotelean view that since man is a political animal that has a perception of good and evil and related virtues, no animal ever qualifies. Similarly, Thomas Aquinas, drawing on Aristotelean philosophy, regards animals—since they lack rationality—as 'appointed for human use'. See Chapter 2 for a more detailed account of these and other philosophical approaches to the moral status of animals.

to Latin America, and it exerted an enormous influence throughout Europe. Justinian's Digest was unequivocal that '*hominum causa omne ius constitutum sit*': all law has been created for the sake of men.[50]

A 'person' under Roman law was an individual who had rights. A 'thing' (*res*), on the other hand, was merely an object of the rights held by a person. Beings that were believed to lack free will—women, slaves, children, the insane, and, of course, animals—were generally classified as property.[51] This assumption was accepted without demurral. The *Institutes* divided the law into the *ius civile*, *ius gentium*, and *ius naturale*. The former applied to all and only human beings, while the *ius naturale* applied to all animals, including human beings. According to leading jurist, Ulpian,[52] all humans were born free by the law of nature; slavery violated the *ius naturale* and existed only under the *ius gentium*.

Even prior to the Twelve Tables,[53] animals were assumed to belong to the human who lawfully controlled them. By the later Republic property law adopted the Stoic view that under natural law, all things were created for our use. Domestic animals and their young were regarded as the descendants of wild animals which had originally been subjugated (by *occupatio*) and then passed from one human owner to another by the civil process. This form of dominion was a logical consequence of the Roman notion that all things were destined to be subject to private ownership.[54]

50 Digest 1.5.2.

51 See generally Alan Watson, ed, *The Digest of Justinian*, four volumes, revised edn (Philadelphia, PA: University of Pennsylvania Press, 2009); Herbert Hausmaninger and Richard Gamauf, transl by George A Sheets, *A Casebook on Roman Property Law* (Oxford: Oxford University Press, 2012).

52 I 1.2.1; D 1.1.1.2-4; D 1.1.1.3-4: *Ius naturale* is that which nature has taught to all animals; for it is not a law specific to mankind but is common to all animals: land animals, sea animals, and the birds. Out of this arises the union of man and woman which we call marriage, and the procreation of children, and their rearing. So we can see that the other animals, wild beasts included, are rightly understood to be acquainted with this law. *Ius gentium*, the law of nations, is that which all human peoples observe. That it is not coexistent with natural law can be grasped simply because it is common to all animals whereas *ius gentium* is common only to human beings among themselves.

53 To resolve disputes between higher- and lower-ranked citizens, the Romans, in about 450 BC, issued, in tablet form, a compilation of laws known as the Twelve Tables. A commission of ten men (*Decemviri*) was appointed in about 455 BC to draft a code of law binding on all Romans—the privileged class (the patricians) and the common people (the plebeians)—which the magistrates (two consuls) were required to enforce. They produced a compilation of numerous statutes, most derived from prevailing custom, which filled ten bronze tablets. The plebeians were unimpressed with the result, and a second commission of ten was appointed in 450 BC. It added another two tablets. See Alan Watson, *Rome of the XII Tables: Person and Property* (Princeton, NJ: Princeton University Press, 2020).

54 Things were divided into at least three overlapping groups of *res extra patrimonium* that belonged to no individual in particular (as opposed to *res patrimonium* which belonged to someone). They were *res publicae* (owned by the State), *res communes* (things owned in common), and *res nullius* (things owned by no one), Alan Watson, *Law of Property in the Later Roman Republic* (Oxford: Oxford University Press, 1969).

Stoic principles of natural law, implemented by classical Roman law, simply assumed that wild animals lived in a 'natural state of freedom' or 'natural state of liberty'. Ownership of a thing owned by no one could, by *occupatio*, become the property of anyone who had the intention to own it. According to the jurist Gaius, everything captured on land, in the sea, or in the air was the captor's by *occupatio*, because they previously belonged to no one. Under the principles of natural law, the natural freedom of wild animals could be lost through *occupatio*, and subsequently regained by their escape. Ownership continued even if the animal was taken by another animal, provided it could be salvaged until it recovered its natural freedom by escaping.

The idea of animals as commodities subsisted through the Middle Ages, and remained unquestioned by English common law. For example, Lord Coke in *The Case of Swans*[55] held that a person could acquire absolute title in domestic animals, but only a qualified or possessory property interest in those wild creatures (*ferae naturae*) not owned by the king. These were susceptible to private ownership by capture or domestication; all property interests were, however, lost if they regained their 'natural liberty' without the intention to return (*animus revertendi*).

While some legal systems have accorded animals a status that marginally exceeds 'simple' property, notably Austria which amended its Civil Code in 1988 to distinguish animals from other things (see Chapter 12), the reality remains that the legal status of animals as property endures up to the present day. This fact constitutes a significant obstacle in the route to the recognition of animal rights.[56]

Legal personhood

The concept of personhood recognises a class of beings that, in effect, correspond to *us*, that is, human beings; the opposite, in other words, of property. Hence, as mentioned in Chapter 2, Kant famously defends personhood as the characteristic that renders a being valuable and therefore morally valuable:

> [E]very rational being, exists as an end in himself and not merely as a means to be arbitrarily used by this or that will.... Beings whose

55 7 Coke Rep. 16, 77 Eng. Rep. 435 (KB 1592).

56 But Visa Kurki claims that 'it is not the case that any physical object must be either property or a legal person'. He gives two examples. The first is the defunct practice of outlawing an individual for a crime; he would be stripped of all legal protection, but could still not be owned even if he was taken as a slave. And his status as property would not be legally recognised as it would in the case of 'real' slaves. The sale of a slave would be legally enforceable, while the sale of an outlaw would not. The other example is of a corporation which is simultaneously property and person. I am not sure that these analogies are likely to dislodge the longstanding orthodoxy that animals are property.

> existence depends not on our will but on nature have, nevertheless, if they are not rational beings, only a relative value as means and are therefore called things.[57]
>
> The fact that the human being can have the representation 'I' raises him infinitely above all the other beings on earth. By this he is a *person* … that is, a being altogether different in rank and dignity from things, such as irrational animals, with which we can dispose of as we please.[58]

The requirement of personhood so conceived thus appears, *prima facie*, to rule out all animals as potential rights-holders. This view, as we shall see later, is contested from a variety of standpoints which seek to defeat its central claim that rests the acquisition of rights on the possession of personhood. As mentioned above, Steven Wise equates *legal* personhood with the capacity to acquire rights. His slave analogy, however, smooths the way for animals to hold rights in the same way as former slaves were able to be regarded as rights-holders through the mechanism of *habeas corpus*, a subject I consider in Chapter 12. For Gary Francione, as discussed in Chapter 8, without legal personhood the interests of animals will always be subordinated to those of humans. He therefore advances the case for abolitionism—the view that we ought not to bring any more domesticated animals into existence.[59]

The question of legal personhood is related directly to the judicial acknowledgement of a 'legal person' for it is only legal persons whose rights and duties are recognised by a court. Thus, despite a number of attempts by the Nonhuman Rights Project (NhRP) in the United States to file petitions for writs of *habeas corpus* on behalf of various animals, the New York State courts have been unwilling to accept that, for example, chimpanzees are legal persons on two grounds: that they are not members of the human

57 Immanuel Kant, *Groundwork of the Metaphysics of Morals*, transl by Mary J Gregor (Cambridge: Cambridge University Press, 1998), 4, 428.

58 *Anthropology from a Pragmatic Point of View*, transl by Mary J Gregor (The Hague: Martinus Nijhoff, 1974), 8, 27. Personhood in and of itself is not, however, a panacea; it does 'not supply the terminological framework we need in the effort to include all sentient beings in a new ethics of replenishment and redemption from harm and injury', Colin Dayan, 'Personhood' in Lori Gruen, ed, *Terms for Animal Studies* (Chicago, IL: University of Chicago Press, 2018), 267, 276.

59 Gary L Francione, *Animals, Property, and the Law* (Philadelphia, PA: Temple University Press, 1995); Francione, 'Animals—Property or Persons?' in Cass R Sunstein and Martha C Nussbaum, eds, *Animal Rights: Current Debates and New Directions* (Oxford: Oxford University Press, 2005), 108. See too David Bilchitz, 'Moving Beyond Arbitrariness: The Legal Personhood and Dignity of Non-Human Animals' (2009) 25 *South African Journal of Human Rights* 38.

community, and that they lack the ability to bear legal duties.[60] On the other hand, an Argentinian court granted a petition on behalf of a chimpanzee, Cecilia, kept in inhumane conditions in a zoo. It ordered her release to a Brazilian sanctuary which provides satisfactory living conditions.[61]

The two requirements that impeded the successful petition of the NhRP in New York might be contested on the basis that human infants are incapable of bearing legal duties. This marginal case is usually rebutted by the contention that they are *potential* members of the human community which animals can never be. What, then, of severely senile adults? Here the argument switches to the fact that they are members of the human community and therefore acquire legal personhood notwithstanding their inability to bear duties.

If legal personhood is the condition for the acquisition of rights, we need to determine what constitutes a 'person'. Is there some acid test by which to distinguish persons from property? An assortment of standards has been proposed including rationality, sentience, language, the capacity for abstract thought, morality, culture, and sophisticated cognitive functioning. Thomas Nagel submits that an organism is conscious 'if and only if there is something that it is like to be that organism—something it is like *for* the organism'; and he argues that, however much we know about an animal's brain and behaviour, we cannot actually put ourselves into its mind and experience its world in the way that it does itself.[62]

The pursuit of a single criterion or group of criteria by which to identify a 'person' seems futile. The starting point of such attempts generally seems to be the faculties that we humans possess. The process tends inevitably to become a tendentious defence of human characteristics. The very term 'personhood' is tainted by this humancentric, speciesist assumption. Donaldson and Kymlicka therefore propose the substitution of 'personhood' with 'selfhood'.[63] As they point out:

> When dealing with sentient humans, we do not assign degrees of basic human rights or inviolability according to differences in mental

60 The petition argued that chimpanzees are autonomous beings with sophisticated cognitive abilities including episodic memory, self-consciousness, self-knowing, self-agency, referential and intentional communication, mental time-travel, numerosity, sequential learning, meditational learning, mental state modelling, visual perspective taking, understanding the experiences of others, intentional action, planning, imagination, empathy, metacognition, working memory, decision-making, imitation, deferred imitation, emulation, innovation, material, social, and symbolic culture, cross-modal perception, tool-use, tool-making, cause-and-effect, P extract from petition of *NhRP v Samuel Stanley* https://www.nonhumanrights.org/wp-content/uploads/Suffolk-Verified-Petition-of-E.Stein-and-S.Wise_.pdf, p 6.

61 I return to this, and similar cases, in Chapter 12.

62 Thomas Nagel, 'What Is It Like to Be a Bat? (1974) 83 *The Philosophical Review* 435. A different view is expressed by Douglas Hofstadter, 'Reflections on "What Is It Like to Be a Bat?"' in Douglas Hofstadter and Daniel Dennett, eds, *The Mind's I* (London: Basic Books), 403.

63 Donaldson and Kymlicka, op cit, 28ff.

> complexity, intelligence, or emotional or moral range. Simple or brilliant, selfish or saint, torpid or vivacious—we are all entitled to basic human rights because we are all vulnerable selves.[64]

Animals, in other words, have inviolable rights by virtue of their selfhood or sentience; the fact that they have a subjective experience of the world.[65] This is not simply semantics; they argue that it moves the discussion away from its pointless preoccupation with identifying some essential characteristic or cluster of attributes that defines humans. Tom Regan reasons that animals, like us, are 'subjects-of-a-life'. They have inherent, not merely instrumental, value or worth. This entitles them to the absolute right to live their lives with respect and autonomy:

> The most reasonable criterion of right-possession ... is not that of sentience or having interests, since neither of these by themselves can account for why it is wrong to treat humans who are not irreversibly comatose merely as means; rather the criterion that most adequately accounts for this is the criterion of inherent value: All those beings (and only those beings) which have inherent value have rights.[66]

Well-meaning attempts to discover a conclusive platform from which to launch our moral journey tend also to generate infinite philosophical and empirical enquiry.[67]

64 Op cit, 30. 'We cannot assume', they aver, 'a priori that only humans will pass attest of personhood', 26. Tomasz Pietrzykowski proposes that animals should be treated as 'non-personal subjects of law' which would accord them the right to be taken into account when decisions are taken that affect their 'most vital interests', 'The Idea of Non-personal Subjects of Law' in V Kurki and T Pietrzykowski, *Legal Personhood: Animals, Artificial Intelligence and the Unborn* (New York: Springer, 2017), 59.

65 Op cit, 31.

66 Tom Regan, *The Case for Animal Rights*, 397. But he would justify sacrificing the lives of a million dogs to save a single human life (351). Singer is to similar effect: since a dog lacks the cognitive ability to imagine the distant future, he asserts, it has less to lose by dying than we do. But Gary Francione counterclaims that a dog's sentience implies an interest in its continued existence, Francione, *Introduction to Animal Rights*, 6, 17. Sentience is best understood as 'a capacity to consciously perceive negative or positive sensations, feelings, emotions or other subjective experiences which matter to the animal', David J Mellor, 'Welfare-Aligned Sentience: Enhanced Capacities to Experience, Interact, Anticipate, Choose and Survive' (2019) 9 *Animals* 440, 449–450.

67 '[T]here is no characteristic that serves to distinguish humans from all other animals for the purpose of denying to animals the one right that we extend to all humans.... In the end, the only difference between humans and animals is species, and species is not a justification for treating animals as property any more than is race a justification for slavery', Gary Francione, 'Animals—Property or Persons' in Cass R Sunstein and Martha C Nussbaum, eds, *Animal Rights: Current Debates and New Directions* (Oxford: Oxford University Press, 2005), 108, 130–131.

But the concept of 'legal personhood' is an unavoidable category that is not so simply displaced.[68] Indeed, as I shall argue in Chapter 13, it may open the door to a fresh way of thinking about the whole question of the moral and legal status of animals. Our efforts are therefore better directed towards elucidating the concept itself. In his analysis, Visa Kurki, drawing on a resemblance with ownership, advances a 'bundle theory' that consists of interconnected incidents which principally endow a putative legal person with certain rights, responsibilities, and/or competences. He distinguishes between active and passive legal personhood. The latter is possessed by infants, while adults of sound mind have both active and passive incidents. Unlike animals', infants' lives, liberty, and property are protected, and they have the standing to be represented in court as well as the capacity to own property. Active incidents of legal personhood, on the other hand, apply predominantly, though not exclusively, to entities with mental abilities roughly corresponding to those of an adult human being of sound mind; they can, for example, enter into contracts and perform other legal acts.[69]

This meticulous dissection of the notion of legal personhood facilitates a greater degree of nuance than the conventional approach. In particular, it supports the view that only sentient beings possess ultimate value and hence can be right-holders. In the NhRP unsuccessful petition of *habeas corpus* on behalf on Tommy, the chimpanzee (see above and Chapter 12), the New York court *a quo* held that 'the ascription of rights has historically been connected with the imposition of societal obligations and duties' thereby thwarting any protection against the maltreatment suffered by the creature. But, as Kurki points out, 'this premise was misguided' because

> Tommy was already protected by legal safeguards that are properly designated as rights. In everyday legal parlance the term 'right' is often used indiscriminately to refer to both interest- theory and will- theory rights, so in this discourse there is no reason to abstain from talking of the legal rights of beings that are unable to exercise their rights—jurists talk about children's rights constantly. Thus, the case was not about whether Tommy ought to be included in the 'rights paradigm' as the court framed it. Animals already hold rights. Rather, the case was about whether a particular incident—which could well be described as a 'fundamental right'—ought to be extended to cover the chimpanzee.[70]

68 But see John Tasioulas who proposes a plurality of human goods—not merely personhood—as the basis of human rights, 'Human Rights, Universality, and the Value of Personhood: Retracing Griffin's Steps' (2002) 10 *European Journal of Philosophy* 88.

69 See generally William Lucy, 'Persons in Law' (2009) 29 *Oxford Journal of Legal Studies* 787; Ngaire Naffine, *Law's Meaning of Life: Philosophy, Religion, Darwin and the Legal Person* (Hart Publishing 2009), 66; Tomasz Pietrzykowski, *Personhood Beyond Humanism: Animals, Chimeras, Autonomous Agents and the Law* (New York: Springer, 2018), 11; Denise Meyerson, 'Persons and their Rights in Law and Morality' (2010) 35 *Australian Journal of Legal Philosophy* 122.

70 Visa AJ Kurki, *A Theory of Legal Personhood* (Oxford: Oxford University Press, 2019), 197. See too Visa AJ Kurki, 'Legal Personhood and Animal Rights' (2021) 11 *Journal of Animal Ethics* 47.

By rejecting the binary concept of legal personhood that draws a line between legal persons with rights, on the one hand, and things, on the other, that are incapable of holding or exercising rights, Kurki's approach recognises that animals have rights. It also explains the position of slaves who enjoyed limited rights without qualifying as legal persons. They lacked adequate passive legal protection—against, for instance, being owned—to be regarded as legal persons. Similarly, animals lack passive incidents: they are susceptible to being owned and, in general, lack protection of their lives, liberty, and bodily integrity. They are therefore not fully legal persons. In other words, it is not the case that the lack of legal personhood is a consequence of their not having legal rights. It is the absence of sufficient passive legal incidents that accounts for their inferior status.

While this account of legal personhood is more congenial towards the recognition of the legal personhood, and hence the rights, of animals, there remains the question of whether this is sufficient to guarantee their protection against abuse. The repudiation of the rationale for animal rights is also based on the claim that they reside outside the boundaries of our human community. I explore this question in Chapter 11.

Relational arguments

The resistance to animal rights theory is sometimes based on the view that, in the case of Donaldson and Kymlicka, points to the negative duties of non-interference rather than the positive relational duties. They argue that rights theorists, as well as Francione's abolitionist approach, fail to develop an account of the ethically desirable relations we can have with nonhumans:

> The inviolable rights of animals not to be killed, caged, or experimented on provide a framework within which humans and animals can then enter into a range of ethically significant interspecies relationships.... If inviolable rights are seen as the sum total of our ethical obligations to animals, this quickly leads to the species apartheid view characteristic of abolitionist/extinctionist position. [But] any plausible relational ethic needs to be supplemented with inviolable rights.[71]

71 Will Kymlicka and Sue Donaldson, 'Rights' in Lori Gruen, ed, *Critical Terms for Animal Studies* (Chicago, IL: Chicago University Press, 2018), 320, 330. They add that when inviolable rights are disavowed in the name of a relational ethic, as Haraway and Rudy allegedly do, 'we end up justifying the killing animals for human benefit', ibid. See Donna Haraway, *When Species Meet* (Minneapolis: University of Minnesota Press, 2007); Kathy Rudy, *Loving Animals: Toward a New Animal Advocacy* (Minneapolis: University of Minnesota Press, 2011). See too Sue Donaldson and Will Kymlicka, *Zoopolis: A Political Theory of Animal Rights* (Oxford: Oxford University Press, 2011).

Rights, they contend, are intrinsically adversarial and antagonistic; they presume and perpetuate indifference or conflict between individuals.[72] We need to 'convert hostility into empathy',[73] an argument advanced by Cora Diamond, especially in relation to vegetarianism.[74] An elaborate, imaginative, and ambitious vision of a 'Zoopolis' is proposed by Donaldson and Kymlicka; I consider its feasibility in Chapter 11.

There is also the associated argument that denies that humans and animals belong on a continuum with a grey area in which it is uncertain whether rights and duties are to be imputed on the basis of what is observable. Roger Scruton opines:

> [T]he distinguishing feature of the moral being [he means humans]—including rationality and self-consciousness—belong to another *system* of behaviour from that which characterises the merely cognitive animal. The transition from the one behavioural system to the other is as absolute a transition as that from vegetable to sentient life....[75]

This is consistent with his general view that animals have no rights because they are non-moral beings who exist outside a 'web of reciprocal rights and obligations ... and it is both senseless and cruel to try to bind them into it'.[76] It does not follow, he adds, that we have no duties towards them: 'Even when no such duty ... has been assumed, our dealings with animals are governed by moral considerations. These ... derive not from the moral law but from the other three roots of moral feeling: virtue, sympathy and piety'.[77]

Animal rights as redundant

Animal rights are occasionally portrayed as 'excess baggage'[78] or as weapons of last resort: 'the really desperate word'.[79] For example, the source of Tom

72 A view held also by revolutionary Marxists who dismiss rights as an expression of a capitalist economy which will be superfluous in a classless, socialist society. See Tom Campbell, *The Left and Rights: A Conceptual Analysis of the Idea of Socialist Rights* (London: Routledge & Kegan Paul, 1983). See Chapter 5.

73 Op cit, 331. The argument that empathy (or compassion) derives from our similarity to animals seems wrong. It surely transcends species correspondence and springs from the capacity to imagine, or even feel, another's pain or suffering. Cf James Rachels, 'Drawing Lines' in Cass R Sunstein and Martha C Nussbaum, eds, *Animal Rights: Current Debates and New Directions* (Oxford: Oxford University Press, 2005), 162. I return to this question in Chapters 12 and 13.

74 Cora Diamond, 'Eating Meat and Eating People' in Cass R Sunstein and Martha C Nussbaum, eds, *Animal Rights: Current Debates and New Directions* (Oxford: Oxford University Press, 2005), 93.

75 Roger Scruton, *Animal Rights and Wrongs*, 2nd edn (London: Demos, 1998), 51–52.

76 Op cit, 123–124.

77 Op cit, 124. I return to his approach, which is not to be dismissed lightly, in Chapter 13.

78 RG Frey, *Interests and Rights: The Case against Animals* (Oxford: Clarendon Press, 1980).

79 Mary Midgley, *Animals and Why They Matter: A Journey Around the Species Barrier* (Harmondsworth: Penguin, 1983), 61–64.

Regan's notion of inherent value has occasionally been depicted as simply a form of sophisticated intuitionism?[80] Though Regan seeks to distinguish his case from that held by classic intuitionists like GE Moore, there is always the danger that your intuition might lead in the opposite direction to mine. How are we to determine who is right? Some rights-sceptics therefore prefer to prescribe duties without recourse to the precarious problems generated by animal rights through the mechanism of a social contract which I discuss in Chapter 10.

Raymond Frey raises a different, but related, point regarding the problem of the assumption of truth that rights-talk makes:

> [I]f a theorist of basic or fundamental moral rights posits such rights; if he also posits that such rights are possessed by all persons equally; and if he further posits that they cannot be relinquished, given up, or forfeited and cannot be ignored, infringed, or violated with impunity; then I just do not see how we can argue with him. And if we cannot argue with him, then I do not see how light is shed on moral problems by positing of this sort.[81]

Nor do I. But it does not follow that to invoke moral rights is to invoke *absolute* moral rights. And I cannot accept that an appeal to *prima facie* rights is necessarily too frail to resist the strength of competing *prima facie* rights.

Ideological objections

The misgivings of the two principal opponents of rights *per se* (communitarianism and critical theory) logically apply no less to this matter than they do to the broader institution of human rights discussed in the following chapter.

Whither rights?

The six impediments sketched above operate to block not only the acknowledgement of limited, inferred rights, but extend to the broader vision of human rights for animals discussed in Chapter 5, augmented by other objections that pertain to both the subject of human rights generally, and to the specific proposal that animal rights are the 'new human rights'. There remain questions about the application and appropriateness of rights such as, for example, to whom are the putative rights owed; are they owed by animals to other animals? These fall to be considered later.

80 See Peter Carruthers, *The Animals Issue: Moral Theory in Practice* (Cambridge: Cambridge University Press, 1992).

81 Frey, 65.

5 Human rights

The idea that animals ought to be candidates for human rights protection will strike many as perverse. Surely, they will protest, human rights are for humans. On what possible grounds can nonhumans be contenders for the benefaction of rights that belong exclusively to us? The very idea appears oxymoronic, or perhaps a misguided Utopian or Procrustean exercise that cannot be taken seriously.

When we ask why it is that humans enjoy these rights, we receive the tautological response: because we are human. The question then arises: what is it about a human that confers upon us this advantage? While it is evidently the case that, unlike animals, we have certain characteristics, capacities, and needs that animals seem to lack, a conspicuous element—discussed in Chapter 4—is personhood. It is also claimed that, unlike us, they are not free agents who are able to choose what we regard as a worthwhile life or imagine a conception of ourselves and a grasp of our past and future. So, for example, James Griffin, while he concedes that there may be creatures other than humans who are capable of this kind of self-awareness and reflection, since they lack personhood or 'human standing', they do not fall within the reach of human rights shelter.[1]

Before addressing the question posed in this chapter, it is important, I think, to appreciate not only the origin, nature, and impact of the concept of human rights, but also the criticisms of the notion, its meaning and application, from various quarters whose attitudes range from the unconvinced to the fervently hostile. This account is followed by an attempt to examine whether the championing of such rights for animals, and, more importantly, its acceptance by the law, is a genuine prospect or merely a fanciful aspiration.

What are human rights?

The concept of human rights has been described as 'one of the greatest inventions of our civilisation [which] can be compared in its impact on human social life to the development of modern technological resources and

1 James Griffin, *On Human Rights* (Oxford, Oxford University Press, 2008), 32–34.

DOI: 10.4324/9781032702575-5

their application to medicine, communication, and transportation'.[2] Though concept (in the form of 'natural rights') emerged in the Middle Ages, the recognition in the seventeenth and eighteenth centuries of the secular notion of human rights was a significant intellectual moment in history. The idea makes little sense unless it is understood as fundamental and inalienable. In classical natural law theory, as expressed, for example, by the Stoic, Cicero, the principles were regarded as emanating from a 'higher' law than the positive law enacted by humans. In *De Re Publica*,[3] he expressed the three main components of any natural law philosophy:

> True law is right reason in agreement with Nature; it is of universal application, unchanging and everlasting.... It is a sin to try to alter this law, nor is it allowable to attempt to repeal any part of it, and it is impossible to abolish it entirely.... [God] is the author of this law, its promulgator, and its enforcing judge.

This stresses natural law's universality and immutability, standing as a superior law, and its discoverability by reason (it is in this sense 'natural').

Natural rights theory achieved its zenith in the early modern era, especially through the writings of Hugo de Groot (Grotius), Hobbes, and Samuel Pufendorf, though its principal adherent was John Locke. He argued that, unlike the nightmare depicted by Hobbes who famously described life before the social contract as 'solitary, poor, nasty, brutish and short', it was, he thought, largely harmonious. A major deficiency, however, was that in this state of nature, property was inadequately protected. For Locke, therefore, in order to rectify this flaw in an otherwise idyllic natural state, people surrendered, under a social contract, some of their freedom. His theory is based on an account of man's rights and obligations under God. When a government is unjust or authoritarian, Locke acknowledges the right of 'oppressed people' to 'resist tyranny' and overthrow the government: 'a tyrant has no authority'.

He attaches considerable importance to the right to property: God owns the earth and has given it to us to enjoy; there can therefore be no right of property. But by mixing his labour with material objects, the labourer acquires the right to the thing he has created.

This view exerted a significant influence on the framers of the American Constitution with its emphasis upon the protection of property. Locke

2 Carlos Nino, *The Ethics of Human Rights* (Oxford: Clarendon Press, 1991), 1. See Charles R Beitz, *The Idea of Human Rights* (New York: Oxford University Press, 2009). See John Tasioulas, 'On the Foundations of Human Rights' in R Cruft, S Liao, and M Renzo, eds, *Philosophical Foundations of Human Rights* (Oxford: Oxford University Press, 2015). I draw here on some of my discussion in Raymond Wacks, *Understanding Jurisprudence: An Introduction to Legal Theory*, 6th edn (Oxford: Oxford University Press, 2021), *passim*.

3 Book 3, Ch 22, sect 33.

believed that the state exists to preserve the natural rights of its citizens. When governments fail in this task, citizens have the right—and sometimes even the duty—to withdraw their support and even to rebel.

The social contract, in his view, preserved the natural rights to life, liberty, and property, and the enjoyment of private rights: the pursuit of happiness engendered, in civil society, the common good. Whereas for Hobbes, natural rights were logically prior (and natural law is derived from them), Locke derives natural rights from natural law—that is, from reason. While Hobbes discerns a natural right of every person to everything, Locke's natural right to freedom is circumscribed by the law of nature and its injunction that we should not harm each other in 'life, health, liberty, or possessions'.

The lofty rhetoric of the Declaration of Independence of 1776 appealed to the natural rights of all Americans to 'life, liberty and the pursuit of happiness'. As the Declaration puts it: 'We hold these truths to be self-evident, that all men are created equal, that they are endowed by their Creator with certain unalienable rights'. Similar sentiments were incorporated into the French 'Declaration of the Rights of Man and the Citizen' of 1789.

The attempt to clothe the positive law with a legitimacy derived from natural law attracted the fury of Jeremy Bentham who described natural law as, amongst other things, 'a mere work of the fancy' and 'bawling upon paper'.[4] In his typically flamboyant style, he describes rights-talk as 'the effusion of a hard heart operating on a cloudy mind. When a man is bent on having things his own way and gives no reason for it, he says: I have a right to have them so'. They are, moreover, a contradiction in terms: 'a son that never had a father', 'a species of cold heat, a sort of dry moisture, a kind of resplendent darkness', 'nonsense on stilts'.[5] Much positivist and non-cognitivist analysis therefore rejects rights-talk as meaningless or, at best, irrational 'emotional ejaculations'.

It was the Catholic Church that gave expression to the full-blown philosophy of natural law as we understand it today. As early as the fifth century, St Augustine asked, 'What are States without justice, but robber bands enlarged?'[6] In about 1140, Gratian published his *Decretum*, a collection of some 4,000 texts dealing with numerous aspects of church discipline which he sought to reconcile. He begins by declaring, in keeping with the medieval conception of natural law: 'Mankind is governed by two laws: the law of nature and custom. The law of nature is contained in the scriptures and the gospel'. But he continues, 'Natural law overrides customs and constitutions.

4 Jeremy Bentham, *Anarchical Fallacies*, quoted in HLA Hart, 'Between Utility and Rights' in his *Essays on Bentham: Studies on Jurisprudence and Political Theory* (Oxford: Clarendon Press, 1982), 199. The next chapter expands on Bentham's utilitarianism.

5 See Jeremy Waldron, ed, *Nonsense upon Stilts: Bentham, Burke and Marx on the Rights of Man* (London: Methuen, 1987), 73.

6 *City of God*, Book 4, iv.

That which has been recognized by usage, or recorded in writing, if it contradicts natural law, is void and of no effect'.

By the seventeenth century in Europe, the exposition of entire branches of the law (notably public international law) purported to be founded on natural law. Grotius is normally associated with the secularisation of natural law. In his influential work *De Jure Belli ac Pacis*, he asserts that even if God did not exist ('*etiamsi daremus non esse Deum*') natural law would have the same content. This proved to be an essential foundation for the emerging discipline of public international law, though exactly what Grotius means when he postulates his *etiamsi daremus* idea is not entirely clear.[7] It would seem that he regarded certain things as 'intrinsically' wrong—whether or not they are decreed by God; for, to use Grotius's own analogy, even God cannot cause two times two not to equal four. In this, he is not denying the existence of God, but underlining that what is right or wrong are matters of natural appropriateness, not of arbitrary divine *fiat*.

In England, the high-water mark of natural law was reached in the eighteenth century with Sir William Blackstone's *Commentaries on the Laws of England*. Blackstone commences his great work by adumbrating classical natural law doctrine—in order, it has been argued,[8] to sanctify English law by this appeal to God-given principles. But, while he makes various claims about positive law deriving its authority from natural law and being a nullity should it conflict with it, these assertions do not actually inform Blackstone's analysis of the law itself.

The legal recognition of human rights in the twentieth century arose when in 1948 the United Nations, in the shadow of the Holocaust, adopted the Universal Declaration of Human Rights. It and the European Convention for the Protection of Human Rights and Fundamental Freedoms of 1952, and the International Covenants on Civil and Political Rights, and Economic, Social and Cultural Rights of 1976, revealed, even to the most sceptical observer, a commitment by the international community to the universal conception and protection of human rights. This so-called International Bill of Rights, with its unavoidably protean and slightly kaleidoscopic ideological character, reflects an extraordinary measure of cross-cultural consensus amongst nations—at least in theory.

In broad terms, the concept of human rights has passed through three generations. The first comprises the seventeenth- and eighteenth-centuries, mostly negative civil and political rights. The second consists in the essentially positive economic, social, and cultural rights that include the right to

7 For differing interpretations contrast A Passerin D'Entrèves, *Natural Law* (London: Hutchinson, 1970), 53–56, and John Finnis, *Natural Law and Natural Rights*, 2nd edn (Oxford: Clarendon Press, 2011), 43–44.

8 See Duncan Kennedy, 'The Structure of Blackstone's *Commentaries*' (1979) 28 *Buffalo Law Review* 205.

housing, education, adequate living standards, and health. They are recognised by various international and regional human rights instruments. The third-generation rights are primarily collective rights which are foreshadowed in Article 28 of the Universal Declaration which declares that 'everyone is entitled to a social and international order in which the rights set forth in this Declaration can be fully realized'. These 'solidarity' rights include the right to social and economic development and to participate in and benefit from the resources of the earth and space, scientific and technical information (which are especially important to the Third World), the right to a healthy environment, peace, and humanitarian disaster relief. Importantly, however, the scope of human rights continues to expand, and this factor is not without relevance to the question of animal rights as human rights.[9]

Certain human rights are doubtless more fundamental, more essential, and more universal, than others. If this is the case, these 'positive', socio-economic rights, though frequently included in human rights declarations and bills of rights, are of a different order from 'negative' political rights, a question that has long plagued the subject.[10]

Human rights scepticism

The concept is not universally venerated. The extent, however, to which any of the following six principal criticisms apply to the extension of human rights beyond our species is a matter to which I return.[11] I shall assume that hostility to rights *per se* may legitimately be interpreted as hostility to the concept of human rights, although this is not the place to disentangle the potential complexities of this assumption.[12]

9 To curb the proliferation of human rights, Philip Alston suggested forty years ago that some form of 'quality control' was required. He proposed that the recognition of new human rights 'should be authoritative (in the sense of giving rise to realistic expectations of compliance by states), and second that the integrity and standing of the existing body of rights is maintained', Philip Alston, 'Conjuring Up New Human Rights: A Proposal for Quality Control' (1984) 78 *American Journal of International Law* 607, 621. The first criterion is plainly pertinent to the extension of human rights to animals.

10 See David Bilchitz, 'Giving Socio-Economic Rights Teeth: The Minimum Core and its Importance' (2002) 118 *South African Law Journal* 484, and David Bilchitz, *Poverty and Fundamental Rights: The Justification and Enforcement of Socio-economic Rights* (Oxford, Oxford University Press, 2008).

11 Some of what follows is adapted from Raymond Wacks, *Understanding Jurisprudence: An Introduction to Legal Theory*, 6th edn (Oxford: Oxford University Press, 2020), Ch 10; Raymond Wacks, 'The End of Human Rights?' (1994) 24 *Hong Kong Law Journal* 372; Raymond Wacks, 'Can Human Rights Survive?' in Raymond Wacks, *Law, Morality, and the Private Domain* (Hong Kong: Hong Kong University Press, 2000), 179.

12 Some pragmatic and principled objections against animal rights are discussed by Will Kymlicka and Sue Donaldson, 'Rights' in Lori Gruen, ed, *Critical Terms for Animal Studies* (Chicago, IL: University of Chicago Press, 2018), 320.

Their imprecision

Notwithstanding its appeal and importance, the idea of human rights remains exasperatingly vague, if not incoherent. It is difficult to disagree with James Griffin:

> The term 'human right' is nearly criterionless. There are unusually few criteria for determining when the term is used correctly and when incorrectly—not just among politicians, but among philosophers, political theorists, and jurisprudents as well. The language of human rights has, in this way, become debased.[13]

This is a problem. When the currency of a concept, especially one as fashionable and influential as 'human rights', is degraded by wanton excess, it not only reduces its utility, but creates a risk that it will generate derision for the idea itself. To assert that a particular pursuit is a human right or that its preclusion is a violation thereof does not, of course, make it so.[14] Nor, of course, is there a necessary connection between what is just and its being a human right.[15] The 'globalisation' of human rights, engendered by the large corpus of United Nations and other international conventions, facilitates the identification and recognition of such rights in diverse societies and cultures.

A degree of liberality, and even perhaps imprecision, is probably inevitable, perhaps even desirable. Yet the danger remains that their amplitude and ambiguity drain human rights of real meaning and hence undermine the very protection such declarations seek to secure. We cannot, it has been justly observed, 'inflate the concept of human rights so much that it covers the whole realm of justice. Human rights would lose their distinctive moral force.'[16] This amplification is particularly worrying in view of the cynicism which the discourse of human rights increasingly attracts, for there is no shortage of detractors and sceptics. Some see human rights as a Machiavellian plot by international capital to enslave the Third World. Others, of a more conservative persuasion, adopt Edmund Burke's view that spurns human rights on the ground that they inspire 'false ideas and vain expectations in men destined to travel in the obscure walk of laborious life'.

13 James Griffin, *On Human Rights* (Oxford: Oxford University Press, 2008), 14–15.

14 This proclivity to munificence arises in other endeavours. I have, for example, argued that the desire to incorporate human rights into the tenets of the rule of law, as proposed most conspicuously by Lord Bingham, 'saps its essential character as a constitutional instrument to contain the exercise of arbitrary power', Raymond Wacks, *The Rule of Law Under Fire?* (Oxford: Hart Publishing, 2021), 46–47. See Tom Bingham, *The Rule of Law* (London: Penguin Books, 2010).

15 'Some international lawyers write as if the domains of justice and human rights are identical. But they are clearly not. Human rights do not exhaust the whole domain of justice or fairness', Griffin, 198.

16 George Letsas, *A Theory of Interpretation of the European Convention on Human Rights* (Oxford, Oxford University Press, 2007), 25.

Their individualism

Communitarians stigmatise rights as individualist. They are seen to operate formally not necessarily to assist those (the poor, oppressed, alienated) who most need them. They are disparaged as 'excess baggage' superfluous in the condemnation of cruelty or exploitation. All we need, it is argued, is a fully developed theory of right and wrong.

Aristotle saw man as a 'social animal' and the community as the central element of any society. Our membership of a community—the town or city where we live, or even our country, where we share a common language, culture, or experience—such as our family, school, or workplace is the driving force of this outlook. Communitarians stress the enhancement of integrity, individual responsibility, and virtues in the public domain, and pursue the development of these values through education, community-based groups, and the family.[17] They reject the Kantian idea that what is *right* has priority over what is *good*. Primacy is given to claims based on the rights of individuals, those based on the good that might be done to them or to others, from violating those claims. For them, justice is inseparable from the practice, beliefs, and traditions of particular societies. For Kant, on the other hand, what is 'right' trumps other values that depend on want-satisfaction because what is right springs from the concept of freedom which is a prerequisite of all human ends. In Kant's words, in his *Critique of Practical Reason*, 'the concept of good and evil must be defined after and by means of the [moral] law'.[18]

The Kantian approach is central to liberal theory and hence fundamental to the communitarian attack on the idea of human rights which is regarded as an atomistic conception of the autonomous individual—which is found in 'those philosophical traditions which come to us from the seventeenth century and which started with the postulation of an extensionless subject, epistemologically a *tabula rasa* and politically a presuppositionless bearer of rights'.[19] In other words, for Kant, the subject of practical reason has an autonomous will which enables him or her to participate in an ideal, unconditioned realm which is independent of our teleological, social, and psychological inclinations.

This conception of the individual is spurned by communitarians who conceive of persons, as Michael Sandel puts it, echoing the arguments of Hegel against Kant, as 'situated selves rather than unencumbered selves'. The communitarian response is that individuals are partly defined by their communities. Moral obligation springs therefore from what Hegel called the '*Sittlichkeit*' of the society. The subject of deontological liberalism is thus a transcendental, detached, independent, and autonomous agent. He or

17 See Alisdair McIntyre, *After Virtue: A Study in Moral Theory*, 3rd edn (London: Duckworth, 1985), 204–205.

18 I discuss Kant in the context of animal rights in Chapter 2.

19 Charles Taylor, 'Atomism' in his *Philosophical Papers*, Volume 2, 210, quoted in Steven Lukes, *Moral Conflict and Politics* (Oxford: Clarendon Press, 1991), 73.

she 'stripped of all possible constitutive attachments, is less liberated than disempowered'.[20] We cannot, in the view of communitarians, be understood as persons without reference to our social roles in the community: as citizens, members of a family, group, or nation.

This is a powerful idea which has exerted considerable influence in moral, political, and legal theory. And it appears to inflict serious damage on the concept of human rights. But is it possible to preserve a broadly Kantian moral system of universal rights without adopting Kant's transcendental idealism? Keep the moral baby and throw out the metaphysical bathwater? This is exactly what John Rawls seems to have attempted in his social contractarian theory of justice in which 'people in the original position' determine principles of justice beneath a veil of ignorance which insulates them from their social condition.[21]

There are a number of versions of communitarianism which I cannot pursue here, but at their heart is a denunciation of the individualism of human rights which, its adherents claim, overlooks community interests, civic virtue, and social solidarity. The essence of the communitarian standpoint lies in our 'moral engagement' with society, its morality and political life. This, in turn, requires us to reflect upon the nature and purpose of the good life. As Sandel puts it, echoing Aristotle, 'It may not be possible, or even desirable, to deliberate about justice without deliberating about the good life'.[22] This may appear slightly Utopian, but there is certainly validity in the communitarian dissatisfaction with liberalism which often seems unable to address effectively the problems of poverty, crime, isolation, the breakdown of family life, selfishness, greed, government incompetence and bureaucracy, corruption, and the general alienation from politics. Our obsession with individual rights neglects the value of participation in the public arena upon which the flourishing of an authentic community rests. Communitarians thus support greater contribution to civic life. Instead of simply disregarding the moral and religious views of others, we should, they maintain, challenge their standpoints so as to gain a better understanding of their perspective and so achieve a profounder sense of justice.

A danger of communitarianism is that it can easily slide into cultural or ethical relativism (see the following section). For example, Michael Walzer argues we should 'look inside' particular societies and social groups to decide whether their practices are just, rather than simply relying on universal abstract principles.[23] Furthermore, each 'sphere' of life generates its own norms of justice. Thus, he argues, the norms that operate in the economic sphere differ from those in the educational domain. 'Justice', he asserts, 'is relative

20 Michael Sandel, *Justice: What's the Right Thing to Do?* (London: Penguin, 2010), 178.
21 John Rawls, *A Theory of Justice* (Harmondsworth: Penguin, 1973). See Chapter 10.
22 Michael Sandel, *Liberalism and the Limits of Justice* (Cambridge: Cambridge University Press, 1982).
23 Michael Walzer, *Spheres of Justice: A Defense of Pluralism and Equality* (New York: Basic Books, 1984).

to social meanings'. This may seem to be a slippage into ethical or cultural relativism; the subject of the next approach.

Relativism

Are human rights truly universal? To what extent are they 'relative' to local culture, morality, history, and social and political conditions? Cultural relativists, claim, for example, that human rights declarations neglect parochial diversity and, although this approach has a fairly long pedigree in philosophy and the social sciences, especially anthropology, it is only recently has it re-joined the assault on the human rights citadel. The doctrine maintains that 'there is an irreducible diversity among cultures because each culture is a unique whole with parts so intertwined that none of them can be understood or evaluated without reference to the other parts and so to the cultural whole, the so-called pattern of culture'.[24]

The thesis implies ethical relativism which claims that 'the moral rightness and wrongness of actions varies from society to society and that there are no absolute moral standards binding on all men at all times'.[25] According the theory's most constructive interpretation, it seems to rest on the view that, since moral beliefs depend on culture, language, economy, and so on, and since such factors vary from society to society, morality is relative to each society. But this standpoint might justify rebarbative practices, customs, or traditions by reference to local culture. We should endeavour sympathetically to understand even barbaric behaviour such as female genital mutilation, 'honour' killings, the murder of homosexuals, and cruelty to animals. Yet in doing so, we risk defending them.

There are two main arguments that may be used in an attempt to defeat the relativist. The first denies that morality depends on social factors at all; this may therefore be described as the absolutist position. The second—universalism—denies the assertion that there has always been a diversity of cultures, and a miscellany of moral beliefs. It holds that certain ideas have universal applicability. The absolutist position was held by Plato and claims that the validity of moral beliefs is logically independent of the social or cultural background of the person who accepts them; ethics is no less a scientific enterprise than mathematics. This so-called cognitivist position arises in two forms: intuitionism (which believes that ethical truths are known by *a priori* cognition—that is, intuition), and naturalism (which holds that ethical truths are known empirically). Cognitivism in ethics has had something of a rough ride from philosophers. It is particularly vulnerable to the charge that it divorces moral thinking from the 'real world'; it compels us to think

24 John Ladd, 'Introduction' in John Ladd, ed, *Ethical Relativism* (Belmont, CA: Wadsworth, 1973), 2. For an excellent account of relativism in its myriad forms, see the entry in the online *Stanford Encyclopedia of Philosophy* by Maria Baghramian and J Adam Carter.

25 John Ladd, 'Introduction', 1.

about morality in a vacuum. Universalism is stigmatised as ethnocentric for its failure to appreciate cultural practices from the perspective of the culture in which a particular practice is transacted.

Utilitarianism

The next chapter examines in greater detail the utilitarian repudiation of the idea of individual rights. The fundamental contradiction between these two viewpoints lingers in political, moral, and legal thinking about rights. The enmity towards rights arises from the utilitarian concern to maximize general welfare. Individual interests may therefore be sacrificed at the altar of utility. Rights are branded as individualist. They operate formally, but do not necessarily help those (the poor, oppressed, alienated) who most need them. They are again regarded as merely 'excess baggage', superfluous in the material condemnation of cruelty or exploitation. All we need, it is argued, is a fully developed theory of right and wrong. Furthermore, as HLA Hart puts it, in unusually blunt terms:

> Except for a few privileged and lucky persons, the ability to shape life for oneself and lead a meaningful life is something to be constructed by positive marshalling of social and economic resources. It is not something automatically guaranteed by a structure of negative rights. Nothing is more likely to bring freedom into contempt and so endanger it than failure to support those who lack, through no fault of their own, the material and social conditions and opportunities which are needed if a man's freedom is to contribute to his welfare.[26]

Utilitarianism's detractors considerably outnumber its supporters, and the attacks take numerous forms. In respect of its approach to individual rights, it is criticised by both free-market libertarians such as Robert Nozick[27] for overriding what John Rawls calls 'the distinction between persons'[28] and liberals like Ronald Dworkin for neglecting individuals' claims to equal concern and respect.[29]

Socialism

The incompatibility of individual rights and socialism has become something of a truism. This argument is typically based on both the irreconcilable conflict between the egoism of liberal theory and the communitarianism of

26 HLA Hart, 'Between Utility and Rights' in HLA Hart, *Essays on Bentham: Studies on Jurisprudence and Political Theory* (Oxford: Clarendon Press, 1982), 207–208.

27 Robert Nozick, *Anarchy, State, and Utopia* (Oxford: Wiley–Blackwell, 2001).

28 John Rawls, *A Theory of Justice* (Harmondsworth: Penguin, 1973), 27.

29 See Chapter 3.

socialism, and the denial that conditions of morality are inherent in human life. Against this position, Steven Lukes has maintained that there are four conditions which combine to make rights necessary: scarcity, egoism, conflicting conceptions of the good, and imperfect knowledge and understanding.[30]

Revolutionary Marxists have little truck with rights (chiefly because they are an expression of a capitalist economy and will be superfluous in a classless, socialist society). This refutation appears to be based on four objections to rights[31]: their legalism—rights subject human behaviour to the governance of rules; their coerciveness—law is a coercive device, and rights are tainted because they protect the interests of capital; their individualism—they protect self-interested atomised individuals, and their moralism—they are fundamentally moral and Utopian, and hence unrelated to the economic base.[32]

Critical theory

An unambiguous assault on the concept of human rights is an important feature of both the critical legal studies movement and of postmodern accounts of society.[33] For example, Costas Douzinas concludes his analysis of the concept of human rights with the following admonition:

> As human rights start veering away from their initial revolutionary and dissident purposes, as their end becomes obscured in ever more declarations, treaties and diplomatic lunches, we may be entering the epoch of the end of human rights and of the triumph of a monolithic humanity. If human rights have become the 'realised myth' of postmodern societies, this is a myth realised only in the energies of those who suffer grave and petty violations in the hands of the powers that have proclaimed their triumph.... The end of human rights comes when they lose their utopian end.[34]

Critical scholarship tends to be ill-disposed towards the concept of individual rights, and, by implication, human rights. The lowest common denominator of this approach is a deconstructive critique of both the indeterminacy

30 Stephen Lukes, *Marxism and Morality* (Oxford: Oxford Paperbacks, 1987), 56–57.

31 Identified by Tom Campbell, *The Left and Rights: A Conceptual Analysis of the Idea of Socialist Rights* (London: Routledge & Kegan Paul, 1983).

32 But see Tom Campbell who suggests that by adopting an interest-based theory of rights (as opposed to power- or contract-based theories), socialist rights are an important element in ensuring democracy. He argues that any form of socialism will require authoritative rules—if only to facilitate cooperative and educational activities, op cit, 123.

33 See generally, Gary Steiner, *Animals and the Limits of Postmodernism* (New York: Columbia University Press, 2013); Jacques Derrida, *The Animal that Therefore I Am*, Mary-Louise Malle, ed, transl by David Wills (New York: Fordham University Press, 2008).

34 Costas Douzinas, *The End of Human Rights* (Oxford: Hart Publishing, 2000).

of rights and their tendency to shore up prevailing social and political hierarchies.[35] Adherents of the Critical Legal Studies (CLS) movement regard rights as one of the features of liberalism which appear to be objective, neutral, and protective of freedom, whereas, in reality, they perpetuate the individualism that is actually destructive of true freedom.[36] This rights-scepticism prompts either an absolute refutation of the concept of rights or the formulation of an alternative vision of rights that extends beyond the communitarian to what Roberto Unger champions as an element in a programme of 'empowered democracy'.[37]

Feminism embraces a wide range of approaches to the oppression of women and, in certain branches of the movement, of members of other oppressed groups. For example, ecofeminists discern a close connection between sexism, speciesism, and racism.[38] It is not always clear (at least to me) the extent to which feminism in general, and, say, radical feminists, in particular, are hostile to the concept of human rights. A good deal of feminist legal theory eschews the idea of rights as formal, hierarchical, and patriarchal. Law in general and rights in particular, reflect, it is contended, a male viewpoint 'characterized by objectivity, distance and abstraction'.[39] In the words of Catharine MacKinnon: 'Abstract rights ... authorise the male

35 There is little support amongst postmodernist writers for animal rights, although some, notably Derrida, denounce the cruelty and violence inflicted on animals. See Derrida, op cit, 88ff; Gary Steiner, *Animals and the Limits of Postmodernism* (New York: Columbia University Press, 2013).

36 See generally Morton J Horowitz, *The Transformation of American Law, 1870–1960: The Crisis of Legal Orthodoxy* (New York: Oxford University Press, 1992); G Edward White, 'The Inevitability of Critical Legal Studies' (1984) 36 *Stanford Law Review* 649; David Kairys, ed, *The Politics of Law: A Progressive Critique* (New York: Pantheon Books, 1982). See too Charles M Yablon, 'The Indeterminacy of the Law: Critical Legal Studies and the Problem of Legal Explanation' (1985) 6 *Cardozo Law Review* 917, Robert W Gordon, 'Critical Legal Histories' (1984) 36 *Stanford Law Review* 270.

37 Rejecting traditional concepts of rights, Unger advances four 'super-liberal rights': 'market rights', 'immunity rights', destabilization rights', and 'solidarity rights' which are supposed to create a society in which individuals are more likely to attain self-fulfilment. See Hugh Collins, 'Roberto Unger and the Critical Legal Studies Movement' (1987) *Law and Society* 387.

38 See Carol J Adams and Lori Gruen, eds, *Ecofeminism: Feminist Intersections with Other Animals and the Earth* (London: Bloomsbury, 2014). There is a strong connection between the feminist and the anti-vivisection campaigns of the nineteenth century in Britain. See Olive Banks, *Faces of Feminism* (Oxford: Blackwell, 1986), 81–82, quoted in Lynda IA Birke, *Women, Feminism and Biology: The Feminist Challenge* (Brighton: Harvester, 1986), 120; Carol J Adams, *Neither Man Nor Beast: Feminism and the Defense of Animals* (New York: Lantern Books, reprint, 2015).

39 EM Schneider, 'The Dialectic of Rights and Politics: Perspectives from the Women's Movement' in Katharine Bartlett and Roseanne Kennedy, eds, *Feminist Legal Theory: Readings in Law and Gender* (Boulder, CO: Westview Press, 1991), 319.

experience of the world'.[40] But, although Elizabeth Kingdom recommends 'abandoning the concept of rights as a means of pressing feminist claims in law',[41] she restricts that rejection to the appeal to women's right to choose and the right to reproduce, resisting 'any extrapolation from that argument a kind of policy essentialism to the effect that every and any mention of rights must be expunged from the feminist dictionary of legal politics'.[42] Her argument is that appeals to rights often conceal inadequate theories of law in respect of women's social position. Such theories tend to be essentialist and therefore unacceptable to many feminist theorists.

Some adherents of Critical Race Theory[43] argue that individual rights often mask racial discrimination and inequalities, and may actually serve to preserve and maintain them.[44]

The postmodern assault on rights lies primarily in its opposition towards the possibility of an autonomous, rational individuated subject. This controlling idea of rights discourse in the liberal tradition is 'trashed' by poststructuralists; it adopts the view that 'what is negated and denied in the process of its construction: a poststructuralist critique of the totalising narratives of liberal political and legal thought would therefore expose how the latter tend to constitute the domain in which the subject may express itself politically in such a way as to effect a closure around the realm of the political itself'.[45] In other words, the rights-bearing subject has been drained both of meaning and authentic existence. The structural, psychological, and linguistic patterns of this approach constitute, through the analysis of social theorists like Michel Foucault, Louis Althusser, and Jacques Lacan, a serious threat to the idea of the universal subject. The poststructuralist onslaught of, in particular, Jacques Derrida, denies the very idea of the subject having an 'essence', and hence the impossibility (indeed, meaninglessness) of rights discourse.

40 C MacKinnon, 'Feminism, Marxism, Method and the State: Toward Feminist Jurisprudence' (1983) 8 *Signs: Journal of Women, Culture & Society* 63.

41 Quoted in Carol Smart, 'Feminism and the Law: Some Problems of Analysis and Strategy' (1986) 14 *International Journal of Sociology of Law* 109.

42 EF Kingdom, *What's Wrong with Rights? Problems for Feminist Politics of Law* (Edinburgh: Edinburgh University Press, 1991).

43 See Angela P Harris, 'The Jurisprudence of Reconstruction' (1994) 82 *California Law Review* 741, 743. Harris's essay is a 'foreword' to a symposium in this number of the journal. See too Symposium, 'Minority Critique of the Critical Legal Studies Movement' (1987) 22 *Harvard Civil Rights—Civil Liberties Law Review* 297 (1987), quoted in Derek P Jinks, 'Essays in Refusal: Pre-Theoretical Commitments in Postmodern Anthropology and Critical Race Theory' (1997) 107 *Yale Law Journal* 1.

44 I discuss these movements at some length in *Understanding Jurisprudence: An Introduction to Legal Theory*, 6th edn (Oxford: Oxford University Press, 2020), Ch 13 and 14.

45 Anne Barron, 'The Illusion of the "I": Citizenship and the Politics of Identity' in Alan Norrie, ed, *Closure or Critique: New Directions in Legal Theory* (Edinburgh: Edinburgh University Press, 1993); see 21.

Animal rights as human rights

As outlined earlier, moral claims are routinely translated into moral rights: humans assert their rights to life, work, health, education, housing, and so on. Communities and putative nations demand a right to self-determination, sovereignty, free trade, and so on. In the legal context, rights have assumed a prominence so great that they are sometimes regarded as synonymous with law itself; declarations of political rights are often conceived to be the hallmark of the modern democratic state. And the inevitable contest between competing rights is one of the self-justifying characteristics of a democratic society.

What of animals? Can we defend human exceptionalism when it comes to the granting of rights? Is it really 'quite inconceivable that the extension of any right should coincide exactly with the boundaries of our species'?[46] Is there any merit in exploring the so-called post-humanist approach which attempts to displace, or at least to reduce, the dominance of the 'human' in our analysis of rights?[47] It distances itself from humanism, arguing that humans do not have innate rights to despoil Nature or to place themselves as superior to it. It rejects, for example, the Cartesian model of human beings and endeavours to locate us within a wider philosophical and social context. We are, it maintains, part of the broader nonhuman realm; different from, but not fundamentally ethically superior to, other creatures that inhabit the natural world. The fact that humans may be more 'intelligent' or possess greater 'knowledge' does not license us to treat other species as we wish. It asserts that animal rights discourse treats animals as lesser creatures—reduced versions of ourselves. By invoking the capacity of animals to experience pain and distress, this approach simply restores the supremacy of humans that it seeks to dislodge. Post-humanists argue that nonhumans are not second-class humans, but that all creatures are worthy of concern and respect in their own right. This analysis has important implications for our attitude towards the protection of animals, and Nature in general.

It is one of the numerous questions that are generated once doubts are expressed about the exclusivity of humans to human rights.[48] But, while it is true that, as we have seen, what might be called constructive or indirect rights are potentially vouchsafed to animals by virtue of welfare

46 Colin Sumner, *The Moral Foundation of Rights* (Oxford: Clarendon Press, 1989), 206.

47 A powerful case in support of this view is made by Cary Wolfe, *What Is Posthumanism?* (Minneapolis, MN: University of Minnesota Press, 2009). See, too, his *Before the Law: Humans and Other Animals in a Biopolitical Frame* (Chicago, IL: University of Chicago Press, 2012).

48 The outstanding work of Saskia Stucki presents a compelling and carefully argued case in support of both limited rights (discussed in Chapter 4), and human rights for animals. See Saskia Stucki, *One Rights: Human and Animal Rights in the Anthropocene* (Cham, Switzerland: Springer, 2023) which I draw on here.

statutes, their claim to the more fundamental rights reserved for humans remains unattainable. Nor have the efforts to invoke human rights before judges met with any success, although the attempts to bring a petition of *habeas corpus* on behalf of captive animals represent a hopeful route to recognition.[49]

Jurists, who adopt a naturalistic approach to human rights, underwrite a humancentric conception that rests on the contribution of such rights to 'human flourishing' or other elements of justice, the common good, or equality.[50] Theirs is a standpoint in which human rights spring from, or are even synonymous with, natural or moral rights. Hence, leading natural law theorist, John Finnis, states:

> Those who propose that animals have rights have a deficient appreciation of the basic forms of human good.... Even if we consider the bodily human goods, and those simply as experienced, we see that the quality of this experience is very different from a merely animal consciousness, since it is experienced as expressive of decision, choice, reflectiveness, commitment, as fruition of purpose, or of self-discipline or self-abandonment, and as the action of a responsible personality.[51]

And to the proposition that very young babies or very old or mentally defective persons lack these faculties and, therefore, that they are no more entitled to rights than a clever, healthy dog is, Finnis replies that respect for human good reasonably extends as far as human beings, and is not to be extinguished by the circumstances that life has not yet provided or has deprived a particular human being of the opportunity of a full flourishing.[52]

But what of the 'full flourishing' of nonhuman beings? That is at the core of Martha Nussbaum's capabilities approach which I review in Chapter 9.

49 Courts in India, Pakistan, Colombia, Argentina, and Switzerland have shown a willingness to open the door to these sorts of actions. See Chapter 12.

50 See John Finnis, *Natural Law and Natural Rights*, 2nd edn (Oxford: Clarendon Press, 2011), 221.

51 Op cit, 194–195.

52 I am grateful to John Finnis for clarifying his position for me. His paradigm, founded on the idea that rights are 'constructed primarily on the implicit model of a relationship between two individuals', would, at first blush, also appear to sound the death knell for animals as right-bearers, and that is how he takes it, though he accepts that one can use the word 'right' as correlative to any use of 'duty to [another]', and therefore speaks not of duties *to* animals but of duties in respect of them (not to be needlessly cruel, etc.), duties with no correlative rights. A Catholic perspective on natural law and rights in general is analysed by John Finnis in 'Grounding Human Rights in Natural Law' (2015) 60 *American Journal of Jurisprudence* 199. For a secular barrier to animal rights, see Shelley Kagan, *How to Count Animals, More or Less*, Uehiro Series in Practical Ethics (Oxford: Oxford University Press, 2022) who defends a hierarchy in which humans count more than animals, and certain animals count more than others.

A political conception of human rights, by contrast, focuses on the practical application of such rights as they operate in society. Stucki treats the two approaches as complimentary; the former being mainly concerned with the nature of human rights, while the latter with their functional and institutional elements.[53]

The central question is what, apart from our humanity, distinguishes us sufficiently from other sentient animals whose vulnerability to pain and suffering resembles our own in non-trivial respects so as to deny them the protection of human rights. It is not enough to invoke the tautology mentioned earlier. Yes, human rights are for humans, but that *petitio principii* only generates the question, what is 'human'? Are there, in other words, characteristics of our humanness that avoid the stigma of speciesism which justify this ethical apartheid? Biological difference merely asserts, without explaining, why the classification *homo sapiens* should govern the rights we enjoy.[54] And an essentialist quest for a litmus test of 'human', as generally undertaken by naturalists, is no less question-begging. It typically deploys a suite of allegedly distinctive features that only humans possess: rationality, personhood, moral agency, dignity.[55]

Not all humans, however, satisfy these criteria; marginal cases such as the mentally ill, the comatose, and infants need to be distinguished from, say, an intelligent chimpanzee. The strategy then shifts to the element of potentiality; human beings may, it is contended, fall short of these sorts of benchmarks, but they have the potential to do so, or they usually do. This manoeuvre cannot entirely eradicate the stain of speciesism for 'there does not seem to be an empirically verifiable feature or capacity that *all and only* humans actually possess *and* that is relevant for grounding human rights'.[56] Nor does the idea that human rights are grounded in the dignity which we humans possess, but which animals lack. This 'new dignitarian'[57] theory, however, is tantamount to a form of hierarchical speciesism.[58]

53 This seems right: 'The Political Conception is not only compatible with the Naturalistic Conception but also incomplete without the theoretical resources that a Naturalistic Conception characteristically provides', S Matthew Laio and Adam Etinson, 'Political and Naturalistic Conceptions of Human Rights: A False Polemic?' (2012) 9 *Journal of Moral Philosophy* 327, 352.

54 How is this to be distinguished from racism? See David Bilchitz, 'Moving Beyond Arbitrariness: The Legal Personhood and Dignity of Non-human Animals' (2009) 25 *South African Journal of Human Rights* 38; Carlos Nino, *The Ethics of Human Rights* (Oxford: Clarendon Press, 1991), 35; S Matthew Laio, 'The Genetic Account of Moral Status: A Defence' (2012) 9 *Journal of Moral Philosophy* 265.

55 See, for example, James Griffin, op cit, 32ff, where he distinguishes humans from animals by pointing to the fact that we 'are agents with a conception of, and the mental abilities to pursue, a good life'. See too S Mattthew Liao, op cit.

56 Stucki, op cit, 28.

57 Will Kymlicka, 'Human Rights Without Human Supremacism' (2018) 48 *Canadian Journal of Philosophy* 763, 768.

58 But see Richard L Cupp, 'Moving Beyond Animal Rights: A Legal/Contractualist Critique' (2009) 46 *San Diego Law Review* 27, for a contrary view that animal rights risks devaluing human dignity.

Paola Cavalieri points out that the emphasis on negative rights implies an 'unjustified minimalist account of human rights':

> Yet it is plausible to maintain that the core of the theory remains protective, and that between the two main sorts of rights—*negative* rights, or rights not to be treated in a certain way, and *positive* rights, or rights to be treated in a certain way—the ones that prevail are always negative rights, and, in particular, the so-called civil liberties, secured by the generalized prohibition against taking life, depriving freedom, and violating bodily integrity.[59]

This is plainly a consequence of pragmatic considerations, nevertheless it does fortify the case for extending the reach of human rights which she was amongst the first to champion.

It is not, I think, unreasonable to conclude that the pursuit of a distinctive human characteristic is fruitless. Moreover, even if a credible yardstick was somehow unearthed, it would likely be highly tendentious since its primary intention would inexorably be to establish an ethical barrier between humans and animals. Progress in this enterprise needs to identify what we *share* with animals, rather than what distinguishes us from them. Alisdair Cochrane has suggested the concept of 'sentient rights':

> The human rights movement cannot consistently turn its eyes away from the suffering and rights violations of non-human sentient creatures. These creatures are sentient like us; these creatures suffer like us; these creatures have interests like us; and these creatures have basic rights like us. To acknowledge these simple points, human rights should be reconceptualized as sentient rights.[60]

However this common disposition is to be designated, the most obvious feature we have in common is our sentient vulnerabilities and needs. We share a susceptibility to pain, suffering, and death, and a need for food and shelter.[61] Is this a sufficient basis on which to extend the fundamental rights incorporated in conventional human rights to

59 Paola Cavalieri, *The Animal Question: Why Nonhuman Animals Deserve Human Rights* (Oxford: Oxford University Press, 2001), 127.

60 Alisdair Cochrane, 'From Human Rights to Sentient Rights' (2013) 16 *Critical Review of International Social and Political Philosophy* 655, 672.

61 See John Tasioulas, 'Human Rights, Universality and the Values of Personhood: Retracing Griffin's Steps' (2002) 10 *European Journal of Philosophy* 79, and John Tasioulas, 'On the Foundations of Human Rights' in R Cruft, S Liao, and M Renzo, eds, *Philosophical Foundations of Human Rights* (Oxford: Oxford University Press, 2015).

animals? [62] Pain, as Christine Korsgaard points out, is cry for help, a reason to end its suffering:

> When you pity a suffering animal, it is because you are perceiving a reason. An animal's cries express pain, and they mean that there is a reason, a reason to change its conditions. And you can no more hear the cries of an animal as mere noise than you can the words of a person. Another animal can obligate you in exactly the same way another person can....[63]

The emergence of 'new humanism', as mentioned earlier, may enhance the prospects of a universal conception of human rights that transcends the artificial borders between us and them.

Traction may also be obtained by appealing to broader ethical and prudential justifications for the extension of fundamental rights to animals. This approach looks to the operation of human rights in the political domain, especially, as alluded to earlier, the manner in which the recognition of fundamental rights is a response to injustice and oppression. The post-apartheid constitution of apartheid South Africa replaced the repressive regime with a liberal democracy, universal adult suffrage, and a bill of rights. Is it too far-fetched to expect that the distress and misery of billions of nonhumans might be alleviated in similar fashion? Some suggest that this would weaken the standing of human rights. But it is arguable that the reverse is the case; it may enhance respect for all life.[64]

The connection between human and animal justice was well described by the social reformer Henry Salt in 1894:

> [R]ights ... cannot be consistently awarded to men and denied to animals, since the same sense of justice and compassion apply in both cases.... It is an entire mistake to suppose that the rights of animals are in any way antagonistic to the rights of men. Let us not be betrayed for

62 '[B]elonging to the human species is [not] a valid ground for human rights. Nor does it mean that all human beings have all human rights, nor that only human beings possess human rights. What it means is that it is true that human beings have human rights simply in virtue of being human if (and only if) within a limited period of time all (but not only) human beings actually possess the features that ground at least one human right', Raffael N Fasel, '"Simply in Virtue of Being Human"? A Critical Appraisal of a Human Rights Commonplace' (2018) 9 *Jurisprudence* 461, 485.

63 Christine M Korsgaard, *The Sources of Normativity* (Cambridge: Cambridge University Press, 1996), 153.

64 Gary Francione, *Introduction to Animal Rights: Your Child or the Dog?* (Philadelphia, PA: Temple University, 2000), 174.

a moment into the specious fallacy that we must study human rights first, and leave the animal question to solve itself hereafter....[65]

There is a growing movement which perceives the human rights of animals to be associated with the wider protection of marginalised minorities, and which also seeks to demonstrate the connection between violence against humans to that which we inflict on animals. Indeed, it is remarked that genocidal propaganda frequently dehumanises victims by branding them nonhuman: rats, cockroaches, monkeys, vermin, and so on.

Another practical benefit of these rights is their amelioration of the possible effects of the abuse and maltreatment of animals on the environment.[66] A conspicuous example is the recent pandemic. Towards the end of 2019, an individual in the notorious Huanan seafood market in Wuhan was reportedly infected with a virus that apparently emanated from an animal. The virus—later identified as COVID-19—spread across the globe. At the time of writing, it has caused (or contributed to) the death of almost seven million people. So-called 'wet' markets (more accurately described as wildlife markets) are common in China. The Huanan market had a section selling wild animals including badgers, wolf pups, snakes, bamboo rats, and porcupines, mostly kept in tiny cages with no apparent concern for their suffering. One stall offered about a hundred varieties of live animals ranging from foxes to peacocks to masked palm civets; the last-mentioned creature is regarded as instrumental in transferring the SARS virus from bats to humans in the 2002/3 epidemic. It has been suggested that an intermediary host between bats and humans may be the pangolin which is described by the International Union for the Conservation of Nature as the most illegally traded mammal in the world. They are prized their meat and the alleged medicinal properties of their scales.[67]

What human rights?

If animals are to be considered right-holders, it is reasonably unproblematic to distinguish the sorts of human rights that are especially beneficial, even

65 Henry S Salt, *Animals' Rights Considered in Relation to Social Progress* (New York: MacMillan, 1894), 19, 21, quoted by Stucki, op cit, 66. Similar sentiments have more recently been expressed by Tom Regan, 'The Case for Animal Rights' in Peter Singer, ed, *In Defence of Animals* (Oxford: Basil Blackwell, 1985); Paola Cavalieri, *The Animal Question: Why Nonhuman Animals Deserve Human Rights* (Oxford: Oxford University Press, 2001).

66 'Our exploitation and extermination of nonhuman animals are not only harming many nonhuman animals but also contributing to public health threats such as pandemics and environmental threats such as climate change', Jeff Sebo, *Saving Animals, Saving Ourselves: Why Animals Matter for Pandemics, Climate Change, and Other Catastrophes* (Oxford: Oxford University Press, 2022), 117.

67 See Andrea Monti and Raymond Wacks, *COVID-19 and Public Policy in the Digital Age* (Abingdon: Routledge, 2021), 3–4.

crucial. They would need to include the right to life, bodily integrity, and freedom from torture, from cruelty, freedom of movement, and perhaps the right to family life. The right to food, shelter, and medical treatment would seem to be necessary to be extended to domesticated animals. The inclusion of political and certain procedural rights (especially *habeas corpus*) is discussed in Chapters 11 and 12.

But it may not have to stop there. The right to privacy may not be an exclusively human need:

> Man likes to think that his desire for privacy is distinctively human, a function of his unique ethical, intellectual, and artistic needs. Yet ... man's need for privacy may well be rooted in his animal origins, and that men and animals share several basic mechanisms for claiming privacy.... [T]he quest for privacy is not restricted to man alone, but arises in the biological and social processes of life.[68]

*

While the proposal to extend human rights to animals is unquestionably a laudable one, the prospect of its realisation is remote. This is not to suggest that the pursuit of this aspiration should be abandoned, but it seems to me that there are less improbable and more practical paths to pursue. I return to the subject in Chapter 12.

68 Alan F Westin, *Privacy and Freedom* (London: The Bodley Head, 1970), 8–11. Whether this conception of 'privacy' is the most constructive one is a subject I have spent almost half a century pontificating upon! See, for example, Raymond Wacks, *Personal Information: Privacy and the Law* (Oxford: Clarendon Press, 1989); Raymond Wacks, *Privacy: A Very Short Introduction*, 2nd edn (Oxford: Oxford University Press, 2015).

6 Utilitarianism vs deontology

How do we decide what is the right thing to do? For a utilitarian, the test is what will increase the 'greatest happiness of the greatest number'. In other words, utilitarianism looks to the consequences of our acts or decisions; it regards pleasure, or the satisfaction of preferences, as the exclusive element in human good, and treats the morality of acts and rules as wholly dependent on the consequences for human welfare. It is therefore consequentialist: it is based on the idea that whether an act is morally right depends exclusively upon its consequences or of some quality related to the act—for example, the motive behind it, or the existence of a general rule requiring acts of the same kind. A deontologist, on the other hand, adopts the view that certain acts are intrinsically right or wrong, regardless of their consequences.

In this chapter, I shall summarise the essentials of each position before examining how the two moral approaches have been applied to the treatment of animals.

Utilitarianism

Utilitarians oppose the metaphysics that characterised much of eighteenth-century political philosophy. Though there are a number of classical utilitarian theories (including those of John Stuart Mill and Henry Sidgwick), it is Jeremy Bentham's formulation that is the most celebrated and influential. While he fulminates against natural rights (which he called 'nonsense on stilts') and, in particular, the views of Blackstone (see Chapter 2), the theory has a serious moral basis which takes as its premise the proposition that the fundamental objective of morality and justice is that happiness should be maximized. This sometimes overlooks the fact that his form of utilitarianism is what has been called 'hedonistic', and may be contrasted with GE Moore's 'non-hedonistic' utilitarianism, and Mill's intermediate position. In practice, however, classical utilitarianism is typically equated with Bentham.

DOI: 10.4324/9781032702575-6

His general view is well captured in this famous passage from *An Introduction to the Principles of Morals and Legislation*[1]:

> Nature has placed mankind under the governance of two sovereign masters, *pain* and *pleasure*. It is for them alone to point out what we ought to do, as well as to determine what we shall do. On the one hand the standard of right and wrong, on the other the chain of causes and effects, are fastened to their throne.... The *principle of utility* recognises this subjection, and assumes it for the foundation of that system, the object of which is to rear the fabric of felicity by the hands of reason and of law. Systems which attempt to question it, deal in sounds instead of sense, in caprice instead of reason, in darkness instead of light.

To this end, Bentham devised his 'felicific calculus' by which we can assess the 'happiness factor' of any action, by identifying 12 pains and 14 pleasures.

Utilitarianism obviously looks to the future in its preoccupation with the maximization of happiness or welfare or some other good. There are two forms of utilitarianism: 'act utilitarianism' and 'rule utilitarianism'. The former adopts the position that the rightness or wrongness of an action is to be judged by the consequences, good or bad, of the action itself. The latter argues that the rightness or wrongness of an action is to be judged by the goodness or badness of the consequences of a rule that everyone should perform the action in like circumstances.[2]

Most discussions of utilitarianism (including this one) concern themselves with act utilitarianism, though it is not uncommon to find appeals made to 'ideal rule utilitarianism' which provides that the rightness or wrongness of an action is to be judged by the goodness or badness of a rule which, *if observed*, would have better consequences than any other rule governing the same action. This version of rule utilitarianism has obvious advantages, for instance, in the context of a judge who is called upon to decide whether a plaintiff should be awarded damages against the defendant: clearly he should ignore the effect of his judgement on the *particular* indigent defendant. It may be contrasted with 'actual rule utilitarianism' which holds that the rightness of an action is to be judged by reference to a rule which is *actually observed* and whose acceptance would maximize utility.

Bentham's version of act utilitarianism is usually considered too quaint for modern tastes, while the 'ideal' act utilitarianism of GE Moore (who, broadly speaking, thought that certain states of mind, such as those of acquiring knowledge, had an intrinsic value independent of their pleasantness) and of John Stuart Mill (who argued that there are higher and lower pleasures—implying that pleasure is a necessary condition for goodness, but that goodness

1 Ch 1, para 1.

2 JJC Smart and Bernard Williams, *Utilitarianism: For and Against* (Cambridge: Cambridge University Press, 1973), 9.

depends on qualities of experience other than pleasantness and unpleasantness) are regarded as somewhat elitist. This is largely because these writers tend to substitute their own preferences for those they think people ought to have. Mill therefore denies the idea that pleasures can be quantified, arguing that some forms of pleasure differ from each other qualitatively. Certain higher (mainly cerebral or highbrow) pleasures are worthier—even though they may be less intense than lower (primarily bodily) pleasures. 'It is better', he famously declared, 'to be a human being dissatisfied than a pig satisfied; better to be Socrates dissatisfied than a fool satisfied'. He does, however, admit that the attainment of happiness is often difficult; therefore, it may at times be morally acceptable to decrease the extent of pain that we experience. Pain, or even sacrificing pleasure, is reasonable only when it produces a greater good. He does not follow Bentham in restricting himself to the external sanctions of punishment, and contends that we are also motivated by internal sanctions like self-esteem, conscience, and guilt. And as we tend to care about others, altruism is frequently sufficient to lead us to act morally. Given that we all want happiness; we must also want everyone to be happy.

In *On Liberty*, Mill argues that individual freedom is really based on utilitarian principles:

> It is proper to state that I forego any advantage which could be derived to my argument from the idea of abstract right, as a thing independent of utility. I regard utility as the ultimate appeal on all ethical questions; but it must be utility in the largest sense, grounded on the permanent interests of man as a progressive being. Those interests, I contend, authorize the subjection of individual spontaneity to external control, only in respect to those actions of each, which concern the interest of other people.[3]

He defends personal freedom also on the basis that it increases general happiness. Thus, he famously advocates freedom of speech and the right to dissent. Only by the free circulation of ideas can the 'truth' be revealed.

Criticism

A fundamental assault on utilitarianism is made by those—including Bernard Williams[4] and John Rawls[5]—who argue that it fails to recognise the 'separateness of persons'.[6] It suggests that utilitarianism, at least in its pure form,

3 John Stuart Mill, in Gertrude Himmelfarb, ed, *On Liberty* (Harmondsworth: Penguin Books, 1974), 1.11.

4 In Smart and Williams, *Utilitarianism: For and Against.*

5 See John Rawls, *A Theory of Justice* (Harmondsworth: Penguin, 1973), 194ff, discussed in Chapters 6 and 10.

6 A common, and justifiable, criticism is that utilitarians regard individuals as 'receptacles' in which to decant pleasure or pain.

treats human beings as means rather than ends in themselves. This important attack consists, in HLA Hart's view,[7] of four main points which may be summarised as follows. First, separate individuals are important to utilitarians only in so far as they are 'the channels or locations where what is of value is to be found'. Secondly, utilitarianism treats individual persons equally, but only by effectively treating them as having *no* worth, for their value is not *as persons*, but as 'experiencers' of pleasure or happiness. Thirdly, why should we regard as a valuable moral goal the mere increase in totals of pleasure or happiness abstracted from all questions of *distribution* of happiness, welfare, and so on? Fourthly, the analogy used by utilitarians, of a rational single individual prudently sacrificing present happiness for later satisfaction, is false for it treats my pleasure as replaceable by the greater pleasure of others.

These four criticisms contain most of the issues that lie at the heart of many of the other attacks, of which the following may be mentioned. Why should we seek to satisfy people's desires? Certain desires are unworthy of satisfaction (for instance, the sadist who wants to torture animals).[8] Rawls argues that utilitarianism defines what is right in terms of what is 'good'; but this means, he says, that it begins with a conception of what is 'good' (for example, happiness) and then concludes that an action is right in so far as it maximizes that 'good'.[9] Moreover, utilitarianism is concerned only with maximizing welfare; many regard the more important question as the just *distribution* of welfare.

Many critics point to the impracticability of calculating the consequences of one's actions: how can we know in advance what results will follow from what we propose to do? Another reproach claims that our wants and desires are often manipulated by persuasion, advertising, and the like. How then can we separate our 'real' preferences from our 'conditioned' ones? Moreover, is it possible (and, if it is, is it desirable) to balance my pleasure against your pain? On a larger scale, can judges or legislators, when faced with a choice between two or more courses of action, realistically (or even sensibly) weigh the majority's happiness against a minority's misery? Finally, how far into the future do (or can) we extend the consequences of our actions? Or to put it slightly differently, as Bernard Williams does, 'No one can hold that everything, of whatever category, that has value, has it in virtue of its consequences. If that were so, one would just go on forever, and there would be an obviously hopeless regress'.[10]

Utilitarianism may be treated as a system of personal morality or as one of social or political decision-making. Bentham, of course, sought to show that,

7 Expressed in his essay, 'Between Utility and Rights', in his *Essays in Jurisprudence and Philosophy* (Oxford: Clarendon Press, 1983), 198, 200–202.
8 Bentham's catalogue includes 'the pleasure of malevolence'.
9 See his alternative, *A Theory of Justice*, 169.
10 In Smart and Williams, *Utilitarianism: For and Against*, 82.

on the basis of the former, we could generalize outwards to the latter. And many of the important law reforms of the nineteenth century are attributable to its influence as a political theory. But it has few supporters today.[11]

Deontology

Deontological theories appraise the morality of choices by standards that differ from the results caused by those choices. Unlike consequentialist theories like utilitarianism, they hold that certain choices cannot be defended by their outcomes—that it matters not how morally good their consequences may turn out to be, some choices are morally wrong. A choice is right in relation to its conformity with a moral norm. One is simply under a moral obligation to abide by such norms. This is typically expressed in the maxim: the right is prior to the good. In other words, if an act does not correspond to what is right, it may not be done—even if it produces good.

The main advantage of deontological morality, as opposed to consequentialism, is that it allows agents to take account of factors such as the wellbeing of their close friends or families. It therefore avoids the demanding characteristics of consequentialism and is more in keeping with our conventional intuition of our moral duties. Moreover, deontological duties are directed to specific individuals rather than, as is the case with consequentialism, designed to improve the lot of people in general.

Deontology is most closely associated with Immanuel Kant who, in his *Groundwork for the Metaphysics of Morals*, states, 'A good will is good not because of what it effects or accomplishes, nor because of its fitness to attain some proposed end; it is good only through its willing, i.e., it is good in itself'.[12] In other words, good will is the basis of moral worth which depends not on the specific act, but on the principle upon which the act is done. Good will is good in itself, not the result of anything else. It is the ability to carry out acts for their sole purpose and duty.

Kant divides these duties between the hypothetical and the categorical. Hypothetical imperatives are those that spring from a particular purpose or end. Categorical imperatives, on the other hand, prompt us to act for the sake of the act itself. They are universal in that they apply to all rational beings: 'Act only according to that maxim whereby you can at the same time will that it should become a universal law'. Its second formulation has a slightly different injunction: 'So act that you use humanity, in your own person as well as in the person of any other, always at the same time as an end, never merely as a means'.

11 Instead, it appears in the nether garments of the so-called 'economic analysis of law'.

12 Immanuel Kant, *Groundwork of the Metaphysics of Morals*, Cambridge Texts in the History of Philosophy, 2nd edn, Christine M Korsgaard, ed (Cambridge: Cambridge University Press, 2012), para 394.

The first formulation captures the idea of acting as if your values should apply to all. The second requires you to treat persons as ends not means to your own objectives. Categorical imperatives, unlike hypothetical imperatives, tell us what to do regardless of our desires. Morality does not state: 'If you want to avoid imprisonment do not steal'. It declares instead: 'Do not steal'. We should refrain from theft whether or not we wish to avoid jail. This means that unless you accept that your moral rule can be applied to everyone, including you, it is not a valid moral rule. For Kant, therefore, the only valid justification for doing the right thing is that you are under a duty to do so. This is the essence of deontology (from the Greek 'deon' meaning 'duty'). When you act from some other motive (for example, fear of the consequences), you are not acting morally.

Duty is thus at the heart of Kant's idea of justice. The claim that we owe a duty of justice to others entails that they have rights against us. In other words, to repeat, it holds that what is right is unrelated to what is good. Justice requires respect for the right, notwithstanding challenging situations and attractive or undesirable outcomes. We all have a right to be respected as individuals—as ends in ourselves. This priority of right stems from the freedom that we have in our relations between us. Justice and right trump all other values because they arise from the idea of freedom which is a precondition of all human goals.

Kant's concept of right is therefore independent of our practical desires, interests, and needs. It rests on the need for a distinct essential principle of duty; the categorical imperative tells us what we ought to do—categorically (i.e., unconditionally). It allows us rationally to distinguish between right and wrong. It is expressed in three different formulae: *universalisability*: we must endeavour to do only what we could reasonably wish to become a universal law; *respect for all persons*: we should always attempt to act so as to respect all persons, including ourselves, as inherently cherished 'ends in themselves', and never consider others as purely instrumental means to other ends; *the principle of autonomy*: as morally autonomous rational agents, we should act as if we were legislating for a (hypothetical) moral republic of all persons. This principle underlines the dignity of all persons, considering them as prized and worthy of respect.

We act morally, Kant maintains, because we are under a duty to do so. When we act from some other motive we do not act morally, but heteronomously (in accordance with our desires) as opposed to autonomously (based on our personal morality). Acting morally requires us to act out of *duty*. Acting in accordance with the categorical imperatives entails treating people with respect—as opposed to in pursuit of an ulterior motive. They are thereby regarded as ends in themselves, unlike utilitarianism which, as outlined above, treats persons as a means to a particular end. It also requires a community to approve a particular model of happiness; this implies imposing one conception of pleasure on all.

Criticism

David Hume famously argued that morality is not based on our rational judgements, but on our emotions. Yet, even if reason really is the foundation of morality, do we still not need to act on our moral convictions? Does reason truly provoke us to act in a certain way? Surely, we also need to *desire* to act. If so, Hume reasons, we need the predisposition to do the right thing. 'Reason', Hume states, 'is and ought only to be the slave of the passions and can never pretend to any other office than to serve and obey them'.[13]

Other criticism relates to the failure to consider the consequences of one's decision or action. Deontology appears to allow one the freedom to decide what is subjectively right, which may simply be what makes one feel good. It is sometimes described as selfish since it fails to reflect upon the effects of one's action on society. There is also the fact that one's moral choice today may change tomorrow giving rise to conflict and inconsistency. Unlike utilitarianism which attempts to improve the world, deontology has the potential morally to worsen the world. For example, suppose my compliance with deontological norms causes calamitous consequences. A standard example is to suppose that there is a concealed nuclear device; unless X violates the deontological duty not to torture Y in order to discover where it is hidden, thousands of innocent people could die when it explodes. This may be a *reduction ad absurdum* of deontology, but it captures the problem of cleaving to an unbending normative prescription. Kant's critics question his view that all duties can be derived from a purely formal principle and argue that his preoccupation with rational consistency neglects the concrete content of moral obligation.

A further criticism has been called 'the paradox of relative stringency'. This refers to the ambiguity of asserting that all deontological duties are to be carried out regardless of the consequences, and yet, at the same time claiming that some of these duties are more stringent than others.

Like Robert Nozick and Ronald Dworkin, John Rawls considers utilitarianism an inadequate means by which to measure justice. His argument, however, differs from theirs. He refuses to accept inequalities even if they secure maximum welfare; his conception of welfare is not concerned with benefits, but 'primary social goods' which includes self-respect. Liberty is non-negotiable—even in order to maximize welfare.[14] His hostility towards utilitarianism is based largely on two features of the theory. First, that it fails to recognise the separateness or distinctness of individual persons. Secondly,

13 David Hume, *A Treatise of Human Nature*, Book III, Part III, Section III (London: Penguin Classics, 1985), 3.

14 Some critics argue that there are fewer differences than Rawls appears to realise. See Frank Michelman, 'Constitutional Welfare Rights and *A Theory of Justice*' in Norman Daniels, ed, *Reading Rawls: Critical Studies on Rawls' A Theory of Justice* (Oxford: Basil Blackwell, 1975), 319.

that questions of justice are *prior to* questions of happiness. In other words, it is only when we regard a particular pleasure as just that we can say whether it has any value. How do we know whether John's enjoyment of torture should be counted as having any value *before* we know whether the practice of torture is itself *just*? Thus, whereas utilitarianism defines what is right in terms of what is good, Rawls regards what is right as prior to what is good.

Animals

Robert Nozick declares that we accept 'utilitarianism for animals, Kantianism for people'.[15] The cogency of this remark should become clear in what follows.

Standard-bearer for the utilitarian cause, Jeremy Bentham, declares:

> The day may come, when the rest of the animal creation may acquire those rights which never could have been withholden from them but by the hand of tyranny. The French have already discovered that the blackness of skin is no reason why a human being should be abandoned without redress to the caprice of a tormentor. It may come one day to be recognized, that the number of legs, the villosity of the skin, or the termination of the os sacrum, are reasons equally insufficient for abandoning a sensitive being to the same fate. What else is it that should trace the insuperable line? Is it the faculty of reason, or perhaps, the faculty for discourse?... [T]he question is not, Can they reason? nor, Can they talk? but, Can they suffer? Why should the law refuse its protection to any sensitive being?... The time will come when humanity will extend its mantle over everything which breathes....[16]

This asseveration is regularly cited in support of the view that we should treat sentient animals has having interests that warrant protection. This principle lies at the heart of Peter Singer's trail-blazing book, *Animal Liberation* (first published in 1975) which adopts a preference utilitarian approach to the moral status of animals.[17] His central argument is that in calculating the consequences of our actions, the pain suffered or pleasure enjoyed by animals counts no less than our own. To regard their experience as in some way

15 Robert Nozick, *Anarchy, State and Utopia* (New York: Basic Books, 1974), 39.

16 Jeremy Bentham, *An Introduction to the Principles of Morals and Legislation*, edited by JH Burns and HLA Hart (London: Methuen, 1982), n283.

17 'Preference' utilitarianism seeks to measure the frustration of preferences rather than the 'pleasure and pain' calculus of the classical version. A 'renewed' edition of *Animal Liberation* was published in 2023 under the title, *Animal Liberation Now* (New York: Harper Collins, 2023).

inferior to ours is 'speciesism'. Animals have moral worth; their lives are not simply expendable or to be exploited for our own ends:

> We ought to consider the interests of animals because they have interests and it is unjustifiable to exclude them from the sphere of moral concern; to make this consideration depend on beneficial consequences for human beings is to accept the implication that the interests of animals do not warrant consideration for their own sakes.[18]

Singer does not claim that the lives of humans and animals have equal worth or that they call for identical treatment—except in respect of the capacity to experience pleasure and pain. Animals need not be *treated* equally, but they are entitled to equal *consideration*:

> The basic principle of equality does not require equal or identical treatment; it requires equal consideration. Equal consideration for different beings may lead to different treatment and different rights.[19]

He argues that, since humans and animals are both capable of suffering and happiness, to treat them differently would constitute speciesism. In the same way as discriminating against people on the grounds of their race or gender is morally wrong, so too is treating animals differentially because they belong to another species.

But, to repeat, his notion of equal consideration of interests does not mean that all sentient creatures—human and animal—must be treated in the same way:

> If I give a horse a hard slap across its rump with my open hand, the horse may start, but it presumably feels little pain. Its skin is thick enough to protect it against a mere slap. If I slap a baby in the same way, however, the baby will cry and presumably does feel pain, for its skin is more sensitive. So it is worse to slap a baby than a horse, if both slaps are administered with equal force. But there must be some kind of blow - I don't know exactly what it would be, but perhaps a blow with a heavy stick - that would cause the horse as much pain as we cause a baby by slapping it with our hand. That is what I mean by 'the same amount of pain' and if we consider it wrong to inflict that much pain

18 Op cit, 271.

19 Op cit, 23. Another feature of utilitarianism sometimes viewed as helpful in developing a sound moral approach towards animals is Mill's view (advanced in a more sophisticated form by RM Hare, *Moral Thinking* (Oxford: Clarendon Press, 1983)) that our primary duty is to develop certain qualities of character which would promote the greatest overall utility. But this may impose unreasonable demands on moral actors. It is not impossible to reconcile consequentialism with rights. See, for example, LW Sumner, *The Moral Foundation of Rights* (Oxford: Clarendon Press, 1987).

> on a baby for no good reason then we must, unless we are speciesists, consider it equally wrong to inflict the same amount of pain on a horse for no good reason.[20]

Not all lives, he asserts, are of equal worth. The key is whether the creature has the capacity for self-awareness and an interest in continued existence. If it does not, their interest is in avoiding a painful death. He does, however, allow that certain animals—whales, the great apes—do have an interest in staying alive. Nevertheless, most animals lack this interest, and therefore it is morally acceptable to sacrifice their lives to save the life of a self-aware human. The opposite is also morally legitimate: the life of a self-aware animal such as a chimpanzee could justifiably be sacrificed to save the life of a human without this capacity such as a person with a serious mental disability.

Singer's act-utilitarianism does not stand in the way of killing for food animals that lack self-awareness provided they suffer no pain, but, because factory farms and other means of animal production cause significant suffering, he argues that there is a moral duty to adopt a vegetarian diet. Again, in keeping with the 'greatest happiness' tenet, he does not in principle object to animal experiments provided that enough humans and animals benefit from them, particularly (in the improbable case) where a single experiment could cure a serious disease.[21] Such experiments are justifiable, provided pain is restricted to a minimum and the research is highly likely to produce aggregate benefits outweighing individual pain. His test is whether it would be morally acceptable to perform such experiments on humans lacking self-awareness, such as mentally retarded human orphans.[22] If it would not, it would be 'speciesist' to inflict pain on animals of similar intelligence.

Critics frequently dismiss the utilitarian position that regards the life of a healthy pig as more valuable than that of a severely retarded human being. As mentioned in Chapter 4, Richard Posner maintains that there is no 'metric' that would enable it to be commensurated, and for conflicts between them to be resolved'.[23]

Not all utilitarians follow Singer's path. RG Frey, for example, argues that, in the case of painful experiments on animals, to rely upon the appeal to benefit to justify such practices, requires some reason which shows that we are not morally entitled to do to humans what we do in our laboratories to animals. And he is unable to find any argument to support the proposition

20 Op cit, 17.

21 Cf Chapter 1. He does concede that the principle of equal consideration of interests would justify experiments on humans lacking self-awareness.

22 See Peter Singer, *Practical Ethics*, 2nd edn (Cambridge: Cambridge University Press 1993), 59. Orphans in order to exclude the possibility of the vicarious suffering of relatives.

23 Richard A Posner, 'Animal Rights: Legal, Philosophical, and Pragmatic Perspectives' in Cass R Sunstein and Martha C Nussbaum, eds, *Animal Rights: Current Debates and New Directions* (New York: Oxford University Press, 2004), 60.

that, no matter how low its quality, a human life is more valuable than an animal life.[24]

The chief attraction of utilitarianism, in short, is its insistence that all sentient beings' interests carry equal weight. But it fails to accord individual animas the protection that their critical predicament demands.

On the other hand, the Kantian deontological approach espoused by Tom Regan is based on a repudiation of utilitarianism which, he argues, is based on aggregating the good generated by an act, and thereby neglects or entirely overlooks the separateness of persons. Their individual identity, experience, and expectations are sacrificed at the altar of the general good. Regan's deontological position treats animals as distinct entities. His major premise is the similarities between a human and an animal life. In particular, animals, like us, are 'subjects-of-a-life'. They have inherent, not merely instrumental, value or worth. This entitles them to the absolute right[25] to live their lives with respect and autonomy:

> [I]ndividuals are subjects-of-a-life if they have beliefs and desires; perception, memory, and a sense of the future, including their own future; an emotional life together with feelings of pleasure and pain; preference-and welfare-interests; the ability to initiate action in pursuit of their desires and goals; a psychophysical identity over time; and an individual welfare in the sense that their experiential life fares well or ill for them, logically independently of their utility for others and logically independently of their being the object of anyone else's interests.[26]

But, asks Paola Cavalieri, what of a being that lacks a sense of future but is endowed, for example, with welfare interests? 'Why should its welfare interests be treated differently from the analogous interests of subjects-of-a-life? What has the sense of future to do with the interest in not suffering?'[27]

24 RG Frey, *Rights, Killing, and Suffering* (Oxford: Basil Blackwell, 1983), 115.

25 I tried to show in Chapter 3 that his argument that animals have an inherent value does not lead ineluctably to a rights-based conclusion. On the other hand, Gary Steiner argues '[g]iven the world in which we live, and given the extraordinary affliction that animals suffer at our hands, the language of rights would appear to be absolutely indispensable in the effort to release animals from their state of affliction'. Gary Steiner, *Animals and the Limits of Postmodernism* (New York: Columbia University Press, 2013), 162. Jacques Derrida, stigmatises the 'stupidity' of the classification of different species under the abstract heading of 'animal', arguing that this is the source of violence towards these creatures, culminating in the industrialised cruelty they suffer. Jacques Derrida, *The Animal That Therefore I Am*, transl by David Willis (New York: Fordham University Press, 2008).

26 Tom Regan, *The Case for Animal Rights*, revised edn (Oxford: Oxford University Press, 2013), 243.

27 Paola Cavalieri, *The Animal Question: Why Nonhuman Animals Deserve Human Rights* (Oxford: Oxford University Press, 2001).

Regan acknowledges that this factor is a sufficient but not a necessary criterion.[28] Importantly, his overarching standard is that of 'inherent value':

> The most reasonable criterion of right-possession ... is not that of sentience or having interests, since neither of these by themselves can account for why it is wrong to treat humans who are not irreversibly comatose merely as means; rather the criterion that most adequately accounts for this is the criterion of inherent value: All those beings (and only those beings) which have inherent value have rights.[29]

Hence, no amount of benefit to humans (from, say, animal experiments) can justify the violation of this absolute right:

> The laudatory achievements of science, including the many genuine benefits obtained for both humans and animals, do not justify the unjust means used to secure them.... [T]he rights view does not call for the cessation of scientific research. Such research should go on—but not at the expense of laboratory animals.[30]

He maintains that mammals that are mentally normal and more than one year old satisfy this condition, including most human beings, with the possible exception of individuals in a persistent vegetative state.[31] It does not follow, he adds, that in the case of babies in the first year of their lives, we may treat them as we like; they have inherent value and we ought therefore to err on the side of their being subjects of a life. In any event, we owe them indirect duties because it benefits those who do fall into this category, such as their parents.

Once Regan's concept of a 'subject-of-a-life' is accepted, hunting, trapping, and battery farming should be abolished since they fail to treat animals with respect:

> What's wrong—fundamentally wrong—with the way animals are treated isn't the details that vary from case to case. It's the whole system. The forlornness of the veal calf is pathetic, heart-wrenching; the pulsing pain of the chimp with electrodes planted deep in her brain is repulsive; the slow, tortuous [*sic*] death of the racoon caught in the leg-hold is agonizing. But what is wrong isn't the pain, isn't the suffering, isn't the deprivation.

28 Op cit, 243.

29 Op cit, 397. But he would justify sacrificing the lives of a million dogs to save a single human life (351). Singer is to similar effect: since a dog lacks the cognitive ability to imagine the distant future, he asserts, it has less to lose by dying than we do. Gary Francione counterclaims that a dog's sentience implies an interest in its continued existence; see his *Introduction to Animal Rights: Your Child or the Dog?* (Philadelphia, PA: Temple University, 2000), 6, 17.

30 Regan, op cit, 397. I considered this vexed subject in Chapter 1.

31 Certain species of birds, and possibly fish also qualify.

> These compound what's wrong.... The fundamental wrong is the system that allows us to view animals as *our* resources, here for *us*—to be eaten, or surgically manipulated, or exploited for sport or money.[32]

This anthropomorphic hubris underpins the abuse and exploitation, and, hence, the suffering of animals. The requirement of respect is a *sine qua non* of our moral obligation to them. It would apply also to animals in the wild; treating them with respect requires that they be left alone as far as possible. Nor can animal experiments be justified whatever their objective. And he rejects the so-called 'replaceability argument'—the view that though the killing of animals diminishes the amount of happiness in the world, this loss is made good by the creation of additional animals, who lead lives roughly as happy as those of the animals eaten. It is often expressed in the form that such animals can be 'refined, reduced, and replaced' (which is the policy in several countries). This is thought to ensure that the total amount of pleasure in the world remains undiminished.

Returning to utilitarianism, it does not require a great deal of perception to recognise its shortcomings in general, and its effectiveness in the defence of animals, in particular. In respect of the first, I have touched on some of these drawbacks or limitations above. Even in the writings of John Stuart Mill and Henry Sidgwick, there is a fairly simple, even simplistic, representation of the nature of 'pleasure and pain'. Moreover, Mill's attention to qualitative (higher and lower) pleasures subordinates his concern for animals, even though he asks:

> Granted that any practice causes more pain to animals than it gives pleasure to man: is that practice moral or immoral? And if, exactly in proportion as human beings raise their heads out of the slough of selfishness, they do not with one voice answer 'immoral', let the morality of the principle of utility be for ever condemned.[33]

The manner in which consequentialist theories look to aggregate pleasure and pain is a constant basis of criticism. As Christine Korsgaard puts it from an unequivocally Kantian standpoint:

> Utilitarians regard the subjects of experience essentially as *locations* where pleasure and pain ... *happen*, rather than beings *for whom* these experiences are good or bad. To put it another way, they think that the

32 Op cit, 13–14.

33 John Stuart Mill, *The Collected Works of John Stuart Mill*, JM Robson, ed (Toronto: University of Toronto Press, 1963), Volume X, 223. Sidgwick's concern for 'the inferior animals' is linked to 'the humane treatment of lunatics' which amount to a 'one-sided restraint of the freedom of action of men with a view to the greatest happiness of the aggregate of sentient beings', Henry Sidgwick, *The Elements of Politics*, 1891 (London: Macmillan, reprinted 1897, 1908, 1919), 141–142.

> goodness or badness of an experience rests wholly in the character of the experience, and not in the way the experience is related to the nature of the subject who has it ... I think that is wrong. We should not care about people and animals because they are the places where good and bad things happen in the world. We should care about people and animals because they are the sort of beings *for* whom things can be good or bad—a fate that we recognize, in our own case at least, to be of the utmost importance. It is our fellow creatures, not their experiences, to whom we should assign moral standing and treat as ends in themselves.[34]

Her interpretation of Kant draws on Aristotle's recognition of the extent to which we share several important characteristics with animals. We have similar cognitive capacities (imagination, desire, and perception) that are deployed to achieve our objectives. She combines this with Kant's fundamental emphasis to arrive at the conclusion that, although the foundation of our moral duties to animals differs from that which we owe to humans, such duties spring, not, as Kant argues, from what we owe ourselves, but rather from direct duties to animals. As discussed in Chapter 2, like Bentham, he nevertheless opposes, blood sports, and cruel 'entertainment' such as cockfighting and bear-baiting. Killing animals for food should be carried out painlessly, and he objects to their slaughter merely on the grounds of their no longer being useful. He is also against animal experiments conducted merely speculatively. In essence, Kant's endorsement of compassion and love for animals is instrumental; it is good because it improves our moral behaviour.

Korsgaard's painstaking, consummate analysis of our ethical obligations to animals spans a wide range of practices that deny animals the dignity to which they are entitled. But at the heart of her Kantian and Aristotelean account is her allegiance to our claim that since we value the fact that we are ends-in-ourselves, we are both committed to combine reciprocally with other autonomous beings, and to regard our treatment of all sentient creatures as of unconditional significance.

Martha Nussbaum, defending her capabilities approach (discussed in Chapter 9), dissents from Korsgaard on the question of the source of our moral duty. She attributes her with the view that 'it's in effect an accident that animals matter; we just happen to pretty much like them'.[35] Instead, she avers:

> But I think that the value of animal lives ought to come from within those lives. Value comes in many varieties in the world, and each

34 Christine Korsgaard, *Fellow Creatures: Our Obligations to the Other Animals* (Oxford University Press, 2018), 159.

35 Martha C Nussbaum, *Justice for Animals* (New York: Simon & Schuster, 2022), 67.

> distinctive sort is valuable because of the sort it is, not because of the likeness to ourselves.[36]

In other words, our moral nature is an aspect of our animal nature, not distinct from it. She is also critical of her alleged view that 'the value of animals is derivative from likeness to humanity'.[37] But this seems to misconstrue Korsgaard's position. As far as I can see, she is entirely neutral on both questions. Moreover, her approach is consistent with Nussbaum's capability preoccupation with the welfare of individual creatures. Korsgaard is explicit:

> [O]n a Kantian account, our duty is not to achieve the good, but to treat individuals in a way that accords with their value as ends in themselves. Those duties are owed not just to abstract representatives of the group 'animals' but to the particular animals with whom we ourselves interact. They are owed not to all of the animals, but to each of the animals, one by one, as individuals.[38]

While several anti-utilitarians are unconvinced by the theory's effort to base justice on the calculation of consequences, there is a recognition that it vouchsafes the principle that all sentient beings' interests deserve equal consideration. On the other hand, deontological approaches value the importance of treating all animals as ends in themselves, not merely as means to our human ends.

36 Ibid.

37 Ibid.

38 Korsgaard, op cit, 218. Similarly, in an earlier work, she says, [W]hat we demand, when we demand … recognition, is that our natural concerns—the objects of our natural desires and interests and affections—be accorded the status of values, values that must be respected as far as possible by others. And many of those natural concerns—the desire to avoid pain is an obvious example—spring from our animal nature, not from our rational nature. Christine M Korsgaard, 'Facing the Animal You See in the Mirror' (2007) 16 *Harvard Review of Philosophy*, 4ff. See too op cit, 160ff.

7 Welfarism

Progressive movements are typically divided between those who advocate moderate reform of injustice, those who adopt a policy of more fundamental improvement, and a group whose goals are substantially more radical that aims to eradicate the inequity altogether. Ruptures along these lines are as inevitable as mitosis. The first approach is the classical welfarist movement which is associated with early campaigners in the nineteenth and twentieth centuries that rejected the standpoint of writers, notably René Descartes, notorious for describing animals as automata. The fact that, according to him, animals lacked a soul rendered them mere machines. Against this callous judgement, welfarists argued that, whether or not nonhumans possessed a soul or the capacity to reason, they were vulnerable to pain and suffering and able to experience pleasure and happiness. This compassionate outlook was famously espoused by Jeremy Bentham (discussed in Chapter 6) who concurred with the view that the crucial condition for attracting empathy was the ability to feel pain. Pleasure and pain are, of course, key factors in the utilitarian calculus employed by utilitarians like Bentham, John Stuart Mill, and, more recently, Peter Singer.

The classical welfarist position is that we are under a duty to treat animals humanely, but they may legitimately be regarded as property and may therefore be owned, used, and killed to satisfy our needs which, they accept, count for more than the interests of the animals. Even Bentham believed that we are morally superior to nonhumans because only we have the capacity to anticipate the future. Without this facility, he maintained, they do not have an interest in avoiding death. In other words, we are free to use animals as we please, provided we do not treat them cruelly. It follows that we may kill, eat, exploit, and experiment on sentient creatures, as long as we avoid cruelty that serves no recognised human ends.

The campaign to reduce the distress of animals was an important catalyst in generating nineteenth-century legislative initiatives to protect animals against cruel treatment. And its influence continues to resonate in contemporary anti-cruelty statutes in many countries. But its limitations are self-evident and have attracted criticism from various quarters, most conspicuously the so-called 'abolitionist' movement (discussed in Chapter 8),

DOI: 10.4324/9781032702575-7

but also by the 'new welfarists'. Exasperated with the failures of classic welfarism, this movement was developed which, like its predecessor, advocates the humane treatment of animals, but repudiates the assumption that all human interests carry greater moral sway than those of nonhumans. Why, it asks, should human interests always trump those of animals? Their programme of reform includes placing limits even on the humane killing and exploitation of animals. This, they argue, is a practicable route to conferring rights on animals. Robert Garner, one of its most prominent champions, questions the classic welfarist view that animals lack the capacity to anticipate the future and therefore that their deaths are not a loss to them.[1] He reasons that even a painless killing of an animal denies it valuable opportunities including the prospect of producing progeny. The fact that animals do not generally seem to comprehend the nature of death and are thus not cognisant of the wish to stay alive, is not a sufficient reason to support the notion that killing them is morally acceptable. At most, it may explain why their lives count for less than ours; it does not render their lives worthless.

There is, he contends, no substantive difference between the manner in which humans and animals experience pain. While he denies that animals have a right to life, he endorses their right against suffering which would abrogate our right to use them for our ends. More controversially, Garner contends that, since animals normally lack an inherent interest in freedom, their status as property does not constitute an impediment to their welfare. They do, he concedes, have an instrumental interest in freedom to, for example, search for food, but they do not enjoy the autonomy to determine how to live their lives, and therefore lack an intrinsic interest in liberty. This leads him to conclude that it is not immoral to own or use an animal, provided it is treated compassionately.[2] Nor, unlike the theorists discussed in Chapter 4, does he consider that the status of animals as property is an obstacle to their being accorded rights. His principal emphasis is on the norm of avoiding 'unnecessary suffering' which, he maintains, is likely to achieve greater success than the more radical approaches which postulate that animals be protected regardless of the human benefits that will be sacrificed as a result.

Since farming and killing animals for food entails unnecessary suffering on a major scale, Garner recognises the need for sweeping transformation, but does countenance the consumption of animals where in impoverished countries it is required to on health grounds, or where animal agriculture is conducted with minimal suffering.

1 Robert Garner, *The Political Theory of Animal Rights* (Manchester: Manchester University Press, 2005).

2 This includes our right to use them for experiments—painlessly, provided they have a genuine scientific purpose, see Robert Garner, *Animal Ethics* (Cambridge: Polity Press, 2005).

Criticism

While recognising that the new welfarist programme pursues the improvement of conditions for many animals, it is criticised for its failure to achieve this objective. Abolitionists, most conspicuously Gary Francione (discussed in Chapter 8), allege that notwithstanding the campaigns and legislative attainments, the promotion of animal welfare has not materially ameliorated the circumstances under which most creatures live, and the 'torture' they endure.

He stigmatises new welfarists as supporters of the property status of animals:

> Animal welfare is not about animals; it is about making humans believe that we take animals seriously as a moral matter. Animal welfare is about making us feel more comfortable about continuing to exploit them. But animal welfare is a moral fantasy. The reality is that, because animals are property, they remain nothing more than things.[3]

Moreover, it is claimed that welfarist groups may sometimes act as an accessory to the abuse of animals by their role in certifying products—meat, eggs, dairy products, and poultry—that are produced humanely. Worse, they may have exacerbated the position by generating the approval of the abuse of animals, and salving the consciences of those who are concerned about their mistreatment.[4]

Nor is he convinced that the statutory and regulatory reforms were introduced in various countries on altruistic grounds. The banning of cruel veal and gestation crates was to increase productivity and economic efficiency rather than to reduce animal suffering.

Donaldson and Kymlicka (whose 'citizenship' model is discussed in Chapter 11) lament the failure of welfarism to achieve real change:

> Welfarism may prevent some truly gratuitous forms of cruelty—literally senseless acts of violence or abuse—but it becomes largely ineffective when confronted with cases of animal exploitation for which there is some recognizable human interest at stake, even the most trivial (such as testing cosmetics), or the most venal (such as saving a few pennies in factory farming). As long as the basic premise of moral hierarchy goes

3 Gary L Francione, 'Animal Welfare and Society—Part 1: The Viewpoints of a Philosopher' (2022) 12 *Animal Frontiers* 43, https://www.ncbi.nlm.nih.gov/pmc/articles/PMC8929975/ (accessed 7 June 2023). *In Rain Without Thunder: The Ideology of the Animal Rights Movement* (Philadelphia, PA Temple University Press, 1996), Francione asserts that even though animal cruelty was legally declared unacceptable in the West more than three hundred and fifty years ago, and despite increasing awareness of animal abuse, the use of animals in food, science, and entertainment has increased, and is so entrenched that the economy could collapse without it. See too Petra Renee Wicklund, 'Abrogating Property Status in the Fight for Animal Rights' (1997) 107 *Yale Law Journal* 569.

4 Ibid.

> unchallenged, reasonable people will disagree about what constitutes an 'acceptable level' of animal exploitation, and our widespread but vague impulse to limit 'unnecessary' animal cruelty will continue to be overwhelmed by the self-interested and consumerist pressures heading in the opposite direction.[5]

Frustration with the limited gains of both classic and new welfarism has engendered an exchange that is at times petty, parochial, and even personal. The rise of the abolitionist movement is in part a direct consequence of the apparent deadlock that the debate has created. It is this movement that is the subject of the following chapter.

5 Sue Donaldson and Will Kymlicka, *Zoopolis: A Political Theory of Animal Rights* (Oxford: Oxford University Press, 2011), 4.

8 Abolitionism

A deontological approach—as outlined in Chapter 6—lies at the heart of the abolitionist movement led by Gary Francione, particularly in his book, *Animals, Property and the Law.*[1] It is based on two fundamental divergences from the new welfarist position (sketched in the previous chapter). First, it rejects the notion that animals should ever be treated as property. Secondly, it repudiates the view that sentience is an inadequate threshold that animals need to satisfy in order to be vested with rights.

In respect of the first, there can be little doubt that the ascription of the status of property to animals constitutes a major obstacle to the acquisition of rights by nonhumans. Unless they have an absolute right not to be regarded as mere things, animals are prevented from procuring other rights. The utilitarian inclination to permit animal suffering when weighed against a competing human benefit is anathema to the abolitionist standpoint:

> The property status of animals renders meaningless any balancing that is supposedly required under the humane treatment principle or animal welfare laws, because what we really balance are the interests of property owners against the interests of their animal property.... Thus, because animals are our property, the law will require their interests to be observed only to the extent that it facilitates the exploitation of the animal.[2]

Sentience, according to the second departure from new welfarism, is a sufficient criterion by which to admit animals to the full panoply of moral rights. The fact that they may lack the capacity to anticipate and plan for their future, it is argued, cannot be allowed to block their path to rights. Killing sentient creatures painlessly would be abhorrent were those creatures human; the same consideration ought to apply to nonhumans. Equality

1 Gary L Francione, *Animals, Property, and the Law* (Philadelphia, PA Temple University Press, 2007).

2 Gary L Francione, 'Animals—Property or Persons?' in Cass R Sunstein and Martha C Nussbaum, eds, *Animal Rights: Current Debates and New Directions* (New York: Oxford University Press, 2004), 117, 120.

DOI: 10.4324/9781032702575-8

demands that no distinction be drawn on the irrelevant grounds that, unlike us, animals may possess a different conception of life. Reasoning and other intellectual skills may be germane when assessing a human's needs, such as for the franchise or education, but they are immaterial when evaluating vulnerability to pain and suffering.

> Sentience is not an end in itself. It is a means to the end of staying alive. Sentient beings use sensations of pain and suffering to escape situations that threaten their lives and sensations of pleasure to pursue situations that enhance their lives. Just has humans will often endure excruciating pain in order to remain alive, animals will often not only endure but inflict on themselves excruciating pain—as when gnawing of a paw caught in a trap—in order to live. Sentience is what evolution has produced in order to ensure the survival of certain complex organisms.[3]

The abolitionist cause encompasses wider moral obligations towards animals—and the world. Francione has identified six principles that are part of the moral campaign:

1 Every sentient being has a right not to be used as property.
2 Abolitionists should never promote welfare reform campaigns or single-issue campaigns.
3 Abolitionists should promote veganism as a moral imperative.
4 Sentience and no other cognitive characteristic is necessary to have the moral right not to be used exclusively as a resource.
5 Abolitionists should reject all forms of discrimination—human and nonhuman.
6 Abolitionists should reject violence and promote non-violence.

These conscientious, one might say revolutionary, aspirations understandably attract imputations of utopianism or naïve sanguinity. And their implications will strike many as highly impractical and unrealistic. For instance, the proposal that all uses of animals—food, sport, entertainment, clothing, research—should be prohibited is unlikely to be welcomed even by those who are sympathetic to the plight of animals. And Francione's radical plea that no new domesticated animals ought to be brought into existence has been widely criticised despite its logical premise that domestication is intrinsically unjust because it selectively breeds animals that are wholly and perpetually dependent on humans for their welfare. The phasing out of future animals is described by Donaldson and Kymlicka as an infringement of individual liberties:

> The abolitionist position implies that if humans stopped 'creating' domestic animals, they would cease to exist. But this isn't the case. For

3 Op cit, 127.

> domesticated animals to be 'phased out of existence' would not just require a cessation of human creation of animals, but a massively increased (and probably impossible) human effort to forcibly sterilize and/or confine all domesticated animals. It would mean not just limiting the procreation of domesticated animals, but preventing it entirely—denying them the opportunity ever to mate and raise a family. It would, in short, involve precisely the sort of coercion and confinement that [animal rights theorists] say makes domestication unjust, and in that sense compounds rather than remedies the original injustice.[4]

Cass Sunstein raises three objections to Francione's case.[5] First, he claims that he fails to demonstrate that the use of animals, as opposed to their ill-treatment, is *ipso facto* morally objectionable, or that property status is inconsistent in providing animals with improved treatment or recognising their moral value.[6] Secondly, Sunstein doubts that a theory of animal rights can be based on sentience alone; such theories, he says, are consequentialist and not deontological, and that rights theories require that animals be moral agents in some relevant sense. Thirdly, he argues that even if animals have rights, they may be outweighed when the benefits of overriding them are considerable.

To the first objection, Francione responds by rejecting his evidently Benthamite position that animals do not have an interest in continued existence; therefore, the use of animal is not morally objectionable. Sunstein's acquiescence to the property status of nonhumans is, of course, dismissed by Francione who maintains that 'the property status of animals ... acts as a blinder that effectively blocks even our perception of their interests as similar to ours because any limitation on property owners is understood to represent significant human "suffering"'.[7] He adds:

> Although Sunstein claims that we can treat animal interests as morally significant even if animals remain human property, it would seem that any recognition that animals have 'intrinsic value' and that respect for

4 Sue Donaldson and Will Kymlicka, *Zoopolis: A Political Theory of Animal Rights* (Oxford: Oxford University Press, 2011), 80–81. It may be more effective to phase out the human race. Christine Korsgaard raises the question of humans deciding to go extinct, and expresses surprise that 'friends of the animals were not more inclined to advocate this', Christine M Korsgaard, *Fellow Creatures: Our Obligations to the Other Animals* (Oxford University Press, 2018). The Lakota Indian tribe have a saying: 'If all green things that grow were taken from earth there could be no life. If all four-legged creatures were taken from earth there could be no life. If all the winged creatures were taken from earth there would be no life. If all our relatives who crawl or swim and live within earth were taken away there would be no life. But if all humans were taken away life on earth would flourish'.

5 Cass R Sunstein, 'Slaughterhouse Jive' (2001) 40 *New Republic*.

6 Gary L Francione, 'Equal Consideration and the Interest of Nonhuman Animals in Continued Existence: A Response to Professor Sunstein' (2006) 1 *University of Chicago Legal Forum* 231.

7 Op cit, 244.

> animal interests is a 'good in itself' would necessarily require a departure from property status because we regard property as having only an extrinsic value.[8]

Sunstein asserts that the owners of pets 'are unlikely to think that their animals are mere commodities' and that these owners are likely to regard themselves as having 'the sorts of rights and duties that make sense for human beings entrusted with the care of living creatures'.[9] He maintains also that 'the fact of ownership even protects animals in important ways' because owners are morally and legally obligated to protect their animals. Non-owners are also under a duty to refrain from damaging the animal property of others, and 'this makes it less likely that such harm will occur'.[10] The wellbeing of domestic animals, and not the benefit to humans, requires that we have the legal right and the duty to control the lives of these animals. Francione naturally finds himself unable to agree.

The abolitionist project is compared by Martha Nussbaum to the campaign for reparations for past iniquities which she dismisses as 'useless handwringing'.[11] Her analogy is somewhat oblique, although there is certainly truth in the observation that there is little justification for those 'who may intensely love dogs and cats, or may respect them even if they do not love them' having to 'atone for their very creation by humans so remote in time that we cannot even imagine them'.[12] Nussbaum, of course, is dedicated to improving the conditions under which existing creatures live by means of her capabilities approach (see Chapter 9):

> The only possible justification for deliberately causing the extinction of a species is that its individual members cannot have lives worth living. But dogs and cats can have flourishing and healthy lives, if humans treat them as they should—a big 'if'....[13]

A better comparison than reparations for past wrongs might be to any radical liberation movement whose dominant purpose is to destroy the existing order and replace it with an entirely new, just system. The injustice of apartheid, for example, called for its comprehensive substitution by a political constitution founded on equality. By the same token, one can see the rationale for eliminating an evil regime that condemns most animals to wretched lives. The difficulties in this case, however, lie in the absence of a simple means by which to terminate the suffering. Even if the means existed

8 Ibid.
9 Sunstein, op cit, 44.
10 Ibid.
11 Martha C Nussbaum, *Justice for Animals* (New York: Simon & Schuster, 2022), 199.
12 Ibid.
13 Op cit, 200.

to enact a constitution—domestically or internationally—that provided resilient defences against the abuse of nonhumans, its enforcement would remain questionable, and the practical problems of eradicating millions of animals by sterilisation would be unimaginably immense.

Defending the aims of new welfarism, Robert Garner (discussed in Chapter 7) points to the legal and regulatory reforms that have both improved the lot of animals, and raised consciousness of their plight.[14] The ambitious abolitionist venture is, he argues, a Utopian moral crusade that is unrealisable, and is unlikely to win popular political backing. Moreover, as Donaldson and Kymlicka allege, it may actually alienate potential supporters of the very cause that abolitionism seeks to advance. Nor, they claim, is the position intellectually sustainable:

> It rests on a series of fallacies and misunderstandings about human-animal relationships.... Consider Francione's claim that 'it makes no sense to say that we have acted immorally in domesticating nonhuman animals but we are now committed to allowing them to continue to breed'. But this is an obvious fallacy.... [T]here is no reason to assume that the remedy to the original injustice of domestication is to extinguish domesticated species. Indeed, we might well think that this abolitionist proposal compounds the original injustice, since it can only be achieved by coercively restricting animals further (e.g. by preventing them from reproducing). The remedy rather, is to include them as members and citizens of the community.[15]

Eating animals

The mainspring of the abolitionist movement is its disquiet regarding the abuse and exploitation of farm animals. It is therefore committed to promoting veganism as a moral obligation. Ending the consumption of meat and, hence, the cruelty of many forms of farming, has long been a feature of animal rights campaigns. The scale of the factory farming, particularly in advanced countries, is chastening. In the United States alone:

> Approximately 9.5 billion animals die annually in food production.... This compares wth some 218 million killed by hunters and trappers and in animal shelters, biomedical research, product testing, dissection, and fur farms combined. Approximately 23 million chickens and some

14 Gary L Francione and Robert Garner, eds, *The Animal Rights Debate: Abolition or Regulation?* (New York: Columbia University Press, 2010), 147.

15 Sue Donaldson and Will Kymlicka, *Zoopolis: A Political Theory of Animal Rights* (Oxford: Oxford University Press, 2011), 79–80. They, of course, propose that animals be regarded as members of the political community, as outlined in Chapter 11.

> 268,000 pigs are slaughtered every 24 hours in the United States. That's 266 chickens per second, 24 hours a day, 365 days a year. From a statistician's point of view, since farmed animals represent 98 per cent of all animals (even including companion animals and animals in zoos and circuses) with whom humans interact in the United States, all animals are farm animals; the number that are not is statistically insignificant.[16]

The overcrowding of animals into small often unsanitary cages and sheds in which they are unable to turn around, the widespread use of antibiotics which can generate resistant bacteria, the genetic manipulation of creatures to increase their size, the harsh conditions of transport to abattoirs where they may be inhumanely killed: these and other elements of the maximization of output and profit are nothing new.[17] Nor are the effects of factory farming on the environment and biodiversity. As one-third of the world's arable land is given over to the cultivation of livestock feed, and more than a quarter is utilised for grazing, factory farming diminishes habitat for animals in the wild.

The moral case for vegetarianism or veganism is fairly straightforward:

> Given that we do not need to eat animals for reasons of health, how, then, can our consumption of animal products be considered as necessary? That's easy; it can't be. If we take seriously the conventional wisdom that we all claim to embrace and we believe that animals have some moral value, then, even without any consideration of animal rights, we cannot justify consuming animal products in any situation in which we have a meaningful choice.[18]

Francione explains our general reluctance to adopt a vegan diet by reference to our treatment of animals as property. This enables us to turn a blind eye to the suffering involved in the production of meat. '[B]ecause animals are property, we do not ask whether the suffering of animals used for food is necessary; we ask whether it is necessary given a use that is not necessary. This is not anything that can be called a moral principle. It is nonsense but it's convenient and it allows us to continue happily consuming animal foods'.[19]

16 David J Wolfson and Mariann Sullivan, 'Foxes in the Hen House, Animals, Agribusiness, and the Law: A Modern American Fable' in Cass R Sunstein and Martha C Nussbaum, eds, *Animal Rights: Current Debates and New Directions* (New York: Oxford University Press, 2004), 206.

17 'Perhaps those who die early are the lucky ones, since their hardier companions have nothing in store for them except another few months of crowded discomfort', Peter Singer, *Animal Liberation*, 2nd edn (New York: Harper Collins, 2009), 118.

18 Gary L Francione, 'Is It Acceptable to Eat Animals? If Yes, Why? If Not, Why Not?' (2022) 12 *Animal Frontiers* 43, 45. See too Cora Diamond, 'Eating Meat and Eating People' in Sunstein and Nussbaum, eds, op cit, 93.

19 Ibid.

Robert Nozick queries whether we have a right to sacrifice animals for our human pleasure. Imagine, he says, if snapping your fingers to music increased your happiness, and you know that the same snap could kill 10,000 contended cows in great pain and suffering or even painlessly. Would it be morally wrong to snap your fingers? Or suppose that you like swinging a baseball bat, and suppose that a cow's head happens to be in the direct path of your bat and you smash its skull? Is this, he asks, any different from hunting for pleasure? What if you hired someone to do the killing for you? Eating meat is not essential for our health, and merely gives carnivores enjoyment. Is it therefore possible to justify killing animals in order to maximize our pleasure? Is there a moral distinction between killing a cow to eat it for pleasure, on the one hand, and killing it in order to enjoy the pleasure of swinging a baseball bat, on the other? Nozick's point is that we should not regard individual rights as an end; we should rather recognise rights negatively as 'side constraints' on our conduct. He does not go so far as to advance the view that animals possess equal moral status to us. It is part of his wider case against utilitarian explanations in support of liberalism.[20]

But there are other more direct arguments against vegetarianism that ought to be taken seriously. RG Frey launches an incisive and spirited attack against moral vegetarianism from an act-utilitarian standpoint[21] (see Chapter 6). Central to his argument is the following reasoning:

1 The only valid argument for animal welfare is the one from pain and suffering (moral rights are 'excess baggage', and the argument from killing overlooks the pain that might be involved).
2 Pain and suffering are not a necessary part of the rearing of farm animals.
3 Therefore, there is no need to adopt vegetarianism in order to prevent pain and suffering.

As an act-utilitarian, Frey also seeks to show that even if the case for moral vegetarianism were accepted, the consequences of the demise of meat-eating (its economic, social, cultural, and culinary effects) render any calculus that holds that the consequences of vegetarianism are preferable to the status quo, deeply implausible. Nor is Frey persuaded that to become a vegetarian remotely ensures that the meat industry will, in fact, disintegrate. Not only is such a tactic likely to prove ineffective ('my individual act of giving up ham sandwiches and fried chicken will make no impression whatever, either on the way pigs and chickens are treated, or the number of pigs and chickens reared for food').[22] But if we are genuinely concerned to improve the lot of

20 Robert Nozick, *Anarchy, State, and Utopia* (Oxford: Wiley-Blackwell, 2001), 317–318.
21 RG Frey, *Rights, Killing, and Suffering* (Oxford: Basil Blackwell, 1983). I draw here on my review in (1986) 49 *Modern Law Review* 403.
22 Op cit, 208.

food animals, he maintains, we should devote our energy to the improvement of farming methods.

This is tendentious. The widespread practice of meat-eating cannot be evaluated in a vacuum (a point implicitly acknowledged by Frey when he comes to consider the consequences of its possible demise). To argue that it does not follow that if it is wrong to be cruel to animals, it is therefore wrong to eat them, neglects the central relationship between meat-eating and meat-farming. He says:

> [E]ven if we allow that most abattoirs would not exist if most people did not eat meat, it does not follow that the wrongness of the slaughterer's act of killing, if it is wrong, somehow mystically transfers to the consumer's act of eating. It is true that animals are killed in order to be eaten; but it is killing, not eating, which carries the moral force in the argument from killing and which is being condemned.[23]

Though he rejects the argument from killing, Frey resists the conflation of killing and eating (and this supplies his principal objection to this argument). But even if the 'transivity' from killing to eating is 'mystical', it nevertheless accounts for the moral turpitude that attends our participation in injustice. This is, admittedly, a complex and difficult issue, but granted that such claims are frequently rhetorical and notoriously slippery, Frey (though he argues ingeniously against it) does not wholly refute the proposition that to kill an animal is *prima facie* to harm it—even if it is slaughtered humanely. Analogies drawn with the taking of human life (he refers to abortion, euthanasia, and capital punishment) seem to be of limited utility since they do not form part of a process that has as its exclusive objective, killing to satisfy wants. Nevertheless, Frey constructs a powerful argument against the assertion (advanced, in particular, by Peter Singer) that moral vegetarianism is a rational outcome of act-utilitarianism.

It may be, therefore, that in order to give a proper ethical account of meat-eating (and its attendant practices), the indispensability of moral rights is established. If this is the case, then Frey has demonstrated the central vulnerability of Singer's *Animal Liberation*, which is essentially what he sets out to do. As I explained in Chapter 5, I am willing to countersign his view that 'our alleged moral rights have proliferated to such an extent that they now run to every corner of our lives',[24] yet when such rights are transposed into legal rights by legislation they are often not the most effective method of securing protection against alleged wrongs.

Frey's painstaking investigation of the possible effects of a widespread adoption of vegetarianism, more than discharges the act-utilitarian's onus of proof in the matter of preferable consequences, even if his account lapses into

23 Op cit, 28–29.
24 Op cit, 43.

the occasional banality: 'Teenagers would be deprived of carousing at the local hamburger establishment',[25] 'The delicatessen trade ... would find itself in trouble, and a wonderful part of New York and other cities throughout the world would virtually disappear'.[26]

By contrast, a non-utilitarian strategy in favour of meat-eating is pursued by Roger Scruton:

> I find myself driven by the love of animals to favour eating them. Most of the animals which graze in our fields are there because we eat them. Sheep and beef cattle are, in the conditions which prevail in English pastures, well-fed, comfortable and protected, cared for when disease afflicts them and, after a quiet life among their natural companions, despatched in ways which human beings, if they are rational, must surely envy. There is nothing immoral in this.... [I]t is not just permissible, but positively right, to eat these animals whose comforts depend on our doing so.[27]

This idyllic image is, of course, worlds away from the horrors of modern factory farming. None the less it raises the question whether genuinely humane farming methods provide moral justification for eating the meat thereby produced. Does it return to Frey's claim that the real issue is not the eating, but the killing of animals? If so, the focus switches to the abattoir. Here Scruton seems to rely on the assumption that the process is humane, and this is, of course, open to serious doubt. He does not, however, resist the moral imperative of treating farm animals compassionately. In rejecting utilitarianism, he states:

> Sympathy and piety are indispensable motives in the moral being and their voices cannot be silenced by mere calculation. Someone who was indifferent to the sight of pigs confined in batteries, who did not feel some instinctive need to pull down these walls and barriers and let in light and air, would have lost sight of what it is to be a living animal.... It seems to me, therefore, that a true morality of animal welfare ought to begin from the premise that this way of treating animals is wrong, even if legally permissible.[28]

It is safe to conclude that the utilitarian case for the moral significance of animal suffering in meat production is not, in fact, an argument for vegetarianism. This is surely true in circumstances under which an animal has lived a contented life and is killed painlessly and then eaten by those who would

25 Op cit, 199
26 Op cit, 197.
27 Roger Scruton, *Animal Rights and Wrongs*, 3rd edn (London: Metro Books, 2000), 100.
28 Op cit, 102.

otherwise suffer hunger or malnutrition. Painlessly killing and eating the animal would be morally justifiable. This situation obtains in many countries where economic, cultural, or climatic conditions make it practically impossible for humans to sustain themselves on plant-based diets.

There is also, as Scruton is not the first to remind us, 'the danger of self-righteousness in criticisms offered from a comfortable armchair by people who do not have the trouble of looking after farm animals and see only their soft and endearing side'.[29]

> Farmers are human beings and no less given to sympathy than the rest of us. And a good farmer, rearing sheep and cattle on pasture, keeping dogs, cats and horses as domestic animals, and free-range chickens for eggs, contributes more to the sum of animal welfare than a thousand suburban dreamers, stirred into emotion by a documentary on television.[30]

Naturally, one must fervently hope and believe that those who are concerned about the suffering of animals base their conviction on rational, non-sentimental grounds.

29 Op cit, 105.
30 Ibid.

9 Capabilities

Why establish principles of justice if they are beyond the reach of individuals to enjoy? If they lack the capacity to benefit from the rights and opportunities guaranteed by these arrangements, they are empty promises. To take the most celebrated example (which I describe in greater detail in Chapter 10), the just society as postulated by John Rawls' social contract is little more than words if one is unable to realise its pledges. We should therefore 'concentrate on the actual behaviour of people, rather than presuming compliance by all with ideal behaviour'. These are the words of Nobel Prize laureate, Amartya Sen, who over a period of several decades has brought to bear his extensive scholarship—Eastern and Western—economic and philosophical, on the subject of justice. Others, notably, the American philosopher, Martha Nussbaum, have pursued a similar 'capabilities' approach which, most germane for present purposes, she has applied to the wellbeing of animals.[1]

Our focus, they claim, should therefore be on what people actually experience rather than assuming conformity with the ideals promised in theories such as Rawls'.[2] Sen's argument is that there is no single, perfectly just social arrangement that could win universal support. The concept of justice is much more nuanced and complex. We need to recognise the limitations of an overarching theory of justice *à la* Rawls, and concentrate on the injustices suffered by millions on our planet. With its emphasis on personal welfare, health, and general wellbeing, this multifaceted approach appraises measures and policies that advance social change. It therefore accentuates the freedom that individuals actually have to do certain things and achieve certain objectives. It thus attempts to treat persons 'in the round', or holistically, seeking, as people typically do, a better life, health, education, social relationships, and other elements of the 'good life'. This distinguishes its concerns from those theories that concentrate wholly on subjective categories such as happiness or wealth. Consequently, it is embraced not only by

1 Martha C Nussbaum, *Justice for Animals: Our Collective Responsibility* (New York: Simon and Schuster, 2022).
2 See Amartya Sen, *The Idea of Justice* (London: Penguin Books, 2010).

DOI: 10.4324/9781032702575-9

philosophers but by those engaged in development studies, welfare economics, and social policy.

Central to this analysis is that if we wish to create a just society, capabilities should be pursued for every person, treating them as an end, and not merely as a means to some end. It rejects the utilitarianism implicit in, for example, determining the quality of life by reference to a country's per capita gross national product (GNP). This metric fails to reveal how income and wealth are actually distributed. Nor does the GNP reflect conditions that are not necessarily related to wealth such as life expectancy, infant mortality, educational opportunities, and other important features of a society. As discussed in Chapter 6, a utilitarian calculus is based on the accumulation of happiness or welfare. This approach begins from a different standpoint:

> In contrast with the utility-based or resource-based lines of thinking, individual advantage is judged in the capability approach by a person's capability to do things he or she has reasons to value. A person's advantage in terms of opportunities is judged to be lower than that of another if she has less capability—less real opportunity—to achieve those things that she has reason to value. The focus here is on the freedom that a person actually has to do this or be that—things that he or she may value doing or being.[3]

As formulated particularly by Martha Nussbaum, it is founded on the conception of the dignity of a human being with a life worthy of that dignity, so as to enable a person to flourish. She identifies the following ten 'central human capabilities'[4]:

1 *Life*: the ability to live to the end of a human life of normal length.
2 *Bodily health*: the ability to enjoy good health, including reproductive health; to be adequately nourished; to have adequate shelter.
3 *Bodily integrity*: the ability to move freely from place to place; to be secure against violent assault, including sexual assault and domestic violence; having opportunities for sexual satisfaction and for choice in matters of reproduction.
4 *Senses, imagination, and thought*: the ability to use the senses, to imagine, think, and reason in a 'truly human' way, informed and cultivated by an adequate education, including, literacy and basic mathematical and scientific training.
5 *Emotions*: the ability to have attachments to things and people outside ourselves; to love those who love and care for us, to grieve at their absence; one's emotional development not being blighted by fear and anxiety.

3 Amartya Sen, op cit, 231–232.

4 Martha C Nussbaum, *Creating Capabilities: The Human Development Approach* (Cambridge, MA: Harvard University Press, 2013). See too her *Frontiers of Justice: Disability, Nationality, Species Membership* (Cambridge, MA: Harvard University Press, 2006). She cites neither Aquinas nor Finnis.

6 *Practical reason*: the ability to form a conception of the good and to engage in critical reflection about the planning of one's life, which entails protection for the liberty of conscience and religious observance.
7 *Affiliation*: The ability to live with and towards others, to recognise and show concern for other human beings, to engage in various forms of social interaction; to be able to imagine the situation of another; self-respect and non-humiliation; to be treated as a dignified being whose worth is equal to that of others.
8 *Other species*: the ability to live with concern for and in relation to animals, plants, and the world of nature.
9 *Play*: the ability to laugh, to play, to enjoy recreational activities.
10 *Control over one's environment*: the ability to participate effectively in political choices that govern one's life; having the right of political participation, protections of free speech and association, and the ability to hold property and have property rights on an equal basis with others; to have the right to seek employment on an equal basis with others; the freedom from unwarranted search and seizure; to work as a human being, exercising practical reason, and entering into meaningful relationships of mutual recognition with other workers.

Nussbaum's inventory echoes the works of the eminent Catholic philosopher, St Thomas Aquinas, who was himself influenced by Aristotle's ethics. Reviving Aristotle's idea of political life of the *polis*, he regards the state as the natural and superior form of association, but one that is subordinate to divine guidance of the world. Natural law, according to Aquinas, is 'participation' in the eternal law—the rational plan that governs creation. When we 'receive' natural law, it comprises the principles of practical rationality by which human action is to be judged as reasonable or unreasonable. They are binding on us because, as rational beings, we are directed towards them by nature; they steer us towards the good, and several specific goods. Intuitively we understand what these goods are: they include life, knowledge, procreation, society, and reasonable conduct. Like Aristotle, Aquinas believes that the good is prior to the right. Whether an act is right matters less than whether it achieves or is some good.

Aquinas' philosophy has its most persuasive contemporary champion in John Finnis who advances his ideas along with those of Plato and Aristotle, to postulate seven 'basic forms of human flourishing' and nine 'basic requirements of practical reasonableness'.[5] Human reason guides us how best

5 John Finnis, *Natural Law and Natural Rights*, 2nd edn (Oxford: Clarendon Press, 2011). See too John Finnis, *Aquinas: Moral, Political and Legal Theory* (Oxford: Oxford University Press, 1998); John Finnis, 'Natural Law: The Classic Tradition' in Jules Coleman and Scott Shapiro, eds, *The Oxford Handbook of Jurisprudence and Philosophy of Law* (Oxford: Oxford University Press, 2002).

to achieve our desires. He starts with the Aristotelian question: what constitutes a worthwhile, valuable, desirable life? These are the 'basic forms of good':

Life:	The drive for self-preservation we all have, it includes health, freedom from pain, and the procreation of children.
Knowledge:	It is good in itself to be well-informed rather than ignorant or muddled.
Play:	Recreation, enjoyment, fun.
Aesthetic experience:	An appreciation of beauty in art or nature.
Sociability (friendship):	Acting in the interests of one's friends.
Practical reasonableness:	Employing one's intelligence to solve problems of deciding what to do, how to live, and shaping one's character.
'Religion':	Our concern about an order of things that transcends our individual interests.

In contrast to Nussbaum, Sen favours a more rounded, organic, and less categorical description of capabilities, arguing that they depend on the context in which they arise. In fact, a good deal of Sen's analysis rests on the significance he attaches to the role of 'public reasoning' that encourages 'different voices' from diverse sections of the community to be heard. The question remains how freedom or human dignity is actually connected to the actual life people choose to lead. The argument then turns to what he calls 'functionings': 'beings and doings': the various conditions and actions of a person. The former includes being properly fed, on the one hand, or malnourished, on the other; living in a satisfactory environment or sleeping rough; being educated or illiterate; being a law-abiding citizen or a criminal, and so on. The second category, 'doings' comprise, for example, child-caring, travelling, voting, debating, drug-taking, hunting, and so on. Our capabilities are the genuine opportunities that we possess to achieve functionings.[6]

The theory enables us to test government policy to see whether it affects people's capabilities and functionings. So, for example, we might ask whether a community enjoys good health without access to clean drinking water, or how can they be healthy without sufficient food, secure without good government, or function effectively without a good education?

6 I investigate the theory in greater detail in Raymond Wacks, *Justice: A Beginner's Guide* (London: Oneworld, 2017), Ch 7. See too Sabina Alkire, *Valuing Freedoms: Sen's Capability Approach and Poverty Reduction* (Oxford: Oxford University Press, 2002); Christopher A Riddle, *Disability and Justice: The Capabilities Approach in Practice* (Blue Ridge Summit, PA: Lexington Books/Rowman & Littlefield, 2014).

The capabilities approach is outcome-oriented; unlike social contractarianism, it looks to the actual content of an outcome to see whether it appears to be compatible with a life that affords dignity, and therefore creates a more just society. It is therefore able to offer a richer, more refined, and more compassionate account of human needs. Nussbaum therefore stresses that we must recognise the requirements of the sick, the elderly, the disabled, and of other species. Where a society accepts that there is a serious deficit in people's capabilities, justice demands that it makes every effort to rectify this shortcoming.[7]

Sen's analysis has been criticised for 'under theorising' the concept of justice. Nussbaum, on the other hand, offers a more philosophical foundation which comprises human dignity associated with human flourishing in the Aristotelian sense. But she abjures any attempt to impose a universal theory that would apply to all societies. Sen repudiates the need for a 'canonical' checklist of capabilities, selected by theorists in the absence of public reasoning, and therefore finds it difficult to accept Nussbaum's enumeration. Ingrid Robeyns resists any endeavour to prescribe a particular catalogue of capabilities to be applied across the board, proposing instead a procedural method by which to choose a list of appropriate capabilities for specific purposes, such as appraising gender inequality in terms of capabilities.[8]

Their quarrel with Rawls is not entirely convincing. His social contract is treated as if it were an actual, rather than a hypothetical agreement between the 'people in the original position' (the meaning of which will be explained in the following chapter). But it was conceived by Rawls as an ideal, a heuristic tool by which to specify the principles of justice that those stripped of their identities would choose. Sen and his followers build a powerful case for promoting justice at grassroots level. This engenders opposition to a Rawlsian approach on two main grounds: the social contract is regarded as both transcendental and hypothetical, and it allegedly neglects the importance of reasoned public discussion and agreement on the principles of justice. But these elements seem to be inevitable features of any social contractarian approach. Moreover, is this not a comparison between apples and oranges? Rawls proffers an ideal theory of justice; the capability approach steers the debate towards the practical or empirical. His theory specifies the just institutions required in a liberal democratic state in order to protect individual citizens. The capability approach, on the other hand, is considerably more ambitious,

7 The approach has stimulated several significant practical applications, especially by the United Nations. It has provided a valuable alternative to the conventional metrics of Gross Domestic Product (GDP) and GNP to measure levels of development in societies—the so-called Human Development Index (HDI). This index incorporates factors such as life expectancy, adult literacy, and school enrolment to identify the degree of poverty, inequality, and other capability deficiencies that exist in spite of a country's high GDP. Other applications have been developed by the UN to assess gender inequality such as the Gender Empowerment Measure (GEM) and the Gender Inequality Index.

8 Ingrid Robeyns, *Wellbeing, Freedom and Social Justice: The Capability Approach Re-Examined* (Cambridge: Open Books Publishers, 2017).

extending to all individuals wherever they live, and to general social norms and conventions, not merely institutions.[9]

The capabilities of animals

Applying this approach to animals, Nussbaum rejects the utilitarianism, particularly of Peter Singer (as discussed in Chapter 6), Rawls' conception of justice, and Kant's view of animals as underserving of both.[10] The capabilities approach is founded on the principle that 'no sentient animal should be cut off from the chance of a flourishing life, a life with the type of dignity relevant to that species, and that all sentient animals should enjoy certain positive opportunities to flourish'.[11] Unlike contractarianism, it endorses *direct* obligations of justice to animals; duties that do not derive from those we owe to humans. And it accepts that animals are subjects with an entitlement to flourishing, and who are therefore subjects of justice *in their own right*, not merely objects of compassion. Unlike utilitarianism, it respects each individual creature, declining to aggregate the good of different lives and forms of lives. Animals are not used as a means to the ends of others or of society as a whole.

But for an animal to thrive, different considerations apply. In the case of humans, the capabilities approach does not seek to draw norms directly from facts about human nature. We evaluate, says Nussbaum, the innate powers of human beings, enquiring which are good, and which are central to a decently

9 Rawlsians, in turn, dislike the presupposition of a specific ethical position that the theory adopts. Nor do they agree with its public conception of justice entailing the provision of information upon which claims of injustice can be made. They insist that social stability requires a common standard of the principles of justice. Capabilities cannot, they contend, be easily evaluated or calculated in this public manner, the capabilities approach is not a practicable theory of justice. I cannot see why Rawls' principles of justice cannot be successfully deployed to resolve problems in 'the real world'. See Chapter 10.

10 She nevertheless supports certain aspects of Christine Korsgaard's interpretation of Kant which I discussed in Chapter 2.

11 Martha C Nussbaum, *Frontiers of Justice: Disability, Nationality, Species Membership* (Cambridge, MA: Harvard University Press, 2006), 351. In his book, *Justice for Hedgehogs* (Cambridge, MA: The Belnap Press, 2011), 419–420, Ronald Dworkin develops the idea of 'living well'. I asked him why he appeared to exclude, at least implicitly, respect for creatures other than humans. Does a person who devotes his life to the care of a pet, or to rescuing a maltreated animal, not live well? Does his or her kindness and sacrifice not constitute equivalent ethical virtue? I recognised, of course, that Dworkin's conception of living well is premised on the respect with which we treat other *humans*, but I could not see why concern for nonhumans does not render a life equally authentic or worthy. It seemed to me that he intentionally avoids this aspect of obligation or responsibility in his moral reckoning. He replied: 'It follows from what I say that animals can't live well. But not that living well doesn't require concern for animals'. It is ironical that the cover brandishes an appealing image of a hedgehog which, given the book's title, might be mistaken for a tract on animal rights. It refers instead to a line by the ancient Greek poet, Archilochus, made famous by Isaiah Berlin: the fox knows many things, but the hedgehog knows one big thing, Isaiah Berlin, *The Hedgehog and the Fox: An Essay on Tolstoy's View of History* (London: Weidenfeld and Nicolson, 1953), 3.

flourishing human life, a life with dignity. An *ethical* appraisal is therefore primary. Her list of capabilities in respect of humans (above) plainly requires some adaptation in the case of animals. Thus, for example, the first requirement, 'life' and its continuation is extended to all animals regardless of whether they have such a conscious interest. All sentient animals have an entitlement against gratuitous killing for sport, or luxury items such as fur. In the case of food, the approach seems unclear: animals may be killed painlessly following a healthy and free-ranging life, but what of the termination of the lives of very young animals? The second requirement, bodily health, requires the legal prohibition of cruelty and neglect. In regard to the capability of 'emotions', it is obvious that sentient creatures experience a range of feelings, including fear, anger, gratitude, grief, and pleasure. Some animals, ethologists have shown, demonstrate compassion. They are, like us, entitled to lives that enable them to have attachments to others, to love and care for others.

Each species is different and therefore warrants differential treatment to ensure that it receives the treatment that is appropriate to its particular needs. She repudiates the *scala naturae* which classifies animals according to their similarity to us:

> The Capabilities Approach (CA) does not rank animals by likeness to humans or seek special privileges for those deemed most 'like us', as do some other popular theoretical approaches. The CA has concern for the finch and the pig as much as the whale and the elephant. And it argues that the human form of life is simply irrelevant when we think about what each type of each animal needs and deserves. What is relevant is *their own* forms of life.... [E]ach sentient creature (capable of having a subjective point of view on [sic] the world and feeling pain and pleasure should have the opportunity to flourish in the form of life characteristic for [sic] that creature.[12]

She therefore criticises Stephen Wise's approach (discussed in Chapter 2) for basing itself on the similarity between humans and animals, and chiding his lawyerly attitude to the question. As a 'shrewd lawyer', his focus is strategic rather than philosophical, and it is fundamentally anthropocentric. Moreover 'it cuts most of the animal kingdom adrift' because of its focus on chimpanzees and bonobos.[13]

When the CA is applied to animals, the same ten capabilities ought to be extended to them with, of course, somewhat different implications. So, for example, their lives ought to be protected against gratuitous killing for

12 Martha Nussbaum, *Justice for Animals*, xxiv.

13 Op cit, 28, 29. Stephen M Wise, *Rattling the Cage: Toward Legal Rights for Animals* (New York: Perseus Books, 2000). She refers too to his 2016 documentary, *Unlocking the Cage* which was screened at the Sundance Film Festival.

sport or their fur. Bodily health requires the banning of cruelty and neglect, confinement, ill-treatment, and the regulation of zoos and aquariums. In the case of 'senses, imagination, and thought', an analogous extension of free movement in an environment that stimulates and pleases the senses is required along with other comparable entitlements. Animals' emotions do not significantly differ from our own; they experience, as mentioned above, similar feelings.

The capability of practical reason is unlikely to be found in many nonhuman beings, but in each case 'we need to ask to what extent the creature has the capacity to frame goals and projects and to plan its life'.[14] In the case of 'affiliation', animals should be able to form attachments and engage in bonding with each other as well as with humans; they are also entitled to self-respect as dignified beings which means they ought to be accorded 'political rights and the legal status of dignified beings'.[15] They should be able to form lives with other species and nature in general. The need for play is no less important to animals than humans. They need adequate space, light and sensory stimulation, as well as with members of other species. Finally, animals ought to have control over their environment. Politically this means they are entitled to just treatment; materially it means respect for the territorial integrity of their habitats, domestically or in the wild.

Conclusion

It is difficult to imagine any rational objection to the ten capabilities that Nussbaum extends to animals. To anyone genuinely concerned to protect the welfare of animals, they seem almost obvious. Nevertheless, she has been criticised for ignoring 'the fact that humans and domestic animals already form mixed societies, and as a result she misses the implications of this shared sociopolitical context for animal justice'.[16] This, according to Donaldson and Kymlicka, is a consequence of the manner in which she links her approach to what she calls 'the species norm':

> According to Nussbaum, individuals thrive in ways typical for members of their species. Therefore justice requires that we enable individuals to achieve (insofar as possible) the capabilities as defined for typical members of their species. The question on her approach is not, what does this *individual* require in order to flourish, but what do individuals of *this type* (i.e. species) typically require in order to flourish?[17]

14 Martha C Nussbaum 'Beyond "Compassion and Humanity: Justice for Nonhuman Animals"' in Cass R and Martha C Nussbaum, eds, *Animal Rights: Current Debates and New Directions* (New York: Oxford University Press, 2004) 299, 316.

15 Ibid.

16 Sue Donaldson and Will Kymlicka, *Zoopolis: A Political Theory of Animal Rights* (Oxford: Oxford University Press, 2011), 95.

17 Op cit, 96. My italics.

This observation is, of course, consistent with their 'citizenship' approach (discussed in Chapter 11). It is premised on the objection that Nussbaum employs the notion of 'species norm' to safeguard the interests of individuals who are incapable of enjoying a 'normal' life such as a severely disabled person. Justice, she argues, requires that we provide such an individual with the means to live a life that is as close to normal as possible. In the case of animals, this requires that they are given access to those capabilities that are typical for members of their species. In reality, however, domesticated animals live in a shared community; we need to establish a just system of coexistence rather than a society in which each species flourishes independently.

It may be, they suggest, that in the case of animals in the wild, the concept of flourishing attached to a particular species makes sense. With domesticated creatures, however, our duties towards them are not fully encapsulated by this discrete qualification:

> We have made domesticated animals part of human society, and we have a duty to ensure that they can flourish in the interspecies context, which will involve capabilities not relevant to their feral or wild cousins.[18]

Our lives are certainly inextricably linked to those of animals, especially those with whom we live in close proximity.[19] And, as they maintain, the situation may cut both ways; our conception of *human* should acknowledge we live in mixed communities, and that we have a duty to act fairly with other species. The idea of flourishing should recognise that we have important relationships with individuals of other species.[20] Moreover, we are not only members of a particular species, we belong to society. In this respect, it seems fair to characterise Donaldson and Kymlicka as communitarian in outlook (see Chapter 4), while Nussbaum cleaves to an individual rights position. At least, the latter seems to be the case, although curiously, while she indicates her support for animal rights (in several places), she seems to offer no analysis of how the capabilities approach connects to such rights, save perhaps via the legislation she proposes. This again raises the question, discussed in Chapter 3, of how and whether, rights may be properly inferred from the statutory protection of animals.

18 Op cit, 97.

19 See John Bradshaw, *The Animals Among Us: The New Science of Anthrozoology* (London: Penguin Books, 2018).

20 Op cit, 97. John Finnis would not deny this. He has assured me that his basic human goods include having good relationships with 'subpersonal realities'.

10 Contractarianism and contractualism

Contractarianism, as should be evident from my several references to John Rawls' theory of justice, seeks to derive the substance of morality from the notion of an agreement that determines the moral principles that are to apply between the parties to the contract. Its origins may be found in Hobbes, whose version is based on mutual self-interest. Morality comprises cooperative behaviour that it is mutually beneficial for self-interested agents to engage in. Contractarianism is also a feature of the philosophy of Rousseau.

The concept of contractualism is founded on the equal moral status of persons, based on their capacity for rational autonomous agency. It adopts the view that morality consists in what would result if binding agreements were struck from the standpoint that respects persons' equal moral importance as rational, autonomous agents. It is an alternative to contractarianism in which parties attempt to maximise their own interests in an agreement with others. Contractualists, by contrast, seek to pursue their interests in a manner that they can defend to others who are pursuing their own interests. Although it has a certain Kantian aspect, its normative focus is on a relationship of mutual respect.

By far the most important contractarian model was developed by John Rawls. In his celebrated, highly influential *magnum opus*, he paints an imaginary picture of the people in the 'original position' each shrouded in a 'veil of ignorance', debating the principles of justice.[1] This ignorance prevents them from knowing to which gender, class, religion, or social position they belong. Each person represents a social class, but they do not know whether they are clever or stupid, strong or weak. Nor do they know in which country or in what period they are living. They possess only certain elementary knowledge about the laws of science and psychology. In this state of blissful ignorance, they must unanimously decide upon the general principles that will define the terms under which they will live as a society. And, in so doing, they are moved by rational self-interest: each seeks those

1 John Rawls, *A Theory of Justice* (Harmondsworth: Penguin, 1973).

DOI: 10.4324/9781032702575-10

principles which will give him or her (they do not know their gender) the best chance of attaining his or her chosen conception of the good life (whatever that happens to be).

As rational individuals, Rawls concludes, they would choose principles which guarantee that the worst condition one might find oneself in, when the veil of ignorance is lifted is the least undesirable of the available alternatives. In other words, they will select those principles which, should they turn out to be at the bottom of the social pile, will be in their best interests. So, argues Rawls, they would choose the following two principles:

First principle: 'Each person is to have an equal right to the most extensive total system of equal basic liberties compatible with a similar system of liberty for all'.

Second principle: 'Social and economic inequalities are to be arranged so that they are both:

1 to the greatest benefit of the least advantaged, consistent with the just savings principle, and
2 attached to offices and positions open to all under conditions of fair equality of opportunity'.

The first has 'lexical priority' over the second. Or, to put it simply, they will put liberty above equality—because of what he calls the 'maximin' strategy: no one would wish to risk his or her liberty when the veil of ignorance is removed, and it is then revealed they are among the least well-off members of society. By the same token of maximin reasoning, they will opt for clause (a) of the second principle—the so-called 'difference principle'. This ensures that the worst anyone could be is 'least advantaged' and, if they do belong to this group, they will benefit from this clause. It would be rational for them to choose this principle rather than either total equality or some form of greater inequality, because of the respective risks of being worse off or reducing the prospects of improving their lot. And, they will be better able to 'improve their lot' in a society which places liberty above equality; this is because various 'social primary goods' (which Rawls defines to include rights, liberties, powers, opportunities, income, wealth, and especially self-respect) are more likely to be attained in a free society.

Contractualism, on the other hand, does not contain a veil of ignorance. Each party is aware of his or her interests, and it is not ignorance of who they are or self-interest that leads them to pay heed to others' welfare, but their concern to justify themselves to everyone else. This is a fundamental element in the moral theory of foremost contractualist, TM Scanlon:

> An act is wrong if its performance under the circumstances would be disallowed by any set of principles for the general regulation of

> behaviour that no one could reasonably reject as a basis for informed, unforced, general agreement.[2]

But the theory goes further; it examines which reasons and forms of reasoning are justifiable. Whether a principle can be reasonably rejected is determined by reference to the implications of individuals having the authority or being directed to reason in the way required by the principle. Scanlon's version offers an account of both the authority of moral standards and what constitutes rightness and wrongness.

All social contract theorists, including contractarians, agree that agents wish to justify themselves to others. Contractarians, however, regard this as merely strategic: justification is instrumentally convenient because it enables the agent to act in accordance with his or her interests. For the contractualist, on the other hand, agents are motivated morally by an inherent wish to justify themselves to others. This motive is part of what being a moral agent is. Notwithstanding these divergences, the two approaches share a number of ideas. In particular, contractualism offers a non-utilitarian theory that bases moral status on rational moral agency; it therefore provides universal general principles of moral conduct.

Animals and contracts

Contractarian theories, such as Rawls', offer little assistance to nonhumans. He explicitly excludes animals as rational agents. This is because they lack two essential attributes that entitle them to be treated in conformity with the principles of justice. First is the capacity to hold a conception of the good and a sense of justice. The second is the power to be a fully cooperating member of society. Only humans possess these. He acknowledges, however, that as animals are sentient, they are owed moral duties:

> Certainly it is wrong to be cruel to animals and the destruction of a whole species can be a great evil. The capacity for feelings of pleasure and pain and for the forms of life of which animals are capable clearly impose duties of compassion and humanity in their case.... They are outside the scope of the theory of justice, and it does not seem possible to extend the contract so as to include them in a natural way.[3]

But is it entirely implausible that in pursuit of objectivity (even though we do not ask them to imagine themselves to be members of another species), the people in the original position, behind their veil of ignorance, might choose a

2 Thomas M Scanlon, *What We Owe to Each Other* (Cambridge, MA: Harvard University Press, 1998), 153. See too David Gauthier, *Morals by Agreement* (Oxford: Clarendon Press, 1986).

3 John Rawls, op cit, 512.

moral system which includes respect for animals? At most, the social contract may require indirect duties to animals because of the (contingent) characteristics of the social contract struck in any particular society, or out of respect for the feelings of humans. But this seems too fragile a foundation upon which to construct a protective framework for nonhumans.[4]

Robert Carruthers proposes a version of contractarianism which, unlike Rawls' essentially political model, presents it as a general theory of morality. But, while he excludes non-rational humans, he concedes that they, unlike nonhumans who have acquired a similar mental level, should be accorded basic rights because 'a rule that accorded rights in proportion to a degree of rational agency would be open to wide and creeping abuse' and could place the rights of the contractors at risk.[5] But, as Cavalieri remarks of this 'slippery slope' argument:

> Carruthers's argument ... is open to the classic challenge made to all arguments of this kind, which lies in questioning their actual applicability to the cases under discussion. And, as has often been emphasized, it is not always the case that when dealing with questions of moral status rational agents cannot draw sharp lines that can prevent the slope from becoming slippery.... If this is so, Carruthers does not succeed in showing that the self-interest of rational agents should lead to a different treatment for humans and nonhumans at the same mental level.[6]

Not only, according to Carruthers, should parties to the contract have the capacity to reflect rationally on their needs and comprehend the world, they ought to be able to reciprocate others' rights and duties. Because they lack these abilities, they are outside of the agreement. Nevertheless, he allows for them to be recipients of indirect duties on the same grounds that Kant specified: if cruelty towards them would render humans less moral towards other humans, or if such cruelty would offend humans. He concludes:

> [T]here is no basis for extending moral protection to animals beyond that which is already provided. In particular there are no good moral grounds for forbidding hunting, factory farming, or laboratory testing on animals. [S]ome version of contractualism provides us with the most acceptable framework for moral theory, and from such a perspective animals will be denied moral standing. There are then only two possible

4 Scanlon suggests that through the concept of trustees, acting on behalf of the animals, they might be asked to accept certain proposed principles, op cit, 183.

5 Peter Carruthers, *The Animals Issue: Moral Theory in Practice* (Cambridge: Cambridge University Press, 1992), 116.

6 Paola Cavalieri, *The Animal Question: Why Nonhuman Animals Deserve Human Rights* (Oxford: Oxford University Press, 2001), 82–83.

> indirect reasons for outlawing the sorts of activities listed above. One pertains to the qualities of moral character revealed in their practitioners.... The other turns on the likely offence caused to animal lovers.... This is not to say, of course, that there is anything wrong with admiring animals, or enjoying their company. Nor is it to deny that there are powerful moral reasons for wishing to preserve endangered species of animal, similar to, but considerably more powerful than, the reasons for preserving great works of art. But what it does mean, is that those who are committed to any aspect of the animal rights movement are thoroughly misguided.[7]

One obvious response to this argument, apart from questioning his slippery slope implication allegation, is to point out that the terms of the hypothetical contract are drafted by humans. Since we are dealing with an imaginary agreement, it is not irrational to enquire what terms an animal might regard as valuable were they to be asked. Nor is it unreasonable to conceive of animals as having certain duties: guide dogs for the blind, sheep dogs, draught animals, including horses, donkeys, camels, and oxen, falcons.[8] Moreover, why, merely because animals are incapable of signing a contract, should they forfeit rights under it? Children are in a similar position but do not suffer a similar loss of contractual rights.

Richard Cupp endorses the view that since animals lack moral agency and cannot be held accountable for their actions, they do not qualify for rights under any fictional contract.

> When an animal bites a human or another animal without provocation, we do not have the offending animal arrested and put on trial. We view courts having done so in the Middle Ages with a sense of absurdity or dark humor, perhaps with the feel of a Monty Python sketch. *New Scientist* derided assigning rights to animals on this basis: If animals have rights which protect them against humans, it is only logical that they should have rights that protect them from each other. If a chimp kills another chimp in the wild, or a human, do we really want to hire a fleet of lawyers? And if we extended honorary personhood to all animals, would the gazelle be entitled to rights against the lion?[9]

This *reductio ad absurdum* is also illogical; it does not follow that the ostensible rights putatively extended to animals would necessarily be rights

7 Op cit, 196.
8 See Chapter 1.
9 Richard L Cupp, 'Moving Beyond Animal Rights: A Legal/Contractualist Critique' (2009) 46 *San Diego Law Review* 27, 66.

in rem. In other words, such rights (as explored in Chapters 3 and 5) are normally proposed as rights *in personam*: rights against specific persons, namely humans.

The hostility of contractualism towards animal rights springs from the inexorable, but harsh, reality, that contracts presume capacity—the ability of an individual to enter into a binding agreement and in so doing benefit from the rights, and expose themselves to the duties, that flow therefrom.

11 Citizenship

Almost every action we take touches the lives of other creatures. The decision to declare war, build a highway, hospital, or housing inevitably affects animals, birds, and other inhabitants of the planet. The activities, decisions, and attitudes of humans have a direct impact upon their wellbeing. The depredation of the environment—greenhouse gases, air and water pollution, habitat loss, poaching—the list goes on, is merely one aspect of the consequences our lives have on theirs. To mention only one current example, the situation in war-torn Ukraine and Gaza has left many abused animals and pets without homes or proper care.[1]

It therefore makes perfect sense to broaden the debate to embrace a political approach to the subject of animal welfare. The idea that animals are—or ought to be—members of the political community, is advanced by Sue Donaldson and Will Kymlicka.[2] Their imaginative and ambitious proposal seeks to demonstrate how the question of animal wellbeing is a political rather than an exclusively ethical one:

> Animals have variable relationships to political institutions and practices of state sovereignty, territory, colonization, migration, and membership, and determining our positive and relational obligations to animals is, in large part, a matter of thinking though the nature of these relationships.[3]

Exasperated by the three dominant moral frameworks—'welfarist', 'ecological', and 'basic rights'—they propose instead an approach that 'connects the treatment of animals more directly to fundamental principles of liberal-democratic justice and human rights'.[4] They are dismissive of the first (which places humans above animals), unhappy with the second (which focuses on the health of ecosystems rather than individual animals), and doubtful of the third

1 See the remarkable work undertaken by the charity, *Warriors of Wildlife*, to relocate these animals from Ukraine to a sanctuary in South Africa: https://www.warriorsofwildlife.org/

2 Sue Donaldson and Will Kymlicka, *Zoopolis: A Political Theory of Animal Rights* (Oxford: Oxford University Press, 2011).

3 Op cit, 12.

4 Op cit, 3.

DOI: 10.4324/9781032702575-11

(which has little support among the general public). Their elaborate project involves adapting human social and political structures to the lives of animals. Regarding animals as citizens generates rights and responsibilities beyond the universal human rights owed to all persons. In the same way that humans exist in a nation state which constitutes an 'ethical community', a 'relational' model of citizenship by which domesticated animals are treated as full citizens, animals in the wild as occupying separate sovereign communities, and 'liminal opportunistic animals' who live among us as migrants or denizens.

They are also critical of the emphasis by animal rights theorists on negative rights, and espouse positive rights to certain goods such as care, safety, and satisfactory habitats. Their principal focus, however, is on the 'relational' duties that we owe to animals which spring from specific relationships that have developed between us and them. In respect of animals in the wild in their sovereign communities, they draw an analogy with international relations between sovereign states. This requires that the inhabitants—the wild animals—govern their own territory. It would therefore be unlawful for humans to colonise or relocate them, but where they are endangered by disease or suffer injury, humans would be under an obligation to assist them. On the other hand, no such duty would arise to prevent predators acting according to their instinct, for this would undermine their self-determination.

In the case of liminal animals who are neither domesticated nor truly wild—foxes, squirrels, rats, mice, birds, and so on—their status as denizens are compared to migrant workers who are neither foreigners nor full members of the political society. Once living among us, they acquire the right to remain and not to be unreasonably interfered with. Their welfare, they suggest, ought to be protected by, for instance, establishing animal corridors to avoid the dangers of crossing roads. The use of pesticides should be controlled along with safe systems of rubbish disposal and other measures to avoid disturbing them.

Domesticated animals ought to be treated as full citizens with the appropriate equivalent rights enjoyed by human citizens. This is because we brought them into our society and have bred them to correspond to our requirements. Nor do they have realistic prospects to depart our community. They therefore deserve to be considered as members of a multispecies society.[5]

A similar appeal for membership is made by Alistair Cochrane who, rejecting a Rawlsian model of social contractarian reciprocity (since animals cannot be expected to reciprocate), postulates instead a 'cosmozoopolis', a mixed human/animal state with group-differentiated political rights for animals. He is critical of the zoopolis which, he believes, unjustly promotes the interests of nonhuman citizens above those of other nonhuman animals,

5 Citizenship entails duties imposed on animals: 'not to bite people or other animals, not to urinate or defaecate in inappropriate places, not to be a nuisance at airports. If animals are cited for violations, their human companion must bear the cost, but it seems right to cite the animal, since holding accountable is a sign of respect', Martha C Nussbaum, *Justice for Animals: Our Collective Responsibility* (New York: Simon & Schuster, 2022), 206.

despite their having similar comparable interests. He also criticises Donaldson's and Kymlicka's idea of extending sovereignty to wild animals which, he suggests, negates the importance of nonhuman animal mobility:

> [W]e cannot draw a simple line between wild and domesticated animals, claiming that the former have no interest in social provision, while the latter always do. What we can say, however, is that all of these individuals have an interest in being included in the political community; that is, in having their interests shape the political agenda and in being *eligible* for certain social provisions.[6]

How might animals' interests 'shape the political agenda'? Rejecting the reliance on sympathetic policy makers or a 'committee of experts' to represent or determine the best interests of animals, Cochrane proposes an animal right to democratically accountable representation:

> Must we resign ourselves to only being able to offer animals ineffectual representation, which treats them as passive and mute? No … it is in fact possible to represent animals effectively without assigning them rights to participation. To do so, we must ensure that the representatives of animals are attentive to the agency, voice and complex interests of animals.… [T]he intrinsic value of animals means they have a right to be included as members of our communities; and respect for their membership requires recognition of their rights to democratic representation within our political institutions.[7]

These worthy schemes represent an idealised picture of the world. They presume a society with institutions both suited to and capable of adopting policies that recognise the status of animals as members of the community. Indeed, most of the approaches considered in these pages proceed on the questionable assumption that the social and political structure is genuinely sensitive to the needs of animals. Some go further and posit a liberal democratic state with what I have elsewhere called morally sound institutions.[8] Unhappily, the fate of billions of animals in the greater part of the world is

6 Alisdair Cochrane, *Should Animals Have Political Rights?* (Cambridge: Polity Press, 2020), 90. Donaldson and Kymlicka defend their position by stressing the significance of the interests of nonhuman animals in their territory and the legitimacy of providing benefits to actual members of society, Sue Donaldson and Will Kymlicka, 'A Defense of Animal Citizens and Sovereigns' (2013) 1 *Law, Ethics and Philosophy* 143.

7 Op cit, 108

8 Raymond Wacks, *The Rule of Law Under Fire?* (Oxford: Hart Publishing, 2021). It has been argued that since animals are potential victims of arbitrary power, they require protection by the requirements of the rule of law so as to ensure that they suffer no harm without the legal accountability to which humans are subject: John Adenitire,'The Rule of Law for All Sentient Animals' 35 *Canadian Journal of Law and Jurisprudence* 1.

very different. Authoritarianism, poverty, populism, and corruption undermine or extinguish the prospects for animals to be regarded as members, let alone citizens, of their societies. Anyone who has visited a live animal market in China, or seen images of puppies crammed in cages for sale as meat in South Korea, or of elephants and rhinos violently killed for their tusks or horns must recognise the gap between Western conceptions of animal justice and the cruel reality of many parts of the world. I described some of these horrors in Chapter 1.

This, of course, is neither to deprecate these ideas nor to doubt their aspirational value. The political turn in animal rights thinking is critically important in acknowledging the manner in which our lives are inextricably linked to our fellow creatures. It would, however, seem to require a stable political order with at least some of the elements of a liberal, democratic system under the rule of law.[9]

Perhaps here lies the dominant message of this strategy; the welfare of animals cannot be detached from the social, economic, and political structure. Impoverished humans are unlikely to treat their donkeys with compassion. Dictatorships are more concerned to consolidate their power and perpetuate their rule than welcome animals into the polity. Corruption destroys the good governance that is a prerequisite of the defence of animals. Unfortunately, fidelity to integrity, democracy, and legality with which these designs bristle, can never be assumed. There is no scarcity of dictatorships across the globe. Populist cant and mendacious demagoguery are always near, especially in a fractured economy. The abuse of power debilitates democratic institutions and compromises good government. It is impossible to ignore the disturbing growth in populism, authoritarianism, and extremism across the globe. Divided societies are less responsive or amenable to the spirit of the political and institutional values that are the lifeblood of a free society.

Any country fragmented by ideological, economic, or social factors is easy prey for totalitarian capture. It is no easy task to inculcate and foster an authentic acceptance of the need to contain the abuse of power by institutional mechanisms. It obviously requires time, persistence, and the political will to confront the excesses of autocracy and its countless vices. It entails also trust in the integrity of the institutions themselves. Cynicism, suspicion, and mistrust are febrile engines of antidemocratic sentiment that plays into the hands of agitators and autocrats. Under these circumstances, what hope for animals?

The solution, I suggest, may lie elsewhere. And I explore that approach in Chapter 12.

9 What follows is drawn from Wacks, note 8.

12 The law

Manifold moral questions arise in almost any legal system. Confronting them is amongst the important characteristics of a free society. Although we cannot easily evade ethical question marks, the identification, or even the acknowledgement, of moral values by which to live is always contentious. A conspicuous example is the decision of the US Supreme Court in 2022[1] overruling its fifty-year-old judgment in *Roe v Wade*[2] which recognised that the Constitution protects a woman's right to an abortion. Feelings on this sensitive subject have always run high in the United States. Long before the current brouhaha, Ronald Dworkin described the intensity of the dispute as 'America's new version of the terrible seventeenth-century European civil wars of religion':

> Opposing armies march down streets or pack themselves into protests at abortion clinics, courthouses, and the White House, screaming at and spitting on and loathing one another. Abortion is tearing America apart.[3]

Nor is it likely to dissipate; presidential elections may be won or lost on the strength of feeling the issue engenders. Many, especially Christians, claim to speak for the foetus which would otherwise have no voice. Nor, of course, have animals. Yet the vehemence and passion that drives the desire to protect the lives of the unborn humans is substantially diminished when the subject is the wellbeing of living animals. Pressure on the legislature and judiciary to respect the rights of either the mother or the foetus is incomparably greater. The explanation for this disparity is obvious; when human interests are affected, public feelings are more easily aroused and more forcefully expressed:

> Killing people outside war is the most seriously-regarded crime ordinarily committed. The only thing more strongly forbidden by our culture is

1 *Dobbs v Jackson Women's Health Organization*, No. 19-1392, 597 US (2022).
2 *Roe v Wade*, 410 US 113 (1973).
3 Ronald Dworkin, *Life's Dominion: An Argument about Abortion and Euthanasia* (New York, NY: Harpercollins, 1993), 4, 103.

DOI: 10.4324/9781032702575-12

> eating people (even if they are already dead). We enjoy eating members of other species, however. Many of us shrink from judicial execution of even the most horrible human criminals, while we cheerfully countenance the shooting without trial of fairly mild animal pests. Indeed we kill members of other harmless species as a means of recreation and amusement. A human foetus, with no more human feeling than an amoeba, enjoys a reverence and legal protection far in excess of those granted to an adult chimpanzee. Yet the chimp feels and thinks ... and may even be capable of learning a form of human language. The foetus belongs to our own species, and is instantly accorded special privileges and rights because of it.[4]

Both sides in these ethical arguments inevitably look to the law which is the ultimate arbiter in these disagreements, and it is to the law that I turn in this chapter for, however, loud the clamour for animal justice, and whatever the arguments in its support, only through legal change can this be achieved.[5]

Legislation exists in a majority of countries that, to a greater or lesser extent, protect animals either against cruelty or, more generally, seeks to secure their welfare.[6] In respect of the latter, an important turning point in the development of legal protection came in 1965 with the publication by the British government's Brambell Committee that studied farming practices.[7] It formulated the 'Five Freedoms' which, amongst other similar reports in various jurisdictions, have established the fundamental conditions of animal welfare that have influenced legislation in many countries. In 1993, the original Five Freedoms were updated with brief descriptions of how each freedom was to be met[8]:

Freedom from hunger and thirst: by ready access to fresh water and a diet to maintain full health and vigour.
Freedom from discomfort: by providing an appropriate environment including shelter and a comfortable resting area.
Freedom from pain, injury, or disease: by prevention through rapid diagnosis and treatment.
Freedom to express normal behaviour: by providing sufficient space, proper facilities, and company of the animal's own kind.
Freedom from fear and distress: by ensuring conditions and treatment which avoid mental suffering.

4 Richard Dawkins, *The Selfish Gene* (Oxford: Oxford University Press, 2003), 10.
5 The subject is admirably canvassed by Raffael N Fasel and Sean C Butler, *Animal Rights Law* (Oxford: Hart Publications, 2023), Chapters 1, 6, and 7, and its accompanying website.
6 For the current situation across the world, see the comprehensive Global Animal Law (GAL) database: https://www.globalanimallaw.org/database/index.html
7 FWR Brambell, *Report of the Technical Committee of Enquiry into the Welfare of Livestock Kept under Intensive Conditions* (HMSO: London, 1965).
8 *Second Report on Priorities for Research and Development in Farm Animal Welfare. Farm Animal Welfare Council* (DEFRA, London, 1993).

While the anti-cruelty statutes of most jurisdictions are limited to delineating examples of mistreatment of various kinds, animal welfare legislation tends to be more comprehensive by specifying both positive duties and sanctions for their infringement. Some explicitly mention the Five Freedoms, others employ more general provisions. Penalties may be both criminal, including imprisonment, and administrative, such as the revocation of licences. In theory, these laws set a standard for the humane treatment of animals, yet their enforcement is rarely adequate. Moreover, they typically contain exemptions (for instance, by permitting 'generally accepted farming practices') or exclusions (for instance, by omitting certain creatures such as laboratory mice from their purview).[9]

The constitutions of a few countries either provide the authority for public bodies to enact animal welfare laws, or declare a commitment, albeit aspirational, to protect nature and its creatures. Rarely are there constitutional provisions that afford direct protection to animals.[10] Nevertheless they have been interpreted by the courts of these countries to support their judgments in a number of cases.[11]

Attempts to introduce international declarations of animal rights have been fruitless.[12] The Universal Declaration of Animal Rights (UDAR) drafted by UNESCO first appeared in 1978 and was revised in 1990.[13] It is a projected inter-governmental agreement to prevent cruelty and reduce suffering, and promote welfare criteria applicable to farm animals, companion animals, their use in scientific research, draught animals, wildlife, and animals used for recreation. Its reach is substantial as it applies to all animals whether sentient or not. Controversially it affirms that 'any act compromising the survival of a wild species ... [is] tantamount to genocide, that is to say, a crime against the species',[14] and 'the massacre of wild animals, and the pollution and destruction of biotopes are acts of genocide'.[15] Another effort to enact an international declaration is the 2010 Declaration of Rights for Cetaceans (whales and dolphins)[16] which provides far-reaching protection for these animals, and includes a statement that no cetacean be considered property.

While there is no extant international treaty protecting animal welfare, there are a number of conventions such as the 1973 Convention on

9 See Raffael N Fasel and Sean C Butler, op cit, 23–25.

10 The Swiss Constitution of 1999 and the Brazilian Constitution of 1988 are notable examples.

11 Federal Supreme Court of Brazil, No. 153.531-8/SC, 3 June 1997; Federal Supreme Court of Switzerland, No. 2C_421/2008; *Animal Welfare Board of India v A Nagaraja and* Others, Supreme Court of India, 7 SCC 547, 7 May 2014.

12 But see Ankita Shanker and Eva Bernet Kempers, 'The Emergence of a Transjudicial Animal Rights Discourse and Its Potential for International Animal Rights Protection' (2022) 10 *Global Journal of Animal Law* 1.

13 The text is available at https://constitutii.files.wordpress.com/2016/06/file-id-607.pdf

14 UDAR Article 8 (1).

15 Article 8 (2).

16 It may be found at https://www.cetaceanrights.org/

International Trade in Endangered Species of Wild Fauna and Flora (CITES) agreement to which most states are parties.[17] Its purpose is the protection of species rather than of animals' welfare *per se*. The Council of Europe has produced several regional treaties which afford protection to animals in a number of contexts.[18]

The paucity of effective legislation on both cruelty and welfare is compounded by the paltry extent of the prosecution of offenders, let alone the conviction and appropriate punishment, for violations of the law. Cases tend to languish in the in-trays of prosecutors—assuming they ever reach them. This general indifference is a product of prejudice in favour of the prosecution of proceedings involving human victims, as well as a general lack of commitment to the cause of nonhuman rights. Nor do animal welfare organisations such as the RSPCA have adequate resources to pursue criminal actions against offenders. And even when they do, sentences tend to be derisory.

These factors have led to a number of initiatives in various countries, at both domestic and international level, to fashion legislative measures with greater muscle. Most radical is the Finnish proposal by the Animal Rights Lawyers Society in 2019 to include an animal bill of rights in the constitution.[19] It would protect all sentient creatures, with the proviso—or 'precautionary principle'—that all animals are presumed to be potentially sentient unless it can be otherwise determined.[20] It also accepts that animals have *locus standi* to appear in court represented by a person specifically appointed for the task. Most significantly, the draft endows animals with substantive positive rights, including the right to life, to experience and express positive emotions, to be protected against and free from fear, pain, distress, and suffering caused by humans, to food and drink, to a suitable living environment, to receive appropriate treatment without delay, and if in a condition such that keeping it alive is obviously cruel, the animal has the right to be euthanised in a manner specified separately in law, respecting

17 The text is available at https://cites.org/sites/default/files/eng/disc/CITES-Convention-EN.pdf

18 They include European Convention for the Protection of Animals during International Transport of 1968 revised in 2003; European Convention for the Protection of Pet Animals of 1987; European Convention for the Protection of Vertebrate Animals used for Experimental and other Scientific Purposes of 1986; European Convention for the Protection of Animals for Slaughter of 1979; European Convention for the Protection of Animals kept for Farming Purposes of 1976. Texts may be found at https://www.coe.int/en/web/conventions/full-list. The European Union has also enacted a number of animal welfare instruments; see the conference proceedings: Sophie Hild and Louis Schweitzer, eds, *Animal Welfare: from Science to Law* (La Fondation Droit Animal, Éthique et Sciences (LFDA), 2019).

19 Other attempts at improving the legislative regime have been made in Switzerland, Germany, Spain; none are as broad or non-species specific as the Finnish submission.

20 Chapter 2A, Section 1, proposed Finnish Animal Bill of Rights, available at https://www.elaintenvuoro.fi/english/

the animal as an individual, sentient being.[21] These rights may be limited only when necessary to safeguard the fundamental rights of humans or animals. Whether this impressive project will remain a mere aspiration remains to be seen.[22]

As mentioned in Chapter 3, attempts have been made, either on the basis of statute or the general law, to vindicate the rights of animals judicially. Most recently, the Constitutional Court of Colombia held that recreational fishing violated the prohibition of animal cruelty and the precautionary principle.[23] This remarkable decision (by 8-1) is a far cry from the resistance displayed by the courts of several other jurisdictions.

The principal obstacle, as discussed elsewhere, has been the aversion to granting animals or their putative representatives *locus standi* to appear before any tribunal. Cases brought on behalf of cetaceans (whales, dolphins, and porpoises),[24] a chimpanzee,[25] orcas, [26] and a macaque,[27] based on diverse causes of action, failed on the unwillingness to accept that these creatures had legal standing to sue. Lawyers have therefore looked to the writ of *habeas corpus* (literally 'you have the body') as an instrument by which to assert the rights or interests of animals. This ancient petition was a crucial check on arbitrary power in England, especially in the seventeenth century. It requires the production of a person detained without trial to be brought before a court. In the absence of a legal justification for his or her imprisonment, the judge could order the individual to be liberated. It took a century for civilian jurisdictions to accept this critical attribute of a free society. Because the detainee cannot, by definition, petition the court, and therefore a third party may do so on their behalf, the requirement of legal standing does not impede the action.

Despite this, the record of judicial readiness to grant the petition in a number of jurisdictions (mainly in the United States and Latin America) has been, with some exceptions, disappointing. The first attempt by the Nonhuman Rights Project (NhRP), discussed in Chapter 3, involved a caged

21 Chapter 2A, Section 4.

22 See Birgitta Wahlberg, 'Re-evaluation of Animal Protection by the Finnish Animal Rights Lawyers Society' (2019) 3 *Society Register* 123.

23 See Marcelo Lozada Gomez, 'The Protection of Animal Welfare vis-à-vis Recreational Fishing: The Judgment C-148/22 of the Colombian Constitutional Court' (2023) 35 *Journal of Environmental Law* 285.

24 *Cetacean Community v Bush*, S District Court, District of Hawaii (2003) 249 F Supp 2d 1206; S Court of Appeals, Ninth Circuit, (2004) 386 F.3d 1169.

25 Martin Balluch and Eberhart Theuer, 'Trial on personhood for chimp "Hiasl"' (2007) https://pubmed.ncbi.nlm.nih.gov/18288430/

26 *Tilikum v Sea World*, US District Court, Southern District of California (2012) 842 F Supp 2d 1259.

27 *Naruto v Slater*, US District Court, Northern District of California (2016)15 cv 04324 WHO; US Court of Appeals, Ninth Circuit (2018) 888 F 3d 418.

chimpanzee called Tommy. The judges denied the *habeas corpus* petition on the ground that there was no precedent supporting the notion that an animal could be regarded as a 'person'. It proceeded on the (arguable) assumption that rights are a correlative of duties; since Tommy was incapable of bearing duties, he could not have rights.[28] Nevertheless, on appeal, one of the judges conceded that even though neither human infants nor comatose adults are capable of bearing duties, they are not deprived of rights. The matter, he stated, will eventually have to be addressed: 'Can a non-human animal be entitled to release from confinement through the writ of habeas corpus? Should such a being be treated as a person or as property, in essence, a thing?'[29] A similar preparedness to keep the door open is evident in a judgment of the New York Supreme Court which, though bound by the *Tommy* decision, expressed the view that '[t]he similarities between chimpanzees and humans inspire the empathy felt for a beloved pet. Efforts to extend legal rights to chimpanzees are thus understandable; some day they may even succeed'.[30]

The strategy did succeed in a decision of an Argentinian court which granted a *habeas corpus* petition in support of a chimpanzee, Cecilia, who was confined in solitude in a zoo. The judge ordered that the animal be transferred to a sanctuary on the ground that she was a 'non-human legal person'. In a comprehensive analysis of ecology, philosophy, and the law, Judge Maria Alejandra Mauricio held that, while Cecilia's status was not equivalent to a human, she was entitled to 'fundamental rights'.[31]

28 *Tommy v Lavery*, New York State Supreme Court, Fulton County, Nonhuman Rights Project (2013) No. 02051: Appellate Division, New York Supreme Court (Third Department), Nonhuman Rights Project (2014) WL 6802767. See too *Kiko v Presti*, Appellate Division, New York Supreme Court (Fourth Department), Nonhuman Rights Project (2015) 124 AD3d 1334; *Tommy and Kiko v Lavery*, New York Court of Appeals, Nonhuman Rights Project (2018) Motion No. 2018-286.

29 *Tommy and Kiko v Lavery*, New York Court of Appeals, Nonhuman Rights Project (2018) Motion No. 2018-286, 2, *per* Judge Fahey.

30 New York Supreme Court, New York County, Nonhuman Rights Project (2015) No. 152 736/15, 32 *per* Judge Jaffe.

31 The petition was also successful when the Supreme Court of Columbia decided that a bear called Chucho who was held in unsuitable conditions in a zoo be relocated to a more congenial habitat. It accepted that sentient animals are entitled to freedom, to live a natural life, and to prosper with the least possible pain. It also repudiated the view that a holder of rights is reciprocally bound to comply with a set of duties. The zoo, however, challenged the ruling, arguing that its rights to due process and to filing a defence had been compromised by the judgment which a higher court accepted and the original decision was overruled, and the Constitutional Court concurred. The cases, in order, are reported as follows: Tribunal Superior del Distrito Judicial de Manizales Sala Civ Fam (2017) MS: C Cruz Valencia, Expediente 17001-22-13-000-2017-00468-00; Supreme Court of Justice, Labour Cassation Chamber, (2017) No. STL12651-2017, Dkt 47924; Supreme Court, Civil Cassation Chamber (2017) No. AHC4806-2017; Constitutional Court (2020) No. T-6.480.577, SU-016/20. But see the Court's starkly different conclusion in the recreational fishing case above.

Less impressed were the judges in Connecticut and New York. A judge in the former state called the petition seeking *habeas corpus* to transfer three elephants from a zoo to a sanctuary 'frivolous',[32] and the appeal by the NhRP was discharged on the ground that the animals, as property, had no legal standing.[33] The argument that rights and duties were correlative again reared its head.[34] Nor was the Supreme Court of Connecticut willing to hear an appeal against the Appellate Court's decision.[35] The New York State Supreme Court of Bronx County declared itself bound by the decision in *Tommy v Lavery* (above), and, while accepting that Happy, an elephant, was not mere property but 'an intelligent autonomous being who should be treated with respect and dignity, and who may be entitled to liberty',[36] none the less rejected the NhRP's petition, as did the Appellate Division.[37] A further appeal to the New York Court of Appeals met a similar fate, the Court (by 5-2) citing the familiar linked arguments of nonhumans' lack of personhood and incapacity of bearing duties as impediments to the claim.[38]

Efforts to obtain judicial recognition of the rights of animals have achieved greater success beyond the United States. Courts in India and Pakistan, for example, have demonstrated a striking willingness to entertain applications other than petitions for *habeas corpus*. The Supreme Court of India, in an action brought by the Animal Welfare Board against the cruelty involved in *jallikattu* racing (in which bulls are maltreated), held that the 'sport' infringed both the Prevention of Cruelty to Animals Act 1960, but also Article 21 of the Indian Constitution which declares: 'No person shall be deprived of his life or personal liberty except according to procedure established by law'. But what is 'life'? The judgment is unequivocal; it encompasses animal life. Moreover, 'life' is interpreted to mean 'something more than survival or existence or instrumental value for human beings, but to lead a life with some intrinsic worth, honour and dignity'.[39]

No less significant is the judgment of the Islamabad High Court which involved a number of animals confined in unsatisfactory conditions in a zoo. The decision is notable for the Chief Justice's grounding his decision

32 *Nonhuman Rights Project v Commerford*, Superior Court, District of Litchfield (2017) LLI-CV-17-5009822-S, 9.
33 Appellate Court of Connecticut (2019) 216 A 3d 839.
34 Ibid, 846. See Chapter 3.
35 Supreme Court of Connecticut (2020) LLI-CV-18-5010773-S.
36 *Nonhuman Rights Project v Breheny* (2020) New York State Supreme Court, Bronx County, No. 260441/2019, 16.
37 Appellate Division, New York State Supreme Court (First Department) (2020) No. 260441/2019.
38 New York Court of Appeals (2020) No. 52, but the two dissenting judgments were remarkably sympathetic to the applicants' case, referring to the majority's 'comforting incoherence of its circular logic', at 9-10 *per* Judge Rivera.
39 *Animal Welfare Board of India v A Nagaraja and Others* (2014) 7 SCC 547 at para 62.

on sources outside Pakistani positive law, including the teaching of various religions:

> The emphasis and importance of 'life' and the protection of living beings cannot be overstated in every religion and faith. Be it Islam, Judaism, Christianity, Buddhism, Hinduism or any other religion, there is no dispute that 'life' is the most precious and superior creation of the Creator. There is consensus among all religions of the world that animals are 'sentient' beings i.e. able to perceive and feel.... [A]nimals also have natural rights which ought to be recognized.... It is ... a natural right of every animal to be respected because it is a living being, possessing the precious gift of 'life'.[40]

Notwithstanding this magnanimity, the court stopped short of acknowledging the existence of animals' right to life.

In a number of similar cases (including in India, Argentina, Switzerland, and Ecuador), judges are increasingly confronted by actions on behalf of abused or maltreated animals.[41] This development is likely to continue, but without explicit carefully drafted legislation protecting the interests of animals, the opportunities available to judges to find in their favour will be severely restricted. Judicial decisions upholding the compassionate treatment of nonhumans may, however, resonate with symbolic significance, but ultimately it is the legislature that must end the failure of the law to live up to its essential task of ensuring justice for all.[42]

A way forward?

To state the obvious, amongst the law's purposes is the remedying of wrongs. The criminal law seeks to prevent, deter, and punish anti-social conduct of various kinds. Tort law's principal objective is to compensate victims for the harm they have suffered. At their heart is the wrongness of suffering. When we condemn egregious events, such as the Holocaust, is it not the unspeakable suffering borne by its victims that is its overarching horror? Of course, there are other, mainly social and political dimensions of atrocities

40 *Islamabad Wildlife Management Board v Metropolitan Corporation Islamabad* WP no. (2020) 1155/2019, 47, 60.

41 They are helpfully summarised and reviewed by Fasel and Butler, op cit, 135–146 and online references to the cases are provided on the book's companion website.

42 '[L]egislative decisions ... will have considerable symbolic importance. But they will not only be symbolic, for they will help define the real-world meaning of legal texts that attempt to protect animal welfare—statutes that now promise a great deal but deliver far too little', Cass R Sunstein, 'Can Animals Sue?' in Cass R Sunstein, and Martha C Nussbaum, eds, *Animal Rights: Current Debates and New Directions* (New York: Oxford University Press, 2004), 251, 261.

that provoke our denunciation: racial or religious discrimination, the abuse of power, the denial of fundamental rights and many other elements of the core injustice, but the imperatives of both criminal and tort law spring from our revulsion at the pain suffered by victims. The creation and elaboration of theories of rights, duties, and other legal notions are essentially subsidiary mechanisms by which the law is conceptualised and its procedures devised and formulated. Once we shift our focus from the mechanics of the legal process to the driving force of its objectives, the injustice of the law's selective defence of the suffering of some living beings, and the general neglect of billions of others is suddenly illuminated.

To advance the cause of animals in court, a range of inventive and imaginative legal devices continue to emerge. Most coalesce around the intractable question of legal personhood; this persists, along with property-based notions of animals, as impediments to granting nonhumans legal standing. As described in Chapter 4, they include occasionally Procrustean endeavours to achieve this end which, exploiting analogies of slavery and corporate personality, judges have generally found easy to resist.[43] The simplest way to eliminate, or at least to circumvent, this stumbling block is to legislate it away by enacting a statutory tort that unambiguously endows animals the right—through their representatives—to bring proceedings for injunctions, damages, and other appropriate legal remedies.[44]

In addition, of course, the enforcement of anti-cruelty legislation needs to be strengthened, especially to increase the abysmally inadequate sentences meted out by judicial officers in many jurisdictions. But the epicentre of any genuine attempt to protect animal welfare is the availability of civil actions to compensate individual or groups of animals for harms suffered. Torts (or delicts, as they are called in continental legal systems) include injuries to the person, property, reputation, privacy, even peace of mind. The law confers on victims the right to obtain compensation for their loss. It provides remedies, pre-emptive and compensatory, for conduct that causes harm either intentionally or negligently. Most torts are actionable only when they have

43 Despite the persuasive arguments deployed in their support. See, for example, David Favre's proposal to divide the concept of title of property between legal title (held by the owner of an animal) and juristic personality (held by the animal) which could result in animals being granted 'equitable self-ownership', David Favre, 'A New Property Status for Animals: Equitable Self-Ownership' in Sunstein and Nussbaum, eds, op cit, 234. Or Visa Kurki's 'bundle theory' of interrelated incidents which essentially grant a putative legal person certain rights, responsibilities, and/or competences, Visa AJ Kurki, *A Theory of Legal Personhood* (Oxford: Oxford University Press, 2019), discussed in Chapter 4.

44 Strangely, this solution has attracted negligible support. Indeed, only after I had arrived at my proposal as sketched in the text, did I serendipitously stumble upon two (neglected) essays that echoed some of my thoughts on the subject: David S Favre, 'Judicial Recognition of the Interests of Animals' (2005) 43 *Michigan State Law Review* 333, and Enger McCartney-Smith, 'Can Nonhuman Animals Find Tort Protection in a Human-Centered Common Law?' (1998) 4 *Animal Law* 173.

caused actual injury or damage. The defendant is normally the person who is primarily liable, though, according to the rules of vicarious liability, one person (typically an employer) may be held liable for a tort committed by another person (for example, an employee).

To redress the pain and suffering inflicted on animals—intentionally or negligently—the proposed statutory tort is founded on the unequal relationship between humans and nonhumans. Nothing in the law can alter the nature of that hierarchy, any more than it does in the case of the relationship between what was once called master and servant, now employer and employee. The crucial purpose of the law of tort in these circumstances is to reduce and regulate this imbalance so as to increase the prospect of fairness between the parties. Consider the birth pangs of the tort of negligence. Prior to the seminal ruling of the House of Lords in *Donoghue v Stevenson*,[45] the common law provided no means of obtaining compensation for damages caused negligently in the absence of a contract. Lord Atkin's trailblazing judgment drew on the biblical injunction to love one's neighbour; he famously declared:

> The rule that you are to love your neighbour becomes in law you must not injure your neighbour; and the lawyer's question 'Who is my neighbour?' receives a restricted reply. You must take reasonable care to avoid acts or omissions which you can reasonably foresee would be likely to injure your neighbour. Who then in law is my neighbour? The answer seems to be persons who are so closely and directly affected by my act that I ought reasonably to have them in contemplation as being so affected when I am directing my mind to the acts or omissions which are called in question.[46]

While this *dictum* launched the new tort of negligence which transformed the common law forever, its moral underpinning has wider significance in respect of the notion of duty in general. The concept of 'duty of care' which is central to this tort envisages a relationship or proximity between the parties that is relevant to the suggested tort under discussion here. The judge did not, of course, intend his reference to 'persons' to apply to animals, but that does not undermine the utility of conceptual *nexus* between tortfeasor and victim that offers an essential foundation for the protection against harms inflicted on those who are our nonhuman 'neighbours'.

45 [1932] AC 562 (HL), See Raymond Wacks, *Law: A Very Short Introduction*, 3rd edn (Oxford: Oxford University Press, 2023).

46 At 580 *per* Lord Atkin. The UK's Animal Welfare Act 2006 provides that owners and keepers have a '*duty of care*' to their animals and must make sure they meet their various needs, including a suitable diet, environment, and place to live, and to be protected from pain, injury, suffering, and disease.

This conception of neighbourliness is powerfully captured by the citizenship project developed by Donaldson and Kymlicka[47]:

> Rather than cutting off relations between humans and animals, our long-term vision seeks to explore and embrace the full possibilities of such relations. This entails recognizing animals not just as individual subjects entitled to respect of their basic rights, but as members of communities—both ours and theirs—woven together in relations of interdependency, mutuality, and responsibility.[48]

The enactment of a tort that explicitly imposes a duty both to *take* care and *extend* care to animals would be transformative. It would ensure that courts are open to claims against individuals, and especially, institutions such as factory farms, laboratories, and abattoirs, transport companies engaged in activities that cause material harm or even death to animals under their control.

A statutory tort protecting the interests of animals would need to contain at least the following sections:

- A description of the purpose and scope of the legislation.
- A definition of the harms against which animals are protected.
- A statement of the conditions under which animals are entitled to live.
- A description of the circumstances under which animals are slaughtered for food, including the requirement that killing avoids pain.
- A statement regarding the entitlement to specific needs various individual animals require in order to flourish.
- The precise nature and scope of the defendant's obligations and liability.
- Defences available to the defendant, such as proof that their interests materially outweigh those of the animal or animals, or that the public interest would demonstrably be served by the activity undertaken by the defendant.
- Remedies available which would include damages (which may need to be transferred to a trust or charity), including exemplary damages, injunctive relief, and confiscation of animals in distress.
- A statement recognising that the appointed representatives of the animals have legal standing to sue on their behalf.

47 See Chapter 11.

48 Sue Donaldson and Will Kymlicka, *Zoopolis: A Political Theory of Animal Rights* (Oxford: Oxford University Press, 2011), 255. But Aquinas says '[T]he love of charity extends to none but God and our neighbour. But the word neighbour cannot be extended to irrational creatures, since they have no fellowship with man in the rational life.... Nevertheless we can love irrational creatures out of charity, if we regard them as the good things that we desire for others, in so far, to wit, as we wish for their preservation to God's honour and man's use; thus too does God love them out of charity', *Summa Theologiae*, https://aquinas.cc/la/en/~ST.II-II

This proposal is not, of course, a panacea. Nor is it likely to win the support of lawmakers in many countries. And even if an enlightened legislature were to adopt a measure along these lines, its effective implementation would depend on the willingness of courts to accept the gravity of the litigation, and hand down judgments that both compensate victims and deter the use of cruel or painful practices.

13 Conclusion

> There is no impersonal reason for regarding the interests of human beings as more important than those of animals. We can destroy animals more easily than they can destroy us; that is the only solid basis of our claim to superiority. We value art and science and literature because these are things in which we excel. But whales might value spouting, and donkeys might maintain that a good bray is more exquisite than the music of Bach. We cannot prove them wrong except by the exercise of arbitrary power. All ethical systems, in the last analysis, depend upon weapons of war.
>
> Bertrand Russell[1]

This story has no happy ending. There is no imminent armistice in our war on the animals. Millions of humans are, of course, outraged by the plight of our fellow creatures. Many charities, animal welfare organisations, enlightened farmers, and activists around the world care passionately about their well-being; and legislative measures, international declarations, and conventions contribute to the amelioration of their lot. But these measures fall far short of the revolution that is required. Sympathy, empathy, compassion, and kindness are indispensable, but cannot, on their own, dispel the gloom. Practical steps to end the suffering of billions of creatures across the globe remain agonisingly remote. The system that condemns so many of our fellow creatures to a life—and death—of pain and wretchedness persists tenaciously.

We are all too willing to look the other way. *Homo sapiens* are relative newcomers to the planet; we arrived only approximately two hundred thousand years ago. Gorillas, elephants, and rats predate us by between fifty or sixty-five million years. It is little more than a cliché to observe that our occupation here has wrought devastation upon the earth. While our achievements in several fields are remarkably prodigious, our relationship with nonhuman inhabitants

1 Bertrand Russell, 'If Animals Could Talk' (1932) in H Ruja, ed, *Mortals and Others: Bertrand Russell's American Essays 1931–1935* (London: Allen & Unwin, 1975), Volume 1, 120–121, quoted in Paul AB Clarke and Andrew Linzey, eds, *Political Theory and Animal Rights* (London: Pluto Press, 1990), 92.

DOI: 10.4324/9781032702575-13

has been less than impressive. While we sanitise and 'Disneyfy' animals in nursery rhymes, cartoons, and animated films, we simultaneously subject them to unspeakable suffering. They are lionised in the names of teams in every sport, of athletes, pop groups, pubs, cars, and numerous other manufactured products. Animals adorn flags, describe celestial bodies, embellish heraldry, and permeate our figurative vocabulary, albeit not always complimentarily. We pamper our pets while turning a blind eye to the atrocious treatment billions of creatures endure every day in factory farms, laboratories, abattoirs, and in the course of transporting them—usually to their death—in conditions of extreme cruelty.

The previous chapters traced the various theoretical arguments and practical proposals that seek the most effective means by which to protect and defend animals' lives, wellbeing, and worth. Each has its merits, and each offers a constructive foundation upon which the pressing questions of nonhuman beings' welfare might best be addressed. There is, however, an inescapable reality. Without the recognition by lawmakers of the need for robust legislative provisions, and by judges of the standing of animals to representation before the courts, little substantive is likely to occur.

At the heart of this vexed subject is the obvious, perhaps even the banal, fact of our association with nonhuman beings. Almost every matter canvassed in the preceding pages, as well as the diverse theories examined, turns, expressly or implicitly, on the nature and form of that relationship and its consequences. Virtually everything we do or refrain from doing affects our fellow creatures. We can accurately specify the distinctive needs of animals, thanks to the advances in ethology and zoology, and the experiences of compassionate observers. That is the easy part. The hard part is to persuade the unconvinced—who cleave to an anthropocentric dogma that springs from cupidity, ignorance, indifference, or plain malevolence—that animals deserve justice in a world that denies the claims that humans reserve for themselves. Acknowledging that animals are members of our community must be the first step towards any effective attempt to arrest the atrocities to which they are exposed.

To illuminate the tribulations of animals, writers have looked to the evils of racism[2] and sexism[3] in the search for a fitting analogy. Drawing on those vices, the neologism 'speciesism' was coined more than fifty years ago by psychologist, Richard D Ryder, who wrote:

> Since Darwin, scientists have agreed that there is no 'magical' essential difference between humans and other animals, biologically-speaking. Why then do we make an almost total distinction morally? If all organisms are on one physical continuum, then we should also be on the same moral continuum.[4]

2 See Jonathan W Thurston-Torres, ed, *Animals and Race* (Michigan: Michigan State University Press, 2023).

3 See, for example, Carol J Adams, *Neither Man Nor Beast: Feminism and the Defense of Animals* (New York: Lantern Books, reprint, 2015).

4 Richard D Ryder, 'Speciesism Again: The Original Leaflet' (1971) 2 *Critical Society* 1–2.

He employed the term again arguing:

> In as much as both 'race' and 'species' are vague terms used in the classification of living creatures according, largely, to physical appearance, an analogy can be made between them. Discrimination on grounds of race, although most universally condoned two centuries ago, is now widely condemned. Similarly, it may come to pass that enlightened minds may one day abhor 'speciesism' as much as they now detest 'racism'. The illogicality in both forms of prejudice is of an identical sort. If it is accepted as morally wrong to deliberately inflict suffering upon innocent human creatures, then it is only logical to also regard it as wrong to inflict suffering on innocent individuals of other species.... The time has come to act upon this logic.[5]

The word was popularised in 1975 by Peter Singer in his seminal book, *Animal Liberation*,[6] and is now employed almost as a talisman to describe the governing anthropocentrism that condemns most of our fellow creatures to their wretched state. The institution of slavery has also been invoked to describe how, like slaves, animals are widely viewed as property with the attendant loss of their rights and dignity.[7] Similarly, and more controversially, the Holocaust has been used to portray the horror and scale of animal suffering.[8]

Each analogy encapsulates different elements of the injustice we perpetrate. Like a palimpsest, each reveals its particular cogency. Speciesism, of course, is the manifestation of our human-centric conceit. Amongst its rudimentary components, as I hope I have shown in the preceding pages, is the exclusion of animals from our conception of community, at least in Western societies.[9] I have suggested that it is only by including nonhuman animals in our understanding of society, that we can begin to shake off the abhorrent assumption that they exist primarily for our use.

5 Richard D Ryder, 'Experiments on Animals' in Stanley and Roslind Godlovitch and John Harris, eds, *Animals, Men and Morals* (London: Victor Gollanz), 81. See too Richard D Ryder, *Animal Revolution: Changing Attitudes Toward Speciesism* (Oxford: Basil Blackwell, 1989).

6 See now the 'renewed' edition, Peter Singer, *Animal Liberation Now* (London: The Bodley Head, 2023).

7 See Marjorie Spiegel, *The Dreaded Comparison: Human and Animal Slavery* (London: 1996).

8 See David Sztybel, 'Can the Treatment of Animals be Compared to the Holocaust?' (2006) 11 *Ethics and the Environment* 97: Charles Patterson, *Eternal Treblinka: Our Treatment of Animals and the Holocaust* (Brooklyn, NY: Lantern Books, 2004).

9 This more expansive conception of society may be found in the idea of 'community' derived from the influential dichotomy drawn by Ferdinand Tönnies, between societies which conform to the *Gemeinschaft* type (community) and the *Gesellschaft* type (association). The former is based on shared, common interests in which the public and private are indistinguishable. The latter assumes a society of atomistic individuals with private interests. Adopting the first conception may offer the foundation upon which to enlarge the frontiers of society to embrace animals. See Ferdinand Tönnies, *Community and Association*, transl and supplemented by Charles P Loomis (London: Routledge & Kegan Paul, 1974).

This exclusivity is especially well epitomised by yet another analogy, that of apartheid which, it is frequently forgotten, or conveniently overlooked, was not merely racial segregation. It was an elaborate, intricate project, sustained by a doctrinaire philosophy applied by an authoritarian regime buttressed by draconian legislation. It relied on an unaccountable security force with sweeping powers, a largely enthusiastic legislature and a mostly pliant judiciary. The legal system was the creation of a white minority; the political system disenfranchised every 'non-white' person, and the law discriminated against non-whites in almost every facet of social and economic life: employment, land, housing, education, sex, and freedom of movement.

In other words, this policy (preposterously styled 'separate development' by its architects) did not seek only to treat non-whites as inferior, but forced them outside the white community politically, socially, economically, and geographically. Analogies and similes risk trivialising the oppression endured by those who lived under the system to which they are compared, yet this one strikingly illustrates the practice of exclusion that we inflict on our fellow creatures, and which we need to jettison.

From this point of departure, three further developments need to follow. They are ontological, political, and legal. The first concerns how we perceive our relationship with fellow creatures which lies at the heart of any serious attempt to improve their lives. This, secondly, has political consequences in respect of the manner in which we conceive society itself, and who qualifies for membership. Thirdly, without legal recognition of this transformed view of social and political relations, the fate of animals is destined to linger in the realm of metaphysical pontification.[10]

We do not need to seek in animals the intellect or the consciousness that we ascribe to ourselves. Their value, and the care that they merit, lies simply in their existence, their being. In the words of JM Coetzee:

> Anyone who says that life matters less to an animal than it does to us has not held in his hands an animal fighting for its life. The whole of the being of the animal is thrown into that fight, without reserve. When you say that the fight lacks a dimension of intellectual or imaginative horror, I agree. It is not the mode of being animals to have an intellectual horror: their whole being is in the living flesh.[11]

Where the domestic law of countries fails to advance the just treatment of animals, the same kind of pressure that is exerted on errant governments to comply with human rights norms must be applied here. Compliance with

10 The painstaking analysis of Donaldson and Kymlicka, and Alisdair Cochrane, discussed in Chapter 11, provides the essential groundwork for the political transformation that is required if the relationship model is to be advanced.

11 JM Coetzee, *The Lives of Animals*, Amy Gutmann, ed (Princeton, NJ: Princeton University Press, 1999), 65, spoken by his character, Elizabeth Costello.

existing international treaties and declarations of animal rights needs to be strongly enforced. We cannot, moreover, shy away from the fact that the preponderance of animal rights campaigns, organisations, and literature is generated in the West. Anyone reading the countless books and articles on the subject will be struck by many of the authors' assumptions of Western culture, social mores, and liberal democratic values. Unhappily, most animals do not live in these relatively enlightened societies. This is not to say that their treatment is necessarily worse, but it often is.

As I suggested in Chapter 12, the notion of proximity or neighbourliness is already present in the law of several jurisdictions. The idea that a duty of care is owed to those who, in the Atkinian formula, are our neighbours, is a central feature of any formulation of responsibility for our conduct.

Shakespeare seems to have understood this. In *As You Like It*, Duke Senior declares to one of his exiled Lords:

> Come, shall we go and kill us venison?
> And yet it irks me the poor dappled fools,
> Being native burghers of this desert city,
> Should in their own confines with forkèd heads
> Have their round haunches gored.[12]

The acknowledgement that the deer are 'native burghers' (albeit that they are soon to be killed) is the exemplar that needs to generate our interaction with animals to advance the cause of justice which, as Benjamin Franklin remarked, 'will not be served until those who are unaffected are as outraged as those who are'. Animals cannot express their outrage; it is therefore we who must speak for them to convey the inherent worth of their lives.

12 Act 2, scene 1. Montaigne is to similar effect when he addresses the animals as '*confreres et compaignons*' in his essay, 'An Apologie of Raymond Sebond' published c1592, in EJ Trechman, *Essays of Montaigne* (London: Oxford University Press, 1927), 464–480.

Acknowledgements

Anyone undertaking this harrowing journey owes a huge debt of gratitude to the pioneers of animal justice. Their efforts continue to inspire scholars and activists pursuing an end to the abuse of our fellow creatures. These Sisyphean exertions are reflected in the chapters of this book; while I may dissent from some of their approaches, we are all committed to the same outcome.

I am grateful to Angie Greenaway and Tim Phillips of *Animal Defenders International* for allowing me to use the image of the macaque on the cover of the paperback edition. The creature was among several monkeys imported to Noveprim's facility in Spain from the company's breeding farm in Mauritius, and was photographed awaiting sale to a laboratory in Europe. Its fate is unknown.

Aakash Chakrabarty and Brinda Sen of Routledge have been supportive and sunny collaborators in this project. I am indebted to them both.

Thanks too to my remarkable wife, Penelope, who, not for the first time, has endured protracted periods of my absenteeism as I toiled at this desk.

Our lives on three continents have been greatly enriched over the years by the companionship of many cherished animals. One hopes that this sentiment was—and continues to be—mutual.

Bibliography

Aaltola, Elisa and John Hadley, eds, *Animal Ethics and Philosophy: Questioning the Orthodoxy* (London: Rowman & Littlefield International, 2015).

Aaltola, Elisa, 'The Meat Paradox, Omnivore's Akrasia, and Animal Ethics' (2019) 9 *Animals* 1125.

Aaltola, Elisa, *Corporal Compassion: Animal Ethics and Philosophy of the Body* (Pittsburgh, PA: University of Pittsburgh Press, 2006).

Abdul Rahman, Sira, 'Religion and Animal Welfare: An Islamic Perspective' (2017) 7 *Animals* 11.

Acampora, Ralph R, *Corporal Compassion: Animal Ethics and Philosophy of Body* (Pittsburgh, PA: University of Pittsburgh Press, 2006).

Ackerman-Lieberman, Phillip, 'Comparison Between the Halakha and Shari'a' in Abdelwahab Meddeb and Benjamin Stora, eds, *A History of Jewish-Muslim Relations: From the Origins to the Present Day* (Princeton, NJ: Princeton University Press, 2013).

Adams Carol J and Lori Gruen, eds, *Ecofeminism: Feminist Intersections with Other Animals and the Earth* (London: Bloomsbury, 2014).

Adams, Carol J and Josephine Donovan, eds, *Beyond Animal Rights: A Feminist Caring Ethic for the Treatment of Animals* (New York: Continuum, 1996).

Adams, Carol J, *Neither Man Nor Beast: Feminism and the Defense of Animals* (New York: Lantern Books, reprint, 2015).

Adenitire, John, 'The Rule of Law for All Sentient Animals' (2022) 35 *Canadian Journal of Law and Jurisprudence* 1.

Aftandilian, Dave, 'Toward a Native American Theology of Animals: Creek and Cherokee' (2011) 61 *CrossCurrents* 191.

Agamben, Giorgio, *Homo Sacer: Sovereign Power and Bare Life*, transl by D Heller-Roazen (Stanford, CA: Stanford University Press, 1998).

Agamben, Giorgio, *The Open: Man and Animal* (Stanford, CA: Stanford University Press, 2004).

Agamben, Giorgio, *The Open: Man and Animal*, transl by K Attell (Stanford, CA: Stanford University Press, 2004).

Akhatar, Salman and Vamik D Volkan, eds, *Cultural Zoo: Animals in the Human Mind and Its Sublimations* (Madison, CT: International Universities Press, 2005).

Akhtar, Aysha, 'The Flaws and Human Harms of Animal Experimentation' (2015) 24 *Cambridge Quarterly of Healthcare Ethics* 407.

Akins, Chana F, Sangeeta Panicker and Christopher L Cunningham, eds, *Laboratory Animals in Research and Teaching: Ethics, Care, and Methods* (Washington, DC: American Psychological Association, 2004).

Alkire, Sabina, *Valuing Freedoms: Sen's Capability Approach and Poverty Reduction* (Oxford: Oxford University Press, 2002.

An'Naim, AA, 'Problems of Universal Cultural Legitimacy for Human Rights' in AA An'Naim and F Deng, eds, *Human Rights in Africa: Cross-Cultural Perspectives* (Washington DC: Brookings Institution, 1990).

Anderson, Elizabeth, 'Animal Rights and the Values of Nonhuman Life', in Cass R Sunstein and Martha C Nussbaum, eds, *Animal Rights: Current Debates and New Directions* (New York: Oxford University Press, 2004).

Andrews, Kristen and Jacob Beck, eds, *The Routledge Handbook of Philosophy of Animal Minds* (New York: Routledge, 2018).

Aquinas, St Thomas, 'Summa Theologica' in *The Summa Theologica of St Thomas Aquinas*, 2nd edn (London: Burns, Oates and Washbourne, 1922).

Aquinas, St Thomas, 'Summa Theologica' in *The Summa Theologica of St Thomas Aquinas* (New York: Benziger Bros, 1918).

Aristotle, *Nichomachean Ethics*, transl by WD Ross (Oxford: Oxford University Press, 1980).

Aristotle, *Physics*, transl by PH Wicksteed and FM Cornford (vol 2). (London: Heinemann, 1929–1934).

Aristotle, *Politics*, transl by H Rackham (Cambridge, MA: Harvard University Press, 1950).

Arluke, Arnold and Clinton R Sanders, *Regarding Animals: Animals, Culture, and Society*. (Philadelphia, PA: Temple University Press, 1996).

Arluke, Arnold, *Brute Force: Policing Animal Cruelty* (West Lafayette, IN: Purdue University Press, 2004).

Armstrong, Susan J and Richard G Botzler, eds, *The Animal Ethics Reader* 2nd edn (New York: Routledge, 2008).

Atterton, Peter and Matthew Calarco, eds, *Animal Philosophy: Ethics and Identity* (New York: Continuum, 2011).

Augustine, St, *The City of God*, transl by M Dods (Edinburgh: TT Clark, 1877).

Baird, Robert M and Stuart E Rosenbaum, eds, *Animal Experimentation: The Moral Issues* (Buffalo, NY: Prometheus Books, 1991).

Banks, Olive, *Faces of Feminism* (Oxford: Blackwell, 1986).

Barad, Judith A, *Aquinas on the Nature and Treatment of Animals* (San Francisco, CA: International Scholars Publications, 1995).

Barilan, Y Michael, 'The Vision of Vegetarianism and Peace: Rabbi Kook on the Ethical Treatment of Animals' (2004) 17 *History of the Human Sciences* 69.

Barron, Anne, 'The Illusion of the "I": Citizenship and the Politics of Identity' in Alan Norrie, ed, *Closure or Critique: New Directions in Legal Theory* (Edinburgh: Edinburgh University Press, 1993).

Baur, Gene, *Farm Sanctuary: Changing Hearts and Minds About Animals and Food* (New York: Touchstone, 2008).

Beauchamp, Tom L, 'Rights Theory and Animal Rights' in Tom L Beauchamp and RG Frey, eds, *The Oxford Handbook of Animal Ethics* (Oxford: Oxford University Press, 2011).

Beauchamp, Tom L, F. Barbara Orlans, Rebecca Dresser, David B Morton, and John P Gluck, *The Human Use of Animals: Case Studies in Ethical Choice* 2nd edn (New York: Oxford University Press, 2008).

Beitz, Charles R, *The Idea of Human Rights* (New York: Oxford University Press, 2009).

Bekoff, Marc (with Carron A Meaney), ed, *Encyclopedia of Animal Rights and Animal Welfare* (Westport, CT: Greenwood Press, 1998).
Bekoff, Marc and Jessica Pierce, *Wild Justice: The Moral Lives of Animals* (Chicago: University of Chicago Press, 2009).
Bekoff, Marc, Colin Allen, and Gordon M Burghardt, eds, *The Cognitive Animal*, (Cambridge, MA: MIT Press, 2002).
Bekoff, Marc, *The Emotional Lives of Animals: A Leading Scientist Explores Animal Joy, Sorrow, and Empathy—and Why They Matter* (Novato, CA: New World Library, 2007).
Benson, G. John and Bernard E Rollin, eds, *The Well-Being of Farm Animals: Challenges and Solutions* (Ames, IA: Blackwell, 2004).
Bentham, Jeremy *Anarchical Fallacies* in HLA Hart, 'Between Utility and Rights' in *Essays on Bentham: Studies on Jurisprudence and Political Theory* (Oxford: Clarendon Press, 1982).
Bentham, Jeremy, *An Introduction to the Principles of Morals and Legislation*, edited by JH Burns and HLA Hart (London: Methuen, 1982).
Benton, Ted, *Natural Relations: Ecology, Animal Rights and Social Justice* (London: Verso, 1993).
Berlin, Isaiah, *The Hedgehog and the Fox: An Essay on Tolstoy's View of History* (London: Weidenfeld and Nicolson, 1953).
Berman, Harold J, *Law and Revolution: The Formation of the Western Legal Tradition* (Boston, MA: Harvard University Press, 1995.
Berman, Louis A, 'The Dietary Laws as Atonements for Flesh-eating' in Roberta Kalechofsky, ed, *Judaism and Animal Rights: Classical and Contemporary Responses: Classical & Contemporary Responses* (Tucson, AZ: Micah Publications, 1992), 150.
Bernstein, Mark H, *The Moral Equality of Humans and Animals* (New York: Palgrave Macmillan, 2015).
Bernstein, Mark H, *Without a Tear: Our Tragic Relationship with Animals* (Urbana, IL: University of Illinois Press, 2004).
Bhattacharyya, Ashim K, *Hindu Dharma: Introduction to Scriptures and Theology* (Bloomington, IN: iUniverse, Inc., 2006).
Biggar, Nigel *What's Wrong with Rights?* (Oxford: Oxford University Press, 2020).
Bilchitz, David, 'Fundamental Rights as Bridging Concepts: Straddling the Boundary Between Ideal Justice and an Imperfect Reality' (2018) 40 *Human Rights Quarterly* 119.
Bilchitz, David, 'Giving Socio-Economic Rights Teeth: The Minimum Core and its Importance' (2002) 118 *South African Law Journal* 484.
Bilchitz, David, 'Moving Beyond Arbitrariness: The Legal Personhood and Dignity of Non-human Animals' (2009) 25 *South African Journal of Human Rights* 38.
Bilchitz, David, *Poverty and Fundamental Rights: The Justification and Enforcement of Socio-economic Rights* (Oxford: Oxford University Press, 2008).
Birke, Lynda IA, *Women, Feminism and Biology: The Feminist Challenge* (Brighton: Harvester, 1986).
Blattner, Charlotte E, Kendra Coulter, and Will Kymlicka, eds, *Animal Labour: A New Frontier of Interspecies Justice?* (Oxford: Oxford University Press, 2019.
Blattner, Charlotte E, *Protecting Animals Within and Across Borders: Extraterritorial Jurisdiction and the Challenges of Globalization* (Oxford: Oxford University Press, 2019).

Bleich, J David, 'Judaism and Animal Experimentation' (1986) 22 *Tradition* 1.
Boddice, Rob, 'The End of Anthropocentrism' in Rob Boddice, ed, *Anthropocentrism: Humans, Animals, Environments* (Leiden: Brill, 2011).
Bostock, Stephen St C, *Zoos and Animal Rights: The Ethics of Keeping Animals* (New York: Routledge, 1993).
Bradshaw, John, *The Animals Among Us: The New Science of Anthrozoology* (London: Penguin Books, 2018).
Braithwaite, Victoria, *Do Fish Feel Pain?* (Oxford: Oxford University Press, 2010).
Brambell, Ben and Bob Fisher, eds, *The Moral Complexity of Eating Meat* (New York: Oxford University Press, 2015).
Brambell, FWR, *Report of the Technical Committee of Enquiry into the Welfare of Livestock Kept under Intensive Conditions* (London: HMSO, 1965).
Braverman, Irus, *Zooland: The Institution of Captivity* (Stanford, CA: Stanford University Press, 2013).
Brown, Les, *Cruelty to Animals: The Moral Debt* (Basingstoke: Macmillan, 1988).
Bulliet, Richard W, *Hunters, Herders, and Hamburgers: The Past and Future of Human-Animal Relationships* (New York: Columbia University Press, 2005).
Burgess-Jackson, Keith. 'Doing Right by Our Animal Companions' (1998) 2 *The Journal of Ethics* 185.
Byrne, Richard W Byrne and Andrew Whiten, eds, *Machiavellian Intelligence: Social Expertise and the Evolution of Intellect in Monkeys, Apes, and Humans* (Oxford: Clarendon Press, 1988).
Cahan, Joshua, '*Tza'ar Ba'alei Ḥayim* in the Marketplace of Values' (2014) 65 *Conservative Judaism* 30.
Cahill, Jonathan M, 'Grounded in Love: A Theistic Account of Animal Rights' (2016) 6 *Journal of Animal Ethics* 67.
Calarco, Matthew, *Thinking Through Animals: Identity, Indifference, Indistinction* (Stanford, CA: Stanford University Press, 2015).
Camosy, Charles C, *For Love of Animals: Christian Ethics, Consistent Action* (Cincinnati, OH: Franciscan Media, 2013).
Campbell, Tom, *The Left and Rights: A Conceptual Analysis of the Idea of Socialist Rights* (London: Routledge & Kegan Paul, 1983).
Cao, Deborah and Steven White, eds, *Animal Law and Welfare: International Perspectives* (Cham, Switzerland: Springer, 2016).
Caras, Roger A, *A Perfect Harmony: The Intertwining Lives of Animals and Humans throughout History* (New York: Simon and Schuster, 1996).
Carbone, Larry, *What Animals Want: Expertise and Advocacy in Laboratory Animal Welfare Policy* (New York: Oxford University Press, 2004).
Carruthers, Peter, *The Animals Issue: Moral Theory in Practice* (Cambridge: Cambridge University Press, 1992).
Causey, Ann S, 'On the Morality of Hunting!' (1989) 11 *Environmental Ethics* 327.
Cavalieri, Paola and Peter Singer, eds, *The Great Ape Project: Equality Beyond Humanity* (New York: St. Martin's Griffin, 1994).
Cavalieri, Paola and Will Kymlicka, 'Expanding the Social Contract' 1996) 8 *Etica & Animali* 5.
Cavalieri, Paola, *The Animal Question: Why Nonhuman Animals Deserve Human Rights* (Oxford: Oxford University Press, 2001).
Chapple, Christopher Key, *Nonviolence to Animals, Earth, and Self in Asian Traditions* (Albany, NY: State University of New York Press, 1993).

Chartier, Gary 'Natural Law and Animal Rights' (2010) 23 *Canadian Journal of Law and Jurisprudence* 33.
Cheney, Dorothy L and Robert M Seyfarth, *How Monkeys See the World: Inside the Mind of Another Species* (Chicago: University of Chicago Press, 1990).
Cholbi, Michael, 'A Direct Kantian Duty to Animals' (2014) 52 *The Southern Journal of Philosophy* 338.
Clark, Stephen RL, *Animals and Their Moral Standing* (New York: Routledge, 1997).
Clark, Stephen RL, *The Nature of the Beast: Are Animals Moral?* (New York: Oxford University Press, 1984).
Clarke, Paul AB and Andrew Linzey, eds, *Political Theory and Animal Rights* (London: Pluto Press, 1990).
Clarke, Stephen RL, *The Moral Status of Animals* (Oxford: Oxford University Press, 1977).
Cochrane, Alasdair, *An Introduction to Animals and Political Theory* (New York: Palgrave Macmillan, 2010).
Cochrane, Alasdair, *Should Animals Have Political Rights?* (Cambridge: Polity Press, 2020).
Cochrane, Alisdair 'From Human Rights to Sentient Rights' (2013) 16 *Critical Review of International Social and Political Philosophy* 655.
Cochrane, Alisdair, 'Labour Rights for Animals' in Robert Garner and Siobhan O'Sullivan, eds, *The Political Turn in Animal Ethics* (Lanham MD: Rowan and Littlefied, 2016).
Cochrane, Alasdair *Animal Rights Without Liberation: Applied Ethics and Human Obligations* (New York: Columbia University Press, 2012).
Coetzee, JM (Amy Gutmann, ed), *The Lives of Animals* (Princeton, NJ: Princeton University Press, 1999).
Cohen, Carl and Tom Regan, *The Animal Rights Debate* (Lanham, MD: Rowman & Littlefield, 2001).
Cohen, Carl, 'Do Animals Have Rights?' (1997) 7 *Ethics and Behavior* 103.
Colb, Sherry F and Michael C Dorf, *Beating Hearts: Abortion and Animal Rights* (New York: Columbia University Press, 2016).
Collins, Hugh, 'Roberto Unger and the Critical Legal Studies Movement' (1987) *Law and Society* 387.
Conn, P Michael and James V Parker, *The Animal Research War* (New York: Palgrave Macmillan, 2008).
Coyle, Sean, 'Natural Law in Aquinas and Suarez' (2017) 8 *Jurisprudence* 319.
Cupp, Richard L, 'Moving Beyond Animal Rights: A Legal/Contractualist Critique' (2009) 46 *San Diego Law Review* 27.
D'Entrèves, A Passerin, *Natural Law*, (London: Hutchinson, 1970).
Dalal, Neil and Chlöe Taylor, eds, *Asian Perspectives on Animal Ethics: Rethinking the Nonhuman* (New York: Routledge, 2014).
Dawkins, Marian Stamp, *Animal Suffering: The Science of Animal Welfare* (London: Chapman and Hall, 1980).
De Waal, Frans, *Good Natured: The Origin of Right and Wrong in Humans and Other Animals* (Cambridge, MA: Harvard University Press, 1997).
De Waal, Frans, *The Age of Empathy: Nature's Lessons for a Kinder Society* (New York: Three Rivers Press, 2009).
DeGrazia, David, *Animal Rights: A Very Short Introduction* (Oxford: Oxford University Press, 2002).

DeGrazia, David, *Taking Animals Seriously: Mental Life and Moral Status* (Cambridge: Cambridge University Press, 1996).
DeMello, Margo, *Animals and Society: An Introduction to Human-Animal Studies* (New York: Columbia University Press, 2012).
Denis, Lara, 'Kant's Conception of Duties regarding Animals: Reconstruction and Reconsideration' (2000) 17 *History of Philosophy Quarterly* 405.
Derrida, Jacques, *The Animal That Therefore I Am* Mary-Louise Mallet, ed, transl by David Wills (New York: Fordham University Press, 2008).
Descartes, René, *Discourse on Method*, transl by J Veitch (Assam: East India Publishing Company, 2021).
Diamond, Cora, *The Realistic Spirit* (Cambridge, MA: MIT Press, 2001).
Dizard, Jan E, *Mortal Stakes: Hunters and Hunting in Contemporary America* (Amherst, MA: University of Massachusetts Press, 2003).
Dombrowski, Daniel A, *Babies and Beasts: The Argument from Marginal Cases* (Champaign, IL: University of Illinois Press, 1997).
Donaldson, Sue and Kymlicka, Will, 'Animals and the Frontiers of Citizenship' (2014) 34 *Oxford Journal of Legal Studies* 201.
Donaldson, Sue and Kymlicka, Will, *Zoopolis: A Political Theory of Animal Rights* (Oxford: Oxford University Press, 2011).
Doniger, Wendy, *The Hindus: An Alternative History* (*London*: Penguin Books, 2009).
Donovan, Josephine and Carol J Adams, eds, *The Feminist Care Tradition in Animal Ethics* (New York: Columbia University Press, 2007).
Douzinas, Costas, *The End of Human Rights* (Oxford: Hart Publishing, 2000).
Dundas, Paul, *The Jainas*, (London and New York: Routledge, 2002).
Dworkin Ronald, *A Matter of Principle* (Cambridge, MA and London: Harvard University Press, 1985).
Dworkin Ronald, *Freedom's Law: The Moral Reading of the American Constitution* (New York: Oxford University Press, 1996).
Dworkin Ronald, *Justice for Hedgehogs* (Cambridge, MA and London: Harvard University Press, 2011).
Dworkin Ronald, *Justice in Robes* (Cambridge, MA and London: Harvard University Press, 2006).
Dworkin Ronald, *Law's Empire* (Cambridge, MA and London: Belknap Press, 1986).
Dworkin Ronald, *Taking Rights Seriously*, new impression with a reply to critics (London: Duckworth, 1978).
Edmundson, William A, 'Do Animals Need Rights?' (2015) 23 *Journal of Political Philosophy* 345.
Eisnitz, Gail A, *Slaughterhouse: The Shocking Story of Greed, Neglect, and Inhumane Treatment Inside the U.S. Meat Industry* (Amherst, NY: Prometheus Books, 2007).
Epstein, Richard, 'Animals as Objects, or Subjects, of Rights' in Cass R Sunstein and Martha C Nussbaum, eds, *Animal Rights: Current Debates and New Directions* (Oxford: Oxford University Press, 2005).
Fasel, Raffael N and Sean C Butler, *Animal Rights Law* (Oxford: Hart Publications, 2023).
Fasel, Raffael N, '"Simply in Virtue of Being Human"? A Critical Appraisal of a Human Rights Commonplace' (2018) 9 *Jurisprudence* 461.
Favre, David S, 'Judicial Recognition of the Interests of Animals—A New Tort,' (2005) *Michigan State Law Review* 333.

Favre, David S, 'A New Property Status for Animals: Equitable Self-Ownership' in Sunstein and Nussbaum, eds, qv, 234.

Favre, David, *Animal Law: Welfare, Interests, and Rights*, 3rd edn (New York: Wolters Kluwer, 2020).

Feinberg, Joel, 'Human Duties and Animal Rights' in Richard Knowles Morris and Michael W Fox, eds, *On the Fifth Day: Animal Rights and Human Ethics* (Moreno Valley, CA: Acropolis Books, 1978).

Feinberg, Joel, 'The Rights of Animals and Unborn Generations', in Joel Feinberg, *Rights, Justice and the Bounds of Liberty: Essays in Social Philosophy* (Princeton, NJ: Princeton University Press, 1980), 159.

Feinberg, Joel, 'The Rights of Animals' in T Regan and P Singer, eds, *Animal Rights and Human Obligations* 2nd edn (London: Pearson, 1989).

Fellenz, Marc R *The Moral Menagerie: Philosophy and Animal Rights* (Urbana, IL: University of Illinois Press, 2007).

Finnigan, Bronwyn, 'Madhyamaka Ethics' in D Cozort and JM Shields, eds, *Oxford Handbook of Buddhist Ethics* (Oxford: Oxford University Press, 2017).

Finnis, John, 'Natural Law: The Classic Tradition' in J Coleman and S Shapiro, eds, *The Oxford Handbook of Jurisprudence and Philosophy of Law* (Oxford: Oxford University Press, 2002).

Finnis, John, 'Natural Law: The Classic Tradition' in Jules Coleman and Scott Shapiro, eds, *The Oxford Handbook of Jurisprudence and Philosophy of Law* (Oxford: Oxford University Press, 2002).

Finnis, John, *Aquinas: Moral, Political and Legal Theory* (Oxford: Oxford University Press, 1998).

Finnis, John, *Natural Law and Natural Rights*, 2nd edn (Oxford: Clarendon Press, 2011).

Fischer, Bob, ed, *The Routledge Handbook of Animal Ethics* (New York: Routledge, 2020).

Foer, Jonathan Safran, *Eating Animals* (New York: Little, Brown and Co, 2009).

Foltz, RC, *Animals in the Islamic Tradition and Muslim Cultures* (Oxford: Oneworld Publications, 2006).

Foltz, Richard C, *Animals in Islamic Tradition and Muslim Cultures* (Oxford: Oneworld, 2006).

Fontaine, Nicholas, *Memoires pour server A l'histoire de Port-Royal*, Volume 2 (Cologne, 1738) in L Rosenfield, *From Beast-Machine to Man-Machine: The Theme of Animal Souls in French Letters from Descartes to La Metttrie* (New York: Oxford University Press, 1940).

Fox, Michael Allen, *The Case for Animal Experimentation: An Evolutionary and Ethical Perspective* (Berkeley, CA: University of California Press, 1986).

Fox, Michael W, *St. Francis of Assisi, Animals and Nature* (Washington, DC: Center for Respect of Life and Environment, 1989).

Framarin, Christopher G 'The Moral Standing of Animals and Plants in Manusmṛti' (2014) 64 *Philosophy East and West* 192.

Framarin, Christopher G, 'The Argument forAhiṃsā in the Anuśāsanaparvan of the Mahābhārata' in Neil Dalal, ed, *Asian Perspectives on Animal Ethics: Rethinking the Nonhuman* (London: Routledge 2014).

Framarin, Christopher G, *Hinduism and Environmental Ethics: Law, Literature and Philosophy* (New York: Routledge, 2014).

Francione, Gary and Anna Charlton, *Animal Rights: The Abolitionist Approach* (London: Exempla Press, 2015).

Francione, Gary L and Robert Garner, eds, *The Animal Rights Debate: Abolition or Regulation?* (New York: Columbia University Press, 2010).

Francione, Gary L and Robert Garner. *The Animal Rights Debate: Abolition or Regulation?* (New York: Columbia University Press, 2010).

Francione, Gary L, *Animals as Persons: Essays on the Abolition of Animal Exploitation* (New York: Columbia University Press, 2008).

Francione, Gary L, *Introduction to Animal Rights: Your Child or the Dog?* (Philadelphia, PA: Temple University, 2000).

Francione, Gary L, *Rain without Thunder: The Ideology of the Animal Rights Movement* (Philadelphia, PA: Temple University Press, 1996).

Francione, Gary L, *Why Veganism Matters: The Moral Value of Animals* (New York: Columbia University Press, 2021).

Francione, Gary L, *Animals, Property, and the Law* (Philadelphia, PA Temple University Press, 2007).

Franklin, Adrian, *Animals and Modern Cultures: A Sociology of Human-Animal Relations in Modernity* (London: Sage, 1999).

Franklin, Julian H, *Animal Rights and Moral Philosophy* (New York: Columbia University Press, 2005).

Frey, RG, *Interests and Rights: The Case against Animals* (Oxford: Clarendon Press, 1980).

Frey, RG, *Rights, Killing, and Suffering* (Oxford: Basil Blackwell, 1983).

Garner, Robert 'The Politics of Animal Rights' (2008) 3 *British Politics* 110.

Garner, Robert and Siobhan O'Sullivan, eds, *The Political Turn in Animal Ethics* (Lanham, MD: Rowman & Littlefield, 2016).

Garner, Robert, *A Theory of Justice for Animals: Animal Rights in a Nonideal World* (New York: Oxford University Press, 2013).

Garner, Robert, *Animal Ethics* (Cambridge: Polity Press, 2005).

Garner, Robert, *Animals, Politics, and Morality*, 2nd edn (Manchester: Manchester University Press, 2005).

Garner, Robert, ed, *Animal Rights: The Changing Debate* (Washington Square, NY: New York University Press, 1997).

Garner, Robert, *The Political Theory of Animal Rights* (Manchester: Manchester University Press, 2005).

Garrett, Jeremy R, ed, *The Ethics of Animal Research: Exploring the Controversy* (Cambridge, MA: MIT Press, 2012).

Gauthier, David, *Morals by Agreement* (Oxford: Clarendon Press, 1986).

Gewirth, Alan, *Human Rights: Essays on Justification and Applications* (Chicago, Il: University of Chicago Press 1982).

Gewirth, Alan, *Reason and Morality* (Chicago, IL: University of Chicago Press, 1978).

Gilhus, Ingvild Saelid, *Animals, Gods, and Humans: Changing Attitudes to Animals in Greek, Roman, and Early Christian Thought* (New York: Routledge, 2006).

Gomez, Marcelo Lozada, 'The Protection of Animal Welfare vis-à-vis Recreational Fishing: The Judgment C-148/22 of the Colombian Constitutional Court' (2023) 35 *Journal of Environmental Law* 285.

Gompertz, Lewis, *Moral Inquiries on the Situation of Man and of Brutes*(1824), Peter Singer, ed, (London: Open Gate Press, 1992)

Goodall, Jane, *In the Shadow of Man*, revised edition (New York: Houghton Mifflin Co, 2000).

Gordon, Robert W, 'Critical Legal Histories' (1984) 36 *Stanford Law Review* 270.

Grandin, Temple and Catherine Johnson, *Animals Make Us Human: Creating the Best Life for Animals* (Boston, MA: Mariner Books, 2010).

Grant, Robert M, *Early Christians and Animals* (New York: Routledge, 1999).

Gray, John, *Straw Dogs: Thoughts on Humans and Other Animals* (London: Granta, 2002).

Greek, C Ray and Jean Swingle Greek, *Sacred Cows and Golden Geese: The Human Cost of Experiments on Animals* (New York: Continuum, 2000).

Griffin, Donald R, *Animal Minds: Beyond Cognition to Consciousness* (Chicago, IL: University of Chicago Press, 1992).

Griffin, James, *On Human Rights* (Oxford, Oxford University Press, 2008).

Gruen, Lori, 2016, 'Conscious Animals and the Value of Experience' in Stephen Gardiner and Allen Thompson, eds, *The Oxford Handbook of Environmental Ethics*, (New York: Oxford University Press, 2016).

Gruen, Lori, ed, *Critical Terms for Animal Studies* (Chicago, IL: Chicago University Press, 2018).

Gruen, Lori, *Entangled Empathy: An Alternative Ethic for Our Relationship with Animals* (Brooklyn: Lantern Books, 2015).

Gruen, Lori, *Ethics and Animals: An Introduction* (Cambridge: Cambridge University Press, 2011).

Grumett, David, 'Aristotle's Ethics and Farm Animal Welfare' (2019) 32 *Journal of Agricultural and Environmental Ethics* 321.

Haq, S Nomanul, 'Islam and Ecology: Toward Retrieval and Reconstruction' (2001)130 *Daedalus* 141.

Haque Nadeem and Al-Hafiz Basheer Ahmad Masrib, 'The Principles of Animal Advocacy in Islam: Four Integrated Ecognitions' (2011) 19 *Society & Animals* 279.

Haraway, Donna *When Species Meet* (Minneapolis: University of Minnesota Press, 2007).

Harris, Angela P, 'The Jurisprudence of Reconstruction' (1994) 82 *California Law Review* 741.

Harris, J W, *Legal Philosophies*, 2nd edn (London: Butterworths, 1997).

Harrison, Peter, 'Descartes on Animals' (1992) 42 *The Philosophical Quarterly* 219.

Harrison, Peter, 'Do Animals Feel Pain?' (1991) 66 *Philosophy* 25.

Harrod, Howard L, *The Animals Came Dancing: Native American Sacred Ecology and Animal Kinship* (Tucson, AZ: University of Arizona Press, 2000).

Harrod, Howard L, *The Animals Came Dancing: Native American Sacred Ecology and Animal Kinship*, 2nd edn (Tucson, AZ: University of Arizona Press, 2000).

Hart, HLA, *Essays on Bentham: Studies on Jurisprudence and Political Theory* (Oxford: Clarendon Press, 1982).

Harvey, Peter, *An Introduction to Buddhist Ethics* (Cambridge: Cambridge University Press, 2000).

Hausman, Gerald, *Meditations with Animals: A Native American Bestiary* (Santa Fe, NM: Bear & Co., 1986).

Herzog, Harold A. "'The Movement is My Life:" The Psychology of Animal Rights Activism,' (1993) 49 *Journal of Social Issues* 103.

Hild, Sophie and Louis Schweitzer, eds, *Animal Welfare: from Science to Law* (La Fondation Droit Animal, Éthique et Sciences (LFDA), 2019).

Hobbes,Thomas, '*De Cive*' in William Molesworth, ed, *The English Works of Thomas Hobbes of Malmesbury* (London: John Bohn, 1841).

Hofstadter, Douglas 'Reflections on "What Is It Like to Be a Bat?"'in Douglas Hofstadter and Daniel Dennett, eds, *The Mind's I* (London: Basic Books), 403.

Hohfeld, Wesley N, *Fundamental Legal Conceptions as Applied in Judicial Reasoning*, WW Cook, ed, (New Haven, CN and London: Yale University Press, 1964).

Horsthemke, Kai, 'Animals and African Ethics' (2017) 7 *Journal of Animal Ethics* 119.

Horwitz, Morton J, *The Transformation of American Law, 1870–1960: The Crisis of Legal Orthodoxy* (New York: Oxford University Press, 1992).

Hume, David, *A Treatise of Human Nature* (Oxford: Clarendon Press, 1888).

Hume, David, *A Treatise of Human Nature*, Book III, Part III, Section III (London: Penguin Classics, 1985).

Hursthouse, Rosiland, *Ethics, Humans and Other Animals: An Introduction with Readings* (New York: Routledge, 2000).

Islam, Nazrul and Saidul Islam, 'Human-Animal Relationship: Understanding Animal Rights in the Islamic Ecological Paradigm' (2015) 14 *Journal for the Study of Religions and Ideologies* 96.

Jacobsen, Knut A, 'The Institutionalization of the Ethics of "Non-Injury" toward All "Beings" in Ancient India' (1994) 16 *Environmental Ethics* 287.

Jain, Pankaj 'Dharma, and Environmental Ethics' (2010) *Union Seminary Quarterly Review*, no page numbers stated.

Jasper, James M and Dorothy Nelkin, *The Animal Rights Crusade: The Growth of a Moral Protest* (New York: Free Press, 1991).

Jasper, Margaret C, *Animal Rights Law* 2nd edn (Dobb's Ferry, NY: Oceana, 2002).

Jinks, Derek P, 'Essays in Refusal: Pre-Theoretical Commitments in Postmodern Anthropology and Critical Race Theory' (1997) 107 *Yale Law Journal* 1.

Kagan, Shelley, *How to Count Animals, More or Less*, Uehiro Series in Practical Ethics (Oxford: Oxford University Press, 2022).

Kairys, David ed, *The Politics of Law: A Progressive Critique* (New York: Pantheon Books, 1982).

Kalof, Linda, ed, *The Oxford Handbook of Animal Studies* (Oxford: Oxford University Press, 2017).

Kant, Immanuel, [1785] *Groundwork of the Metaphysics of Morals (Grundlegung zur Metaphysik der Sitten)*, trans by Mary J Gregor (Cambridge: Cambridge University Press, 1998).

Kant, Immanuel, *Critique of Judgment*, transl by WS Pluhar (Indianapolis, IN: Hackett Publishing Company, 1987).

Kant, Immanuel, *Lectures on Ethics*, transl by Louis Infield (New York: Harper and Row, 1963).

Kant, Immanuel, *The Metaphysics of Morals*, transl by Mary Gregor (Cambridge: Cambridge University Press, 1996).

Karp, Adam, *Understanding Animal Law* (Durham, NC: Carolina Academic Press, 2016).

Kean, Hilda, *Animal Rights: Political and Social Change in Britain since 1800* (London: Reaktion Books, 1998).

Kemmerer, Lisa, 'The Great Unity: Daoism, Nonhuman Animals, and Human Ethics' (2009) 7 *Journal for Critical Animal Studies*, 63.

Kemmerer, Lisa, *Animals and World Religions* (New York: Oxford University Press, 2012).

King, Barbara J, *How Animals Grieve* (Chicago: University of Chicago Press, 2013).
Kingdom, Elizabeth F, *What's Wrong with Rights? Problems for Feminist Politics of Law* (Edinburgh: Edinburgh University Press, 1991).
Knight, Andrew, *The Costs and Benefits of Animal Experiments* (New York: Palgrave Macmillan, 2011).
Kohn, Livia, *Cosmos and Community: The Ethical Dimensions of Daoism* (Cambridge: Three Pines, 2004).
Korsgaard, Christine M, 'Facing the Animal You See in the Mirror' (2007) 16 *Harvard Review of Philosophy*, 4.
Korsgaard, Christine M, *Fellow Creatures: Our Obligations to the Other Animals* (Oxford University Press, 2018).
Korsgaard, Christine M, *The Sources of Normativity* (Cambridge: Cambridge University Press, 1996).
Kotzmann, Jane, 'Sentience and Intrinsic Worth as a Pluralist Foundation for Fundamental Animal Rights' (2023) 43 *Oxford Journal of Legal Studies* 405.
Kramer, Matthew H, 'Do Animals and Dead People Have Legal Rights?' (2001) 14 *Canadian Journal of Law and Jurisprudence* 29.
Kramer, Matthew H, 'Getting Rights Right' in Matthew H Kramer, ed, *Rights, Wrongs and Responsibilities* (London: Palgrave 2001).
Kramer, Matthew H, 'Refining the Interest Theory of Rights' (2010) 55 *American Journal of Jurisprudence* 3.
Kramer, Matthew H, 'Rights without Trimmings' in Matthew H Kramer, NE Simmonds and Hillel Steiner, *A Debate Over Rights: Philosophical Enquiries* (Oxford: Oxford University Press, 1998).
Krishna, Dharma, *Mahabharata: The Greatest Spiritual Epic of All Time* (Ashland, OH: Torchlight Publishing, 1999).
Kurki, Visa AJ, *A Theory of Legal Personhood* (Oxford University Press, 2019).
Kurki, Visa AJ, 'Rights, Harming and Wronging: A Restatement of the Interest Theory' (2018) 38 *Oxford Journal of Legal Studies* 430.
Kymlicka, Will, 'Human Rights Without Human Supremacism' (2018) 48 *Canadian Journal of Philosophy* 763.
Ladd, John '*Introduction*' in John Ladd, ed, *Ethical Relativism* (Belmont, CA: Wadsworth, 1973).
Laio S Matthew and Adam Etinson, 'Political and Naturalistic Conceptions of Human Rights: A False Polemic?' (2012) 9 *Journal of Moral Philosophy* 327.
Laio, S Matthew, 'The Genetic Account of Moral Status: A Defence' (2012) 9 *Journal of Moral Philosophy* 265.
Lamb, David, 'Animal Rights and Liberation Movements' (1982) 4 *Environmental Ethics* 215.
Langley, Gill, ed, *Animal Experimentation: The Consensus Changes* (New York: Chapman and Hall, 1989).
Lazare, Jodi, 'Animal Rights Activism and the Constitution: Are Ag-Gag Laws Justifiable Limits?' (2022) 59 *Osgoode Hall Law Journal* 667.
Leahy, Michael PT, *Against Liberation: Putting Animals in Perspective*, 2nd edn (New York: Routledge, 1994).
Leibniz, G W, *A Treatise of Human Nature* (Oxford: Clarendon Press, 1888).
Letsas, George, *A Theory of Interpretation of the European Convention on Human Rights* (Oxford, Oxford University Press, 2007).

Linzey, Andrew and Claire Linzey, eds, *The Routledge Handbook of Religion and Animal Ethics* (New York: Routledge, 2019).
Linzey, Andrew and Dan Cohn-Sherbok, *After Noah: Animals and the Liberation of Theology*. (Herndon, VA: Mowbray, 1997).
Linzey, Andrew and Dorothy Yamamoto, eds, *Animals on the Agenda: Questions about Animals for Theology and Ethics* (London: SCM Press, 1998).
Linzey, Andrew and Paul Barry Clarke, eds, *Animal Rights: A Historical Anthology* (New York: Columbia University Press, 2004).
Linzey, Andrew and Tom Regan, eds, *Animals and Christianity: A Book of Readings* (New York: Crossroad, 1988).
Linzey, Andrew, ed, *The Link Between Animal Abuse and Human Violence* (Eastbourne: Sussex Academic Press, 2009).
Linzey, Andrew, *Why Animal Suffering Matters: Philosophy, Theology, and Practical Ethics* (New York: Oxford University Press, 2009).
Locke, John, *The Second Treatise of Government* in *John Locke: Two Treatises of Government*, Peter Laslett, ed, (Cambridge: Cambridge University Press, 1988.
Loftin, Robert W, 'The Morality of Hunting,' (1984) 6 *Environmental Ethics* 241.
Lucy, William, 'Persons in Law' (2009) 29 *Oxford Journal of Legal Studies* 787.
Lukes, Stephen, *Marxism and Morality* (Oxford: Oxford Paperbacks, 1987).
Lukes, Steven, *Moral Conflict and Politics* (Oxford: Clarendon Press, 1991).
Lyons, David, 'Rights, Claimants, and Beneficiaries' (1969) 6 *American Philosophical Quarterly* 173.
MacCormick, Neil, 'Rights in Legislation' in PMS Hacker and J Raz, eds, *Law, Morality and Society* (Oxford: Clarendon Press, 1977).
MacCormick, Neil, *Legal Rights and Social Democracy: Essays in Legal and Political Philosophy* (Oxford: Clarendon Press, 1982).
Machan, Tibor R, 'Do Animals Have Rights?' (1991) 5 *Public Affairs Quarterly* 163.
MacKinnon, Catharine, 'Feminism, Marxism, Method and the State: Toward Feminist Jurisprudence' (1983) 8 *Signs: Journal of Women, Culture & Society* 63.
Malamud, Randy, *Reading Zoos: Representations of Animals and Captivity* (Washington Square, NY: New York University Press, 1998).
Marris, Emma, *Wild Souls: Freedom and Flourishing in the Non-Human World* (New York: Bloomsbury Publishing, 2021).
Martha C Nussbaum, eds, *Animal Rights: Current Debates and New Directions* (New York: Oxford University Press, 2004), 206.
Mason, Jim and Peter Singer, *Animal Factories*, revised edn (New York: Harmony Books; 1990).
Mason, Jim, *An Unnatural Order: Uncovering the Roots of Our Domination of Nature and Each Other* (New York: Simon and Schuster, 1993).
Masri, al-Hafiz, *Islamic Concern for Animals* (Petersfield, Hants: The Athene Trust, 1987).
Masson, Jeffrey and Susan McCarrthy, *When Elephants Weep: The Emotional Lives of Animals* (London: Vintage, 1996).
McCartney-Smith, Enger, 'Can Nonhuman Animals Find Tort Protection in a Human-Centered Common Law?' (1998) 4 *Animal Law* 173.
McCloskey, HJ, 'The Moral Case for Experimentation on Animals,' (1987) 70 *The Monist* 64.

McIntyre, Alisdair, *After Virtue: A Study in Moral Theory*, 3rd edn (London: Duckworth, 1985).

Mead, SM, *Tikanga Māori: Living by Māori Values* (Wellington: NZ: Huia Publishing, 2003).

Meijer, Eva, *When Animals Speak: Toward an Interspecies Democracy* (New York: NYU Press, 2019).

Meltzer, Milton, *Slavery: A World History* (Boston, MA: Da Capo Press, 1993).

Meyerson, Denise, 'Persons and their Rights in Law and Morality' (2010) 35 *Australian Journal of Legal Philosophy* 122.

Michelman, Frank, 'Constitutional Welfare Rights and *A Theory of Justice*' in Norman Daniels, ed, *Reading Rawls: Critical Studies on Rawls' A Theory of Justice* (Oxford: Basil Blackwell, 1975).

Midgley, Mary, *Animals and Why They Matter* (Harmondsworth: Penguin Books, 1983).

Midgley, Mary, *Beast and Man: The Roots of Human Nature* (New York: Routledge, 2002).

Mill, John Stuart, *On Liberty*, ed Gertrude Himmelfarb (Harmondsworth: Penguin Books, 1974).

Montaigne, Michele de, 'An Apologie of Raymond Sebond' published c1592, in EJ Trechman, *Essays of Montaigne* (London: Oxford University Press, 1927)

Monti, Andrea and Raymond Wacks, *COVID-19 and Public Policy in the Digital Age* (Abingdon: Routledge, 2021).

Muesse, Mark, *The Hindu Traditions: A Concise Introduction* (Minneapolis, MN: Fortress Press, 2011).

Munro, Lyle, *Confronting Cruelty: Moral Orthodoxy and the Challenge of the Animal Rights Movement* (Leiden: Brill Academic, 2005).

Nadsdy, Paul, *Power, Knowledge, and Aboriginal-State Relations in the Southwest Yukon* (Vancouver, BC: University of British Columbia Press, 2004).

Naffine, Ngaire, *Law's Meaning of Life: Philosophy, Religion, Darwin and the Legal Person* (Oxford: Hart Publishing 2009).

Nagel, Thomas, 'What is It Like to Be a Bat? (1974) 83 *The Philosophical Review* 435.

Nino, Carlos, *The Ethics of Human Rights* (Oxford: Clarendon Press, 1991).

Nozick, Robert, *Anarchy, State, and Utopia* (Oxford: Wiley-Blackwell, 2001).

Nussbaum, Martha C, *Justice for Animals* (New York: Simon & Schuster, 2022).

Nussbaum, Martha C, *Creating Capabilities: The Human Development Approach* (Cambridge, MA: Harvard University Press, 2013).

Nussbaum, Martha C, *Frontiers of Justice: Disability, Nationality, and Species Membership* (Cambridge: The Belknap Press, 2006).

Nussbaum, Martha, *Justice for Animals: Our Collective Responsibility* (New York: Simon & Schuster, 2022).

O'Hagan, Emer, 'Animals, Agency, and Obligation in Kantian Ethics,' (2009) 35 *Social Theory and Practice* 544.

O'Neill, Onora, 'Kant on Duties Regarding Nonrational Nature,' (1998) 72 *The Aristotelian Society*, 211.

O'Sullivan, Siobhan, *Animals, Equality and Democracy* (New York: Palgrave Macmillan, 2011).

Oliver A Houck, 'Noah's Second Voyage: The Rights of Nature as Law' (2017) 31 *Tulane Environmental Law Journal* 17.

Orlans, F Barbara, et al, *The Human Use of Animals: Case Studies in Ethical Choice* (New York: Oxford University Press, 1998).
Ortega y Gasset, José, *Meditations on Hunting* (New York: Charles Scribner's Sons, 1972).
Pachirat, Timothy, *Every Twelve Seconds: Industrialized Slaughter and the Politics of Sigh* (New Haven, CT: Yale University Press, 2011),
Page, Tony. *Buddhism and Animals: A Buddhist Vision of Humanity's Rightful Relationship with the Animal Kingdom* (London: UKAVIS Publications, 1999).
Palmer, Clare, *Animal Ethics in Context* (New York: Columbia University Press, 2010).
Patterson, Charles, *Eternal Treblinka: Our Treatment of Animals and the Holocaust* (Brooklyn, NY: Lantern Books, 2004).
Pepperberg, Irene Maxine, *The Alex Studies: Cognitive and Communicative Abilities of Grey Parrots* (Cambridge, MA: Harvard University Press, 1999).
Perkins, David, *Romanticism and Animal Rights* (Cambridge: Cambridge University Press, 2003).
Peters, Anne, 'Liberté, Égalité, Animalité: Human-Animal Comparisons in Law' (2016) 5 *Transnational Environmental Law* 25.
Peters, Anne, ed, *Studies in Global Animal Law* (Heidelberg: Max-Planck-Institute for Comparative Public Law and International Law/Springer Open, 2020).
Peterson, Dale, *The Moral Lives of Animals* (New York: Bloomsbury Press, 2011).
Phelps, Norm, *The Great Compassion: Buddhism & Animal Rights* (New York: Lantern Books, 2004).
Pickering, George, 'Physician and Scientist (1964) 2 *British Medical Journal*. 1615.
Pietrzykowski Tomasz, 'The Idea of Non-personal Subjects of Law' in V Kurki and T Pietrzykowski, *Legal Personhood: Animals, Artificial Intelligence and the Unborn* (New York: Springer, 2017).
Pietrzykowski, Tomasz *Personhood Beyond Humanism: Animals, Chimeras, Autonomous Agents and the Law* (New York: Springer 2018).
Postema, Gerald J, *Bentham and the Common Law Tradition* (Oxford: Clarendon Press, 1986).
Preece, Rod and Lorna Chamberlain, *Animal Welfare and Human Values* (Waterloo: Wilfrid Laurier University Press, 1993).
Preece, Rod, *Brute Souls, Happy Beasts, and Evolution: The Historical Status of Animals* (Vancouver: UBC Press, 2005).
Premack, David, *Gavagai! or the Future History of the Animal Language Controversy* (Cambridge, MA: MIT Press, 1986).
Pu, Chengzhong, *Ethical Treatment of Animals in Early Chinese Buddhism* (Newcastle upon Tyne: Cambridge Scholars Publishing, 2014).
Puskar-Pasewicz, Margaret, ed, *Encyclopedia of Vegetarianism* (Westport: Greenwood Publishing Group, 2010).
Rachels, James, *Created from Animals: The Moral Implications of Darwinism*, (Oxford: Oxford University Press, 1990).
Radhakrishnan, Sarvepalli, 'The Pluralistic Realism of the Jainas' in *Indian Philosophy*, (Oxford: Oxford University Press, 2008).
Ranger, Shelagh, ed, *The Wisdom of Sheba: Animals and Nature in African Religious Thought* (New York: Continuum, 2002).
Rawls, John, *A Theory of Justice* (Oxford: Oxford University Press, 2002).

Raz, Joseph, *Ethics in the Public Domain: Essays in the Morality of Law and Politics* (Oxford: Clarendon Press, 1995).
Raz, Joseph, *The Morality of Freedom* (Oxford: Clarendon Press, 1986).
Raz, Raz, 'Legal Rights' (1984) 4 *Oxford Journal of Legal Studies* 1.
Regan, Tom, *All That Dwell Therein: Animal Rights and Environmental Ethics* (Berkeley, CA: University of California Press, 1982).
Regan, Tom, *Defending Animal Rights* (Urbana, IL: University of Illinois Press, 2001).
Regan, Tom, *The Case for Animal Rights*, 2nd edn (Berkeley, CA: University of California Press, 2004).
Regan, Tom, 'The Case for Animal Rights', in Peter Singer, ed, *In Defence of Animals* (Oxford: Basil Blackwell, 1985).
Regan, Tom, and Peter Singer, eds, *Animal Rights and Human Obligations*, 2nd edn (Englewood Cliffs, NJ: Prentice Hall, 1989).
Regan, Tom, ed, *Animal Sacrifices: Religious Perspectives on the Use of Animals in Science* (Philadelphia, PA: Temple University Press, 1986).
Regan, Tom, *Empty Cages: Facing the Challenge of Human Rights* (Lanham, MD: Rowman & Littlefield, 2004).
Ricard, Max, *A Plea for the Animals: The Moral, Philosophical, and Evolutionary Imperative to Treat All Beings with Compassion* (Boulder, CO: Shambhala Publications, 2016).
Riddle, Christopher A, *Disability and Justice: The Capabilities Approach in Practice* (Blue Ridge Summit, PA: Lexington Books/Rowman & Littlefield, 2014).
Roberts, WA, *Principles of Animal Cognition* (Boston: McGraw-Hill, 1998).
Robeyns, Ingrid, *Wellbeing, Freedom and Social Justice: The Capability Approach Re-examined* (Cambridge: Open Books Publishers, 2017).
Rodd, Rosemary, *Biology, Ethics, and Animals* (Oxford: Clarendon Press, 1990).
Roderigues, H, *Hinduism and Animal Rights* (2015) http://www.mahavidya.ca/2015/06/26/hinduism-and-animal-rights/
Rollin, Bernard E, *Animal Rights and Human Morality*, revised edn (Buffalo, NY: Prometheus Books, 1992).
Rollin, Bernard E, *The Unheeded Cry: Animal Consciousness, Animal Pain and Science* (Oxford: Oxford University Press, 1989).
Rollin, Bernard E, *The Unheeded Cry: Animal Consciousness, Animal Pain, and Science* (Oxford: Oxford University Press, 1989).
Rothschild, Miriam, *Animals and Man* (Oxford: Clarendon Press, 1986).
Rousseau, Jean-Jacques, 'Second Discourse' in *The Social Contract and Discourses* (London: Dent, 1913.
Rowlands, Mark, *Animal Rights: A Philosophical Defence* (New York: Palgrave Macmillan, 2000).
Rowlands, Mark, *Animals Like Us* (London: Verso, 2002).
Rowlands, Mark, *Can Animals Be Persons?* (New York: Oxford University Press, 2019).
Rowlands, Mark, *Can Animals Be Moral?* (New York: Oxford University Press, 2012)
Rudy, Kathy, *Loving Animals: Toward a New Animal Advocacy* (Minneapolis: University of Minnesota Press, 2011).
Ryder, Richard D, 'Experiments on Animals' in Stanley and Roslind Godlovitch and John Harris, eds, *Animals, Men and Morals* (London: Victor Gollanz)
Ryder, Richard D, *Animal Revolution: Changing Attitudes Toward Speciesism* (Oxford: Basil Blackwell, 1989).

Ryder, Richard D, ed, *Animal Welfare and the Environment* (London: Duckworth, 1992).

Saeed, Samier, 'Squashing the Beef: Why American Animal Rights Advocates Should Start Liking Jewish and Islamic Law' (2022) 42 *Columbia Journal of Environmental Law* 521.

Salt, Henry S, *Animals' Rights Considered in Relation to Social Progress* (London: Centaur Press, 1980 (first published in 1892).

Sandel, Michael *Justice: What's the Right Thing to Do?* (London: Penguin, 2010).

Sandel, Michael, *Liberalism and the Limits of Justice* (Cambridge: Cambridge University Press, 1982).

Sangave, Vilas Adinath, *Aspects of Jaina Religion*, 3rd ed, (Madison, WI: Bharatiya Jnanpith, 2001).

Sapontzis, Steve F, 'On Justifying the Exploitation of Animals in Research,' (1988) 13 *The Journal of Medicine and Philosophy* 177.

Sapontzis, Steve F, *Morals, Reason, and Animals* (Philadelphia, PA: Temple University Press, 1987).

Sargent, Tony, *Animal Rights and Wrongs: A Biblical Perspective* (London: Hodder and Stoughton, 1996).

Scanlon, Thomas M, *What We Owe to Each Other* (Cambridge, MA: Harvard University Press, 1998).

Schaffner, Joan E, *An Introduction to Animals and the Law* (New York: Palgrave Macmillan, 2011).

Schneider, EM, 'The Dialectic of Rights and Politics: Perspectives from the Women's Movement' in Katharine Bartlett and Roseanne Kennedy, eds, *Feminist Legal Theory: Readings in Law and Gender* (Boulder, CO: Westview Press, 1991), 319.

Schochet, Elijah Judah, *Animal Life in Jewish Tradition: Attitudes and Relationships* (Brooklyn, NY: Ktav Publishing House, 1984).

Schwartz, Richard H, *Judaism and Vegetarianism*, 3rd edn (New York: Lantern, 2001).

Scruton, Roger, *Animal Rights and Wrongs*, 3rd edn (London: Metro Books, in association with Demos, 2000).

Scruton, Roger, *On Hunting* (London: Yellow Jersey Press, 1998).

Sebo, Jeff, *Saving Animals, Saving Ourselves: Why Animals Matter for Pandemics, Climate Change, and Other Catastrophes* (Oxford: Oxford University Press, 2022).

Sen, Amartya, *The Idea of Justice* (London: Penguin, 2010).

Shevelow, Kathryn, *For the Love of Animals: The Rise of the Animal Protection Movement* (New York: Henry Holt and Co, 2008).

Sidgwick, Henry, *The Elements of Politics*, 1891 (London: Macmillan, reprinted 1897, 1908, 1919).

Simmonds, NE, 'Rights at the Cutting Edge' in Matthew H Kramer, NE Simmonds, and Hillel Steiner, *A Debate over Rights: Philosophical Enquiries* (Oxford: Oxford University Press 1998).

Singer, Peter and Jim Mason, *The Way We Eat: Why Our Food Choices Matter/The Ethics of What We Eat* (New York: Rodale Press, 2006).

Singer, Peter, *Ethics into Action: Henry Spira and the Animal Rights Movement* (Lanham, MD: Rowman & Littlefield, 1998).

Singer, Peter, *Practical Ethics*, 2nd edn (Cambridge: Cambridge University Press 1993).

Singer, Peter, *Animal Liberation*, 2nd edn (New York: Harper Collins, 2009).

Singer, Peter, *Animal Liberation Now* (London: The Bodley Head, 2023).
Skidmore, J, 'Duties to Animals: The Failure of Kant's Moral Theory' (2001) 35 *The Journal of Value Inquiry* 541.
Smart JJC and Bernard Williams, *Utilitarianism: For and Against* (Cambridge: Cambridge University Press, 1973).
Smart, Carol, 'Feminism and the Law: Some Problems of Analysis and Strategy' (1986) 14 *International Journal of Sociology of Law* 109.
Smith, Jane A. and Kenneth M Boyd, eds, *Lives in the Balance: The Ethics of Using Animals in Biomedical Research* (New York: Oxford University Press, 1991).
Smith, Kimberly K, *Governing Animals: Animal Welfare and the Liberal State* (New York: Oxford University Press, 2012).
Sorabji, Richard, *Animal Minds and Human Morals: The Origins of the Western Debate* (Ithaca, NY: Cornell University Press, 1993).
Spiegel, Marjorie, *The Dreaded Comparison: Human and Animal Slavery* (London: 1996).
Sprigge, TLS, 'Non-Human Rights: An Idealist Perspective' (1984) 27 *Inquiry* 439.
Steiner, Gary, *Animals and the Limits of Postmodernism* (New York: Columbia University Press, 2013).
Steiner, Gary, *Animals and the Moral Community: Mental Life, Moral Status, and Kinship* (New York: Columbia University Press, 2008).
Steiner, Gary, *Anthropocentrism and Its Discontents: The Moral Status of Animals in the History of Western Philosophy* (Pittsburgh, PA: University of Pittsburgh Press, 2006).
Steiner, Hillel *An Essay on Rights* (Oxford: Blackwell 1994).
Steven (Musa) Woodward Furber, *Rights and Duties Pertaining to Kept Animals A Case Study in Islamic Law and Ethics* (Abu Dhabi, UAE, Tabah Foundation, 2015).
Stewart, James J, *Vegetarianism and Animal Ethics in Contemporary Buddhism* (Abingdon and New York: Routledge, 2014).
Stucki, Saskia 'Towards a Theory of Legal Animal Rights: Simple and Fundamental Rights' (2020) 40 *Oxford Journal of Legal Studies* 533.
Stucki, Saskia, *One Rights: Human and Animal Rights in the Anthropocene* (Cham, Switzerland: Springer, 2023).
Sumner, Colin, *The Moral Foundation of Rights* (Oxford: Clarendon Press, 1989).
Sunstein, Cass R and Martha C Nussbaum, eds, *Animal Rights: Current Debates and New Directions* (New York: Oxford University Press, 2004).
Sunstein, Cass R, 'Standing for Animals (with Notes on Animal Rights)' (2000) 47 *UCLA Law Review* 133.
Sunstein, Cass, 'Can Animals Sue?' in Cass R Sunstein and Martha C Nussbaum, eds, *Animal Rights: Current Debates and New Directions* (New York: Oxford University Press, 2004).
Swan, James A, *In Defense of Hunting* (New York: HarperCollins, 1995).
Sweeney, Noël, *A Practical Approach to Animal Welfare Law*, 2nd edn (Sheffield: 5M Publishing, 2017).
Sztybel, David, 'Can the Treatment of Animals be Compared to the Holocaust?' (2006) 11 *Ethics and the Environment* 97.
Sztybel, David, 'Marxism and Animal Rights' (1997) 2 *Ethics and the Environment* 169.
Tasioulas, John, 'Human Rights, Universality and the Values of Personhood: Retracing Griffin's Steps' (2002) 10 *European Journal of Philosophy* 79.

Tasioulas, John, 'Human Rights, Universality, and the Value of Personhood: Retracing Griffin's Steps' (2002) 10 *European Journal of Philosophy* 88.

Tasioulas, John, 'On the Foundations of Human Rights' in R Cruft, S Liao, and M Renzo, eds, *Philosophical Foundations of Human Rights* (Oxford: Oxford University Press, 2015).

Taylor, Angus, *Animals and Ethics: An Overview of the Philosophical Debate*, 3rd edn (Ontario: Broadview Press, 2009).

Taylor, Sunaura, *Beasts of Burden: Animal and Disability Liberation* (New York: The New Press, 2017).

Thapar, Valmik, *Land of the Tiger, A Natural History of the Indian Subcontinent* (Berkeley CA: University of California Press, 1997).

Thomas, Hugh, *The Slave Trade: The Story of the Atlantic Slave Trade 1440-1870* (New York: Simon and Schuster, 1997).

Thurston-Torres, Jonathan W, ed, *Animals and Race* (Michigan: Michigan State University Press, 2023).

Tlili, Sarra 'Animals Would Follow Shaf'i'ism: Legitimate and Illegitimate Violence to Animals in Medieval Islamic Thought' in Robert Gleave and Istvan Kristo-Nagy, eds, *Violence in Islamic Thought from the Qoran to the Mongols* (Edinburgh: Edinburgh University Press, 2016).

Tlili, Sarra, *Animals in the Qur'an* (Cambridge: Cambridge University Press, 2012).

Varner, Gary E, *Personhood, Ethics, and Animal Cognition: Situating Animals in Hare's Two Level Utilitarianism* (New York: Oxford University Press, 2012).

Varner, Gary E, *In Nature's Interests? Interests, Animal Rights, and Environmental Ethics* (Oxford: Oxford University Press, 1998).

Višak, Tatjana and Robert Garner, eds, *The Ethics of Killing Animals* (New York: Oxford University Press, 2016).

Voltaire 'Betes' in *Dictionnaire Philosophique* (Wentworth Press, 2019).

Wacks, Raymond, 'Sacrificed for Science: Are Animal Experiments Morally Defensible?' in Gerhold K Becker, ed, in association with James P Buchanan, *Changing Nature's Course: The Ethical Challenge of Biotechnology* (Hong Kong: Hong Kong University Press, 1996).

Wacks, Raymond, *Justice: A Beginner's Guide* (London: Oneworld Publications, 2017).

Wacks, Raymond, *Law: A Very Short Introduction*, 3rd edn (Oxford: Oxford University Press, 2023).

Wacks, Raymond, *Philosophy of Law: A Very Short Introduction*, 2nd edn (Oxford: Oxford University Press, 2nd edn, 2014).

Wacks, Raymond, *The Rule of Law Under Fire?* (Oxford: Hart Publishing, 2021).

Wacks, Raymond, *Understanding Jurisprudence: An Introduction to Legal Theory* 6th edn (Oxford: Oxford University Press, 6th edn, 2020).

Wahlberg, Birgitta, 'Re-evaluation of Animal Protection by the Finnish Animal Rights Lawyers Society' (2019) 3 *Society Register* 123.

Waldau, Paul and Kimberley Patton, eds, *A Communion of Subjects: Animals in Religion, Science, and Ethics* (New York: Columbia University Press, 2006).

Waldau, Paul. 'Buddhism and Animal Rights,' in Damien Keown, ed, *Contemporary Buddhist Ethics* (Richmond, Surrey: Curzon Press, 2000).

Waldron, Jeremy, ed, *Nonsense upon Stilts: Bentham, Burke and Marx on the Rights of Man* (London: Methuen, 1987).

Walker, Rebecca L, 'Animal Flourishing: What Virtue Requires of Human Animals', in *Working Virtue: Virtue Ethics and Contemporary Moral Problems*, Rebecca Walker and Philip J Ivanhoe, eds, (Oxford: Oxford University Press, 2007).

Walzer, Michael, *Spheres of Justice: A Defense Of Pluralism and Equality* (New York: Basic Books, 1984).

Watson, Alan, ed, *The Digest of Justinian*, 4 volumes, revised edn (Philadelphia, PA: University of Pennsylvania Press, 2009).

Watson, Alan, *Law of Property in the Later Roman Republic* (Oxford: Oxford University Press, 1969).

Watson, Alan, *Rome of the XII Tables: Person and Property* (Princeton, NJ: Princeton University Press, 2020).

Wellman, Carl, *Real Rights* (Oxford: Oxford University Press 1995).

White, Alan R, *Rights* (Oxford: Clarendon Press, 1984).

White, Edward G, 'The Inevitability of Critical Legal Studies' (1984) 36 *Stanford Law Review* 649.

Whitfort, Amanda, 'Evaluating China's Draft Animal Protection Law' (2012) 34 *Sydney Law Review* 347.

Wicklund, Petra Renee, 'Abrogating Property Status in the Fight for Animal Rights' (1997) 107 *Yale Law Journal* 569.

Wise, Steven M, 'Animal Rights, One Step at a Time' in Sunstein and Nussbaum, qv.

Wise, Steven M, 'Hardly a Revolution—The Eligibility of Nonhuman Animals for Dignity-Rights in a Liberal Democracy' (1998) 22 *Vermont Law Review* 793.

Wise, Steven M, 'Legal Rights for Nonhuman Animals: The Case for Chimpanzees and Bonobos' (1996) 2 *Animal Law Review* 179.

Wise, Steven M, 'The Legal Thinghood of Nonhuman Animals' (1996) 23 *Environmental Affairs* 471.

Wise, Steven M, *Drawing the Line: Science and the Case for Animal Rights* (Cambridge, MA: Perseus, 2002).

Wise, Steven M, *Rattling the Cage: Toward Legal Rights for Animals* (Cambridge, MA: Perseus, 2001).

Wolfe, Cary, *What Is Posthumanism?* (Minneapolis MN: University of Minnesota Press, 2009).

Wolfe, Cary, *Before the Law: Humans and Other Animals in a Biopolitical Frame* (Chicago, Ill: University of Chicago Press, 2012).

Wolfe, Cary, ed, *Zoontologies: The Question of the Animal* (Minneapolis, MN: University of Minnesota Press, 2003).

Wolfson David J and Mariann Sullivan, 'Foxes in the Hen House, Animals, Agribusiness, and the Law: A Modern American Fable' in Cass R Sunstein and Martha C Nussbaum, eds, qv.

Yablon, Charles M, 'The Indeterminacy of the Law: Critical Legal Studies and the Problem of Legal Explanation' (1985) 6 *Cardozo Law Review* 917.

Zamir, Tzachi, *Ethics and the Beast: A Speciesist Argument for Animal Liberation* (Princeton, NJ: Princeton University Press, 2007).

Index

Note: Page numbers followed by "n" refer to foot notes.

Made in the USA
Monee, IL
12 November 2026

da1ff8fd-14dd-48cb-8685-ba9b0a754646R01